I0188516

Varieties of Religious Authority

The **International Institute for Asian Studies (IIAS)** is a postdoctoral research centre based in Leiden and Amsterdam, the Netherlands. Its main objective is to encourage the study of Asia and to promote national and international co-operation in this field. The geographical scope of the Institute covers South Asia, Southeast Asia, East Asia, and Central Asia. The institute focuses on the humanities and the social sciences and, where relevant, on their interaction with other sciences.

The **Institute of Southeast Asian Studies (ISEAS)** was established as an autonomous organization in 1968. It is a regional research centre dedicated to the study of socio-political, security and economic trends and developments in Southeast Asia and its wider geostrategic and economic environment. The Institute's research programmes are the Regional Economic Studies (RES, including ASEAN and APEC), Regional Strategic and Political Studies (RSPS), and Regional Social and Cultural Studies (RSCS).

ISEAS Publishing, an established academic press, has issued more than 2,000 books and journals. It is the largest scholarly publisher of research about Southeast Asia from within the region. ISEAS Publishing works with many other academic and trade publishers and distributors to disseminate important research and analyses from and about Southeast Asia to the rest of the world.

IIAS/ISEAS Series on Asia

Varieties of Religious Authority

Changes and Challenges in 20th Century Indonesian Islam

EDITED BY
AZYUMARDI AZRA, **KEES VAN DIJK**,
AND **NICO J.G. KAPTEIN**

ISEAS

International Institute for Asian Studies
The Netherlands

Institute of Southeast Asian Studies
Singapore

First published in Singapore in 2010 by ISEAS Publishing
Institute of Southeast Asian Studies
30 Heng Mui Keng Terrace
Pasir Panjang
Singapore 119614

E-mail: publish@iseas.edu.sg
Website: http://www.bookshop.iseas.edu.sg

First published in Europe in 2010 by
International Institute for Asian Studies
P.O. Box 9515
2300 RA Leiden
The Netherlands

E-mail: iias@let.leidenuniv.nl
Website: http://www.iias.nl/

All rights reserved. No part of this publication may be reproduced, stored in a retrieval system, or transmitted in any form or by any means, electronic, mechanical, photocopying, recording or otherwise, without the prior permission of the Institute of Southeast Asian Studies.

© 2010 Institute of Southeast Asian Studies, Singapore.

The responsibility for facts and opinions in this publication rests exclusively with the author and her interpretations do not necessarily reflect the views or the policy of the publishers or its supporters.

ISEAS Library Cataloguing-in-Publication Data

Varieties of religious authority : changes and challenges in 20th century Indonesian Islam / edited by Azyumardi Azra, Kees van Dijk and Nico J.G. Kaptein.
(IIAS-ISEAS series on Asia).
1. Ulama—Indonesia.
2. Authority—Religious aspects—Islam.
3. Islam—Indonesia—History—20th century.
I. Azra, Azyumardi.
II. Dijk, Kees van, 1946–
III. Kaptein, Nico J. G.
IV. Title.
V. Series.
BP63 I5V29 2010

ISBN 978-981-230-940-2 (hard cover)
ISBN 978-981-230-951-8 (E-Book PDF)

Typeset in Singapore by Superskill Graphics Pte Ltd
Printed in Singapore by Utopia Press Pte Ltd

CONTENTS

ABOUT THE CONTRIBUTORS

Arief Subhan received a scholarship under the project "Dissemination of Religious Authority in Twentieth Century Indonesia" sponsored by the International Institute for Asian Studies (IIAS), Leiden University to undertake a doctoral degree. He is a lecturer at the Faculty of Da'wa and Communication, Islamic State University (UIN), Jakarta. He is also a researcher in the Center for the Study of Islam and Society (PPIM) at the same university.

Azyumardi Azra (editor) received his Ph.D. degree in 1992 from Columbia University and is Professor of History at the UIN in Jakarta. From 1998–2006 he was Rector of this university. He has published widely on various aspects of history, religion and politics.

Didin Nurul Rosidin, Java, Indonesia. After finishing his study at the Islamic High School Special Programme (*Madrasah Aliyah Program Khusus* or MAPK) in 1992, he studied Qur'anic Exegesis and Prophet Tradition at the Faculty of Theology, Walisongo State Institute for Islamic Studies (Institut Agama Islam Negeri or IAIN) in Surakarta, Central Java. He received his undergraduate degree in 1996. From 1998 to 2000, he took his Master's Programme in Islamic Studies at Leiden University sponsored by the Indonesian-Netherlands Cooperation in Islamic Studies (INIS). Under the same sponsor and at the same university, he took his Doctor's programme from 2001. In addition to formal education institutions, he has also studied at a number of Pesantren, including Gontor, East Java, Darussalam, Ciamis, West Java, and Jamsaren, Surakarta, Central Java. From 1998 to the present, he has been working as a lecturer on the History of Islamic Civilization at the Faculty of Theology, Walisongo State Institute for Islamic Studies in Semarang, Central Java. In 2002, he was appointed as a vice-supervisor of Pesantren Al-Mutawally, Kuningan, West Java. He continues to hold this position today.

Kees van Dijk (contributing editor) is a researcher at the KITLV/Royal Netherlands Institute of Southeast Asian and Caribbean Studies since 1968. Since 1985, he has held a chair as Professor of the History of Islam in

Indonesia at Leiden University. He studied Non-Western Sociology at Leiden University, and during his study, specialized in Indonesian Studies. He graduated in 1970. He obtained his Ph.D. at Leiden University in 1981. The title of his Ph.D. thesis was "Rebellion Under the Banner of Islam: The Darul Islam in Indonesia" (1991). He also published "A Country in Despair: Indonesia between 1997 and 2000" (2001).

Andrée Feillard is Senior Researcher with the French Public Centre of Scientific Research (Centre National de la Recherche Scientifique, CNRS). She was Representative for the Jakarta bureau of the École Française d'Extrême-Orient, the prestigious French research institution. Her field of research is traditionalist Islam (her Ph.D. dissertation is on the large Islamic organization, Nahdlatul Ulama), and she has more recently worked on new radical groups, and published a book on the emergence of radicalism, titled *La Fin de l'Innocence? L'islam indonésien face à la tentation radicale, de 1967 à nos jours*, Les Indes Savantes, Paris; Irasec, Bangkok. She was a foreign correspondent for *Agence France Presse* and *Asiaweek* in Indonesia from 1981 to 1989.

Marc Gaborieau is attached to the Centre National de la Recherche Scientifique (CNRS) and the École des Hautes Études en Sciences Sociales (EHESS) in Paris.

Jajat Burhanudin (Ph.D. Leiden University 2007; MA 1996 Leiden University) is a lecturer at the Faculty of Adab and Humanities of the UIN in Jakarta and a researcher at the PPIM of the same university. From 2001–05 he conducted Ph.D. research within the framework of the "Dissemination of Religious Authority in Twentieth Century Indonesia" sponsored by IIAS.

Nico J.G. Kaptein (editor) teaches Islamic Studies at the Department for Middle Eastern Languages and Cultures at Leiden University. Moreover, he is Senior Research Fellow at the International Institute for Asian Studies (IIAS), Leiden (where he together with Josine Stremmelaar coordinated the programme "The Dissemination of Religious Authority in Twentieth Century Indonesia" 2001–05). Having coordinated the Indonesian Netherlands Cooperation in Islamic Studies (INIS) Programme which ended in 2005, he is at present Academic Coordinator of the INIS follow-up, the Training of Indonesia's Young Leaders Programme.

Michael Laffan gained his Ph.D. from Sydney University in 2001 and was a Research Fellow at the International Institute for Asian Studies in Leiden until December 2004. Since then he has been an assistant professor with Princeton University's Department of History. He has published various articles on aspects of Islam in the region, ranging from pre-colonial and trans-oceanic connections to issues relating to imperialism and the forms of modernity. While his first book, *Islamic Nationhood and Colonial Indonesia* (2003), dealt with the role of religion in the making of Indonesia, his current project looks at the linkages between Dutch colonial scholarship on Islam and local debates, with specific reference to the place of Sufism in that future nation.

Machasin is Professor of History of Islamic Culture at the Faculty of Letters, UIN Sunan Kalijaga, Yogyakarta, Indonesia. He also teaches for the World Religions MA Programme at Gadjah Mada University, Yogyakarta. At present, he is Director of Islamic Higher Education, Directorate General of Islamic Education, Ministry of Religious Affairs, Republic of Indonesia.

Noorhaidi Hasan is a Senior Lecturer at the Islamic State University (UIN), Sunan Kalijaga, Yogyakarta, Indonesia. His main interest includes various manifestations of political Islam in contemporary Indonesia, on which he has published various articles in international journals. In 2006, he published the book *Laskar Jihad: Islam, Militancy and the Quest for Identity in Post-New Order Indonesia*, which was derived from his 2005 Utrecht University dissertation prepared within the programme "The Dissemination of Religious Authority in Twentieth Century Indonesia".

Abdulkader Tayob teaches Islamic Studies at the University of Cape Town. He was previously ISIM Professor at Radboud University in Nijmegen, Netherlands. He has published a number of books and articles on Islam in South Africa, and the study of religions. Presently, he is working on contemporary Islamic thought, and Islam and the public sphere in Africa.

ACKNOWLEDGEMENTS

The research programme leading to this publication was made possible through financial support from the Royal Netherlands Academy of Arts and Sciences (KNAW) in the framework of the Scientific Programme Indonesia — Netherlands (SPIN). The editors gratefully acknowledge this support.

INTRODUCTION

The twentieth century was a period of profound political, social and religious changes in Indonesia. From a Dutch colony, Indonesia, the country with the largest number of Muslims in the world, was transformed into an independent, semi-secular state, in which "Belief in the One and Only God" (and not Islam) became one of the constitutional "Pancasila" pillars of political and social life. In the first decades of the last century, Islamic leaders and Islamic organizations had to operate in a setting in which the establishment of direct colonial rule was accompanied by strong competition between the state and Muslim authorities. Thereafter, political circumstances changed dramatically. From 1942 to 1945 Indonesia was ruled by Japan, while between 1945 and 1950 the War for Independence was fought and won. After 1950 Muslim religious and political leaders had to take into account different forms of government, each with its own specific ideas about the place of Islam in society; first a democracy modelled along Western lines; then, after 1959 a period of some forty years in which Indonesia was ruled by two successive totalitarian regimes and freedom of expression was curtailed; finally, the present-day situation in which, in reaction to what the country had experienced in the decades before Soeharto had to step down as President in 1998, civic liberties are stressed.

The economy also changed over time, resulting in transformations which posed new challenges to existing religious values and patterns of association. People were drawn into larger social, cultural and economic structures. The Indonesian economy developed from one which was rural-based and geared to the interests of the colonial power, first those of the Netherlands and than those of Japan, to one in which national interests and development became important catchwords. Initially the effort seemed to fail. In the 1960s the Indonesian economy went through extremely bad times. The year 1969 saw the start of the first of a series of Five-Year Development Plans. The result of the development effort was not only economic growth and the emergence of an extremely rich middle class, but also accelerated urbanization with the accompanying social and cultural dislocations and a wide gap between the rich and a great mass of urban and rural poor. Economic development also allowed the government to use money to coopt social, political and religious leaders. The Asian financial crisis at the end of the 1990s hit Indonesia particularly hard. For a moment it seemed that its economy would cave in.

In the course of the last century the religious landscape only became more diverse. As was the case in the rest of the Islamic world, established, traditional Islamic beliefs and leaders got new "modernist" competitors, while at different moments throughout the period, political Islam made its voice heard. Developments in wider society contributed to the diversification of religious opinion. Because of the spread of secular education and the advent of first the printing press and later on other means of mass communication, there emerged a large audience of believers who had access to sacred and other texts and who reflected independently on the meaning and function of religious beliefs and practices. As a result, religious authority was redistributed over an increasing number of actors and increasingly tested and contested, also within the confines of learned tradition. Although many Muslims in Indonesia continued to regard the *ulama* (the "learned") as the principal source of religious guidance, religious authority had become more diffused and differentiated over time. Pious behaviour and persuasive argumentation have become two of the yardsticks qualifying new groups of religious authority in response to the questions of the time.

This fascinating century in the history of Indonesia formed the time frame of the bilateral research programme *Islam in Indonesia: Dissemination of Religious Authority in the 20th Century*. This programme was executed in the framework of the so-called Scientific Programme Indonesia-Netherlands (SPIN). SPIN was launched in the year 2000. It is based on an agreement between the Indonesian and Dutch governments. In the Netherlands the responsibility for the administration and funding falls under the Royal Netherlands Academy of Arts and Sciences (KNAW), while the Indonesian counterpart is the Indonesian Ministry for Research and Technology (RISTEK). The *Islam in Indonesia* programme officially ran from 1 January 2001 to 31 December 2005 and was coordinated by the International Institute for Asian Studies (IIAS) in Leiden, the Netherlands, and the Pusat Pengkajian Islam dan Masyarakat (PPIM) of the Universitas Islam Negeri (UIN) Syarif Hidayatullah in Jakarta, Indonesia. Other institutions which were involved were: the Royal Netherlands Institute of Southeast Asian and Caribbean Studies (KITLV); the International Institute for the Study of Islam in the Modern World (ISIM); the Research School for Asian, African and Amerindian Studies (CNWS), all three in Leiden; and the UIN Sunan Kalijaga in Yogyakarta, Indonesia.

The *Islam in Indonesia* programme aimed at the studying and documenting of changes and continuities in Muslim religious leadership in relation to the shaping of present-day Indonesian nationhood over the last hundred years. The underlying assumptions of this research programme were that Islam, like any other living religious tradition, evolves by constant repositioning of beliefs and practices, and that this repositioning often reflects — or gives meaning to — social, economic and political transformations. One of the ways to analyse this is by looking at the dissemination of religious authority. The concept refers to the development of points of reference and identity within a given religious tradition which evolve around the related notions of belief as religious "knowledge" and symbolic structure as expressed in ritual and community experience.

From these considerations as the overall research subject emerged the question of how religious authority manifested itself in twentieth century Indonesia in the changing national and international context. Sub questions were: What was the relationship between the state and religious authority in its many manifestations? Which institutions play a role in spreading religious authority and what is the role of the state in this? How did the Middle East contribute in shaping and maintaining religious authority in Indonesia? In order to further implement the research questions four themes were defined. These were: *ulama* and *fatwa*; *tarekat* in urban communities; *dakwah* activities in urban communities; and education. The start of the research programme *Islam in Indonesia* in 2001 coincided with a dramatic increase in (or at least increased visibility of) the activities of radical Islamic groups in Indonesia and in the rest of the world. In the last couple of years, terrorist attacks by Islamic groups have taken place all over the world. These and other developments in and outside Indonesia more or less directed the participating scholars to pay attention to the processes of radicalization of Islam in Indonesia.

This book consists of contributions which were presented in the final conference of the research programme, in Bogor on 7–9 July 2005, organized by Azyumardi Azra, Kees van Dijk, and Nico Kaptein, with managerial support from Josine Stremmelaar (IIAS). The conference was jointly organized by IIAS (Leiden) and UIN (Jakarta), in cooperation with the KITLV (Leiden/Jakarta) and ISIM (Leiden). During this conference, a number of the issues related to the concept of religious authority were tackled, mainly in relation to Islam in Indonesia. However, in order to make comparison of the Indonesian case possible, specialists from other regions were also invited.

All contributions in this book deal with the multifaceted and multidimensional topic of religious authority and aim to complement each other. However, the editors have not been so strict in their guidelines that the contributions cannot be read separately. Most chapters deal with Indonesia, but two have been added in order to provide a comparative dimension to the Indonesian case. The order in which the chapters are presented here is partly chronological (from historical to contemporary), while chapters which focus on the same aspects of religious authority have been grouped together.

The first contribution by Marc Gaborieau stresses that the notion of religious authority in Islam is secondary, in the sense that it has always been derived from the ultimate source of authority which is God. After having studied the concept of religious authority in the Indian subcontinent in the period 1919–56, he concludes that the concept has changed in two ways: firstly, the future of the South Asian Muslim community has been determined largely by laymen and not by the traditional holders of religious authority, the *ulama*; and secondly, they derived this authority largely from their own charisma and the messianic aspirations of the Muslim community.

In the second chapter, Michael Laffan examines the debate surrounding *tariqa* practices in Southeast Asia in the early twentieth century and amongst other things, discusses the authority of the local Sufi *shayks* vis-à-vis more sophisticated elitist Sufism. The third contribution links up with this and deals with the role of the *ulama* in twentieth century Indonesia. In this chapter by Jajat Burhanudin, he maintains that despite the rise of an Islamic public sphere, which ended the monopoly of the *ulama* as the sole voices of Islam, the *ulama* are still a powerful force in society, resulting amongst other things from the new technologies which they have embraced to strengthen their position in society. The author of the next contribution, Abdulkader Tayob, thinks along the same lines, but broadens his geographical scope by not only looking at the position of the *ulama* in Indonesia, but also in South Africa and Egypt. The author ends his chapter by suggesting to look more carefully at the organization, role and instruments of the *ulama* in modern society.

The author of the fifth chapter, Didin Nurul Rosidin, deals with a hitherto little-explored Muslim mass organization in Indonesia, the Mathla'ul Anwar, and examines the contest for authority among the elites of the organization in the last years of the Soeharto administration. In the following chapter, Machasin deals with yet another aspect of religious authority in Indonesia and discusses the contest between formal religious institutions and the local *ulama*, which operate on a less formal and more personal level.

The seventh chapter, written by Arief Subhan, gives a broad overview of the Indonesian *madrasahs* and shows that these institutions are very diverse in nature and reproduced and transmit different concepts of religious authority, ranging from a curriculum which gives ample room to secular subjects to a purely Salafi understanding of Islam.

The chapter by Noorhaidi Hasan also examines the presence of the Salafi ideology in Indonesia and offers an interesting case study of a particular form of religious authority by going into the influence of the transnational contemporary Salafi *da'wa* movement. The author shows how the concept of *jihad* served as a vehicle to mobilize the radical Islamic organization Laskar Jihad in Post-New Order Indonesia. Andrée Feillard studies the reactions of the Javanese established holders of religious authority, the *ulama,* on the rise of new forms of this authority. These reactions are very different, ranging from indifference to feelings of incompetence to cope with the new situation.

The concluding chapter by Kees van Dijk underlines that most of the research of the previous contributions approaches the notion of religious authority by means of historical and sociological concepts and as a result tend to downplay the specific theological or "supernatural" dimension of the issues. The author shows how in a number of case studies this supernatural dimension was decisive in the outcome of particular historical events, thus making a plea for including this theological dimension in future research.

1

THE REDEFINITION OF RELIGIOUS AUTHORITY AMONG SOUTH ASIAN MUSLIMS FROM 1919 TO 1956

Marc Gaborieau

PROLOGUE: RELIGIOUS AUTHORITY IN ISLAM

Authority in the abstract sense — as distinguished from shear power, force or violence — can be defined in Weberian terms as the right to impose obedience in the name of common values and rules of conduct, shared by those who exercise this authority and those who are submitted to it (Hardy 1986, pp. 42–43). Religious authority means therefore the right to impose rules which are deemed to be in consonance with the will of God. In Islam, the very notion of authority is problematic, for it is vested in principle only in Allah, Who is the only sovereign, and Who does not delegate His right to frame rules, but only His command to obey His rules as known through revelation (Gardet 2002, p. 281). This situation is therefore different from that which prevails for instance in Christianity, where the Church, and those who rule it, are empowered to frame rules of conduct. In Islam, it is thus only in a secondary sense that those who relay the command of Allah are said to have authority. Therefore in this chapter we will use the term "authority" in this secondary sense.

Now through which channels is this command of Allah relayed? Which are the persons or institutions which transmit it to the believers, and can be considered as the holders of authority? It is not easy to answer this question, since in Islam there is no religious sphere completely separated from the profane sphere, where one could find a church, or a clergy with the exclusive monopoly of religious authority (Gardet 2002, p. 280). In fact, as I have argued elsewhere (Gaborieau and Zeghal 2004, pp. 6–8), the transmission of Allah's command follows three lines of delegation, which are not on the same plane.

The first two, which are more properly religious and can be combined in the same person are distinguished as two opposed ways of knowing God's command; they are traditionally termed exoteric (*zahiri*) and esoteric (*batini*).

The exoteric one is most often placed in the foreground. It is mediate in the sense that God's command is known only through sacred texts, that is to say the Qur'an and the Traditions (*Hadith*) of the Prophet. It is acquired through education in schools of religious sciences called *madrasahs*, where the main discipline taught is the science of jurisprudence (*fiqh*) and not theology as in the case of Christianity (see "Introduction" to Grandin and Gaborieau 1997). Those who master these religious sciences are called *ulama* (sing. *alim*). They are traditionally considered as the successors of the Prophet and as having a kind of monopoly on the transmission and interpretation of the divine law, the *sharia*. They have the triple role of transmitting religious knowledge, managing the cult in the mosques, and administering justice.

The esoteric way, on the contrary, gives immediate access to the divine realm, through mystical experiences which complement Prophetic revelation through dreams or illuminations called unveiling (*kashf*) or inspiration (*ilham*). Those who partake of it are called Sufis and are usually linked to mystical orders (Popovic and Veinstein 1996). All through the Middle Ages and the pre-modern period, the Sufi saint was an indispensable charismatic authority for rulers to establish and legitimize their power (Digby 1986).

The coexistence of these two ways raises problems. In the Middle Ages, they were usually united in the same persons, who could be called *ulama*/sufi and enjoyed a double authority founded on both knowledge of sacred texts and mystical experiences (Gaborieau 1989). In the modern period, with the development of Wahhabisme and modernism, the Sufi way, which has always been optional, came more and more under attack as a blameworthy innovation. One of the questions of this chapter will be about the resilience of the mystical path in the twentieth century.

But before coming to this point, we have to deal with the third line of delegation of Allah's command, political power, which constitutes the third pole of religious authority in Islam. Traditionally, the sovereign Caliph, Sultan or King — was considered as the shadow of God on earth, and was also endowed with religious authority. He had the responsibility of ensuring the smooth functioning of religious institutions, particularly the administering of divine law through the judges (*qadi*) he appointed, as repeatedly emphasized by the historiography of the Mughal empire in India (Hardy 1986, pp. 43–45). He had to repress excesses, fight heresies and arbitrate conflicts between *ulama* and Sufis, who in the last resort, submitted to him. Shall we therefore say that he was the supreme religious authority as I suggested elsewhere (Gaborieau 1989)? An Anglo-American school of South Asian history has developed a full-fledged argumentation investing Muslim kings with religious authority in the pre-modern period (Richards 1978 and 1984 ; Hardy 1986) in a research context where reflections on authority have been pervasive (Metcalf 1984; Gaborieau 1986). Shall we follow this line of thought?

SCOPE OF THE CHAPTER

This chapter will examine the evolution of the relations between the three poles of religious authority among the Muslims of the Indian subcontinent in a more recent period, from 1919 to 1956. The starting point has been chosen for two reasons: it is the second of two crucial periods which marked the religious evolution of the subcontinent in the modern period. The first was the reorganization of religious schools from 1818 onwards following the lead of a charismatic leader, Sayyid Ahmad Barelwi (1786–1831; see Gaborieau 2000b; Matringe 2005, pp. 51–82), both a Sufi and a jihad fighter, whose preaching caused the split of the religious schools between reformists (Deobandis, Ahl-i Hadith), traditionalists (Barelwis) and modernists (Aligarh) (Metcalf 1982; Gaborieau 2003). The second period which is the object of this chapter starts with the interval between the two world wars: this was a time of effervescence in most Muslim countries: a recent publication (Dupont and Mayeur-Jaouen 2002) has shown that the Indian events were part of this wider evolution. To mark the end of this second period, the proclamation of the first constitution of Pakistan in 1956 has been chosen as the time of crystallization of the political institutions of the subcontinent, where the Islamic Republic of Pakistan stands in contrast to the secular state established in India by the 1950 constitution.

Reflections on the evolution of religious authority in South Asia during this period have been scarce. Most of them deal with the religious history of the *ulama* and Sufis (Sanyal 1996, pp. 128–65; Buehler 1998, pp. 1–28), discussing the recent evolution of traditional religious leaders. Only a few study laymen turned politico-religious leaders, namely the Indian nationalist Abul Kalam Azad (1888–1958; see Douglas 1988, pp. 165–71 and 259–63) and the fundamentalist Pakistani leader Maududi (1903–79; see Nasr 1996, pp. 126–40). Professor Nasr raises in Weberian terms the question of a new definition of religious authority as millenarian and charismatic in connection with politics. Can we draw on these precedents to see whether our period has not enlarged the scope of religious authority by introducing a charismatic element?

This chapter has two parts. The first one examines the historical context of the Indian subcontinent after World War I and pinpoints the common trends of evolution. The second part locates, in comparison with the preceding periods, the discontinuities in the three poles of religious authority. The conclusion will try to assess how far did these evolutions and discontinuities alter the concept of religious authority. We will in this way refine and deepen questions already raised by Kenneth Cragg (1965) and Farzana Shaikh (1989) which I outlined in a short paper about this period (Gaborieau 2002).

THE HISTORICAL CONTEXT

General Background

Since it is important to have in mind the main problem facing the Indian Muslims at the time (Hardy 1972; Hasan 1991; Markovits 1994; Gaborieau and Jaffrelot 1994; Long 1998), we will first sketch the broader political context and then detail the more specific developments of the period.

After the repression of the 1857 Mutiny, and the definitive establishment of the *Pax Britannica* around 1872, Muslims had for some decades adopted a low profile. They either took an active loyalist stance, such as the modernists who followed Sayyid Ahmad Khan (1817–98) in the creation of the Aligarh Anglo-Oriental College (Lelyveld 1978); or chose to withdraw to religious studies without overt political involvement, as did the reformist *ulama* of Deoband (Metcalf 1982). Up until World War I, Muslims appeared as loyal subjects. Some of them, assembled in the Muslim League, a party founded in 1906, pushed a non-subversive claim: since Muslims were in a minority (more than 20 per cent), in order to protect their rights they asked, for a distinct political representation through separate electorates, which were granted before the war (Shaikh 1989). Other Muslims, who sided with the Hindus in the Congress Party founded in 1885, did not voice this demand.

After World War I, the situation of Indian Muslims became more complicated, as several claims, which were not entirely compatible, collided. We focus here on the two most important of them. First, the Muslims had to deal with the common claim of all Indians for political autonomy (and later independence): after the war, a new generation of Muslim leaders, notably Muhammad Ali (1878–31), opted to fight the British to gain autonomy; gradually all Muslims opted for this stance. The second question was of that of the place of the Muslim minority, in relation to the Hindu majority, in a politically autonomous India. Two options were defined successively, a process that led to a definitive split in the political attitudes of Muslims.

The first option was to form a joint Hindu-Muslim front, in order to create an undivided Indian nation where all religious communities would be on an equal plane. This solution was proposed first by Abul Kalam Azad, who took as a model the precedent of Egyptian nationalism, in which Muslims and Christians worked together (Douglas 1988, p. 85). It was adopted by the Association of the *Ulama* of India (*Jam'iyyatu'l-'ulama-i Hind*), which was founded in 1919 and soon came under the leadership of the Deoband school; they gave this option a theological justification on the basis of the Madina Pact in which the Prophet allied with the Jews in order to fight the Arab polytheists (Friedmann 1971 and 1986). In the beginning of our period, from 1919 to 1921, this political stance was accompanied by another campaign, the Khilafat Movement, in which Indian Muslims collaborated with Hindu nationalists led by Gandhi: they pressed the Turkish nationalists to maintain the Ottoman Sultan as the universal Caliph, whose authority would extend also to Indian Muslims. In this scheme, the latter would be Indian citizens, but would form a separate religious community, a *millat*, under the authority of the *ulama*, who would themselves obey the Caliph (Hardy 1971; Minault 1982; Bozdemir 1994). This scheme collapsed for two reasons: first on the larger scene, the Turkish eventually deposed the Sultan and no other Caliph could be found; second, after 1921 a series of riots in India between Hindus and Muslims broke their political cooperation. This quasi-medieval scheme of the caliphate, which was resuscitated in order to solve communal tension, was definitively outmoded. The way out was either to keep to it in a modernized form, or to adopt the second option. The *ulama*, keeping their alliance with the Congress Party, chose the first way, fighting for a united secular India, where Muslims would preserve their Personal Law as codified by the British, and would remain under the control of the *ulama*, who would be the supreme religious and quasi-political authority in the absence of a Caliph (Hardy 1971). A minority of lay "Nationalist Muslims" also chose to work with the Congress Party, but propounded more secularized forms of Islam (Troll 1995).

However, the bulk of lay politicians, in the framework of the Muslim League, progressively built a second, so-called "separatist", option, which led eventually to the creation of a separate state for the Muslims. This step was prepared by the protracted communal tensions between Hindus and Muslims throughout the 1920s, with riots, and attempts at conversions and re-conversions (Clementin-Ojha and Gaborieau 1994; Gaborieau 2002). The first formulation of this second option was made by Muhammad Iqbal (1877–1938) in his address to the Muslim League in 1930, and was finally taken up in 1940 as the official programme of the Muslim League by its new president, Muhammad Ali Jinnah (1876-1948) in the famous Lahore Resolution (Jalal 1985).

On the eve of World War II, two questions remained to be solved. First what would be the choice between the two options, i.e. a united India or a separate state for the Muslims? Who was to decide? On whose authority: that of the *ulama*, or of the lay politicians? The answer to this first question was to be given by the partition of the subcontinent between India and Pakistan in 1947. The second question was: what was to be the nature of the state, or the states, which would be set up after the departure of the British? Were they to be secular, i.e. neutral without any official religious authority? Or were they to be religious, with a Hindu state in India according to the model devised by the Hindu nationalists (Jaffrelot 1993) and, in Pakistan, an Islamic state according to the concept created by Abu'l-A'la Maududi as early as 1938 (Ahmed 1987)? Who would exercise religious authority, and which kind of authority in such a state? This second question was to be debated in the parliaments of the respective countries before the promulgation of the constitution of India in 1950 and of Pakistan in 1956.

Specific Politico-religious Trends

In addition to the greater political events outlined above, we may underscore the following evolutions which illustrate discontinuities in politico-religious authority.

In this period when religion invaded politics, in addition to the official apparition of the *ulama* in politics, there was also a growing involvement of lay scholars and politicians who posed as authoritative in religious matters. Most of them were men. We will describe many of them later, for example, Azad, Muhammad Ali, Maududi and finally Jinnah. Let us also mention the curious example of Muhammad Asad (1900–92), an Austrian Jew converted to Islam: after partition he was a civil servant in Pakistan and a rival of Maududi in propounding a theory of the Islamic state; he was later to influence Sayyid Qutb (Binder 1961; Heymann 2005). We have finally to mention, in the Indian context, another category of laymen, the modernist thinkers who produced innovative works on the place of Islam in a secular state, and on the modernization of religion (Troll 1995): the particular Indian context, where Muslims are in a minority, prompted them to more creative reflections than the Pakistan situation which is less conducive to original thinking. We may also notice from that time the progressive involvement of women, not only in politics, but also in religious questions, which were first dealt with by "secluded scholars" (Minault 1998), and progressively by more and more outspoken and unveiled ladies (Dedebant 2003). The rise of proselytizing movements, like Tablighi Jama'at in the 1920s, and the Jama'at-i Islami of Maududi in 1941, also enhanced the religious role of both lay men and women, who had to supplement the *ulama* in preaching, and partake somewhat of their authority (Ahmad 1991).

A second characteristic evolution of this period mainly under the influence of laymen was the return to an offensive theory of jihad. In the previous century, to counteract the accusation of having propagated Islam through the sword, the Indian Muslim had built an apologetic theory of jihad as a purely defensive war. With the growing confrontation of the Indian Muslims with the British and then with the Hindus (Jaffrelot 1993), the classical theory of jihad as an all-out, offensive as well as defensive war, was revived first by Azad and then by Maududi; the latter became famous with his 1927 book in Urdu called *Al-jihad fi'l-Islam*, which was warmly applauded by the Deobandi *ulama* and praised for having restored the broken pride of Indian Muslims (Nasr 1996, pp. 22–23).

A third legacy of the troubled period of the 1920s was what has been called the "rise of proselytism" (Clementin-Ojha and Gaborieau 1994) with a flowering of Muslim and Hindu missionary organizations, one of which, the Tablighi Jama'at, has spread all over the world post-1947 (Gaborieau 1997; Masud 2000). Other religious movements, as different as the traditionalist Barelwis (Sanyal 1996 and 2005) and the fundamentalist Jama'at-i Islami (founded by Maududi), have been deeply involved in proselytism (Ahmad 1991; Troll 1994).

This leads us to the fourth characteristic evolution of this period: the reversal relations with the Middle East. Whilst up to the 1920s Indian Muslim would look to the Middle East for religious as well as political inspiration, after the end of the Khilafat movement the trend was reversed. Indian Muslims became conscious of their creativity and tried to export it either by spreading their organizational skill, as was the case for Tablighi Jama'at after 1947, or by diffusing their thought through translations in Arabic: Maududi started to do so from the early 1940s and was to be a great inspiration for Middle Eastern Islamists; Abu'l-Hasan Ali Nadwi (1914–99), who was incidentally the first translator of Maududi into Arabic and was later instrumental in the diffusion of the Tablighi Jama'at in the Arab world, did so for his own writings (including his criticism of Maududi).

EVOLUTION OF RELIGIOUS AUTHORITY

In order to gauge the evolution of religious authority during this period we will examine successively the three categories of holder of this authority as defined in the prologue of this chapter and see how they fared.

Sufis Recede to the Background

Sufism in South Asia is in a paradoxical situation. On the one side, traditional practices at Muslim shrines are still very alive (Troll 1989; Ernst and Lawrence 2002). Sufism is also an important ideological asset to counteract the accusation of spreading Islam through the sword: conversions are believed to have been peacefully achieved by Sufi "missionaries". On the other side, criticisms of Sufi devotions have been continuously pouring out for two centuries, voiced by the Wahhabis, the modernists and the fundamentalists (Gaborieau 1999; Metcalf 1982: *passim*). External manifestations of Sufi devotions are condemned, or at least despised. The reformists like the Deobandis who have retained a minimal Sufi practice keep it in the private sphere (Metcalf 1982, pp. 157–97).

The only reformist school which has vindicated the full Sufi heritage, is that of the Barelwis (Sanyal 1996 and 2005) who have been joined by the Naqshbandis (Buehler 1998); their practice of Sufism may be compared to that of the Indonesian Nahdlatul Ulama. However, they do not have the same political importance, for the Barelwis did not actively participate in the political process, except rather recently and marginally in Pakistan. Such self-avowed Sufis remain very influential in the private sphere, but are kept in the background of the public sphere.

Ulama Come to the Foreground

One of the great events of the twentieth century, as Wilfred Cantwell Smith has underlined long ago (Smith 1963), has been the coming to the foreground of the *ulama* in their capacity as experts of the exoteric knowledge. This trend started in the second half of the nineteenth century in India with the foundation of the three great schools of *ulama* which put a greater emphasis on exoteric knowledge, namely the Deobandis, the Ahl-i Hadith and the Nadwatu'l-'*Ulama* (Metcalf 1982; Matringe 2005, pp. 62–82). This trend became more manifest from 1919 when the *ulama* officially entered politics with the Khilafat movement. The lead was given by the older school of Farangi Mahall, which was instrumental in the foundation of the Association of the *Ulama* of India in 1919 (Robinson 1980 and 2001), an organization that posed as the official religious authority for Indian Muslims in the political field. The leadership of this organization was soon captured by the Deobandis, who kept it till the end of the British Raj. They publicized a very elaborate doctrine of the role of the *ulama* in an United India, and of their control of the religious and social life (Hardy 1971 and 1972).

Post-1947, the Association of the *Ulama* of India remained the official interlocutor for the Indian Union, in connection with Deoband and the Nadwatu'l-'Ulama, to preserve the Muslim institutions, particularly the personal law (Gaborieau 1996; Matringe 2005, pp. 38–46). The most famous spokesman for the *ulama* in India and abroad was the famous Abu'l-Hasan 'Ali Nadwi. In Pakistan, after Partition, two rival associations arose (Binder 1961): the Barelwi one (Association of the Ulama of Pakistan) remained marginal; the Deobandi one (Association of the Ulama of Islam) was prominent and tried to influence the Islamization of the state; its principal spokesman was Muhammad Shafi' (1897–1976), a former mufti of Deoband.

It would therefore seem that the *ulama*, who were so well organized for political action in both India and Pakistan, should stand as the final religious authority and have the last say on the question of the place of Islam in the political institutions. But that was not the case. They were outdone by a new kind of charismatic leaders.

Rise of Charismatic Religio-political Leaders

Actually, more innovative than the coming of the *ulama* to the foreground, was the apparition of charismatic political leaders with religious pretensions. The tone had been set as early as 1919 by the strange alliance of the most charismatic of the Hindu leaders, Gandhi, and a traditional Muslim scholar turned politician, Abdul Bari (1878–1926; see Robinson 1980) to launch simultaneously the Khilafat movement and the non-cooperation movement as a prelude to the independence of India.

Most of the other charismatic leaders were laymen. We may mention Muhammad Ali (1878–1931; see Hasan 1981) who was the main organizer of the Khilafat movement and posed also as a religious man; although he died prematurely in 1931, he had a lasting influence on several generations of Muslim leaders, notably on Maududi who attributed his "conversion" to him. Muhammad Iqbal (Matringe 2005, pp. 83–86), poet, lawyer, philosopher and political man, laid the theoretical foundation of Muslim separatism and of the creation in the subcontinent of a separate Islamic state which was to be called Pakistan. But before and after them the two most striking examples, who have been the objects of recent detailed biographies, were Azad and Maududi on whom we will concentrate now.

Abul Kalam Azad (Douglas 1988; Hasan 1992) was born in 1888 in Madina from an Indian Sufi father and an Arabian mother. He was educated in India by private tutors and was a child prodigy with a wide knowledge of the intellectual life in the whole Muslim world which he could acquire through his mastery of Arabic, his mother tongue. He entered public life before World War I through his Urdu journal *Al-Hilal*, in which he aroused the enthusiasm of Indian Muslims to fight for the independence of their country and the glory of Islam. It is in this context that he rehabilitated the offensive jihad; he was congratulated for that by the Deobandi *ulama*. He was interned by the British during the war; after the end of hostilities, he emerged as a charismatic leader. He joined hands with the Congress Party and the *ulama* to launch the Khilafat movement: he was its main theorist. He also aspired to be its leader: to this end he forged the concept of a new position, that of *amir-i Hind*, Amir of India, destined to be the sole chief, with wide religious and judicial prerogatives, of the Indian Muslim community, and its sole representative before the Caliph in Istanbul. To prove that he was worthy of this role, he posed as possessed of extraordinary gifts as the renovator (*mujaddid*) of the age, and even as the promised *mahdi* who was to bring back perfection at the end of the world. Under pressure of *ulama*, he regained his composure and from then on led a more serene life as Congress leader, commentator of the Qur'an and finally Education Minister of India from 1947 to his death in 1958. But he had set the tone for a new kind of charismatic leadership.

As emphasized by the biographer of Azad (Douglas 1988, pp. 262–63), Abu'l-A'la Maududi (Adams 1966 and 1983; Nasr 1994 and 1996) took on as his lifelong ambition, the charismatic programme of the young Azad. Born in 1903 of a Sufi father, at an early age he had to earn his living as a journalist managing a newspaper of the Association of the Ulama of India; he took this opportunity to acquire a training in religious sciences. In mid-1920, a sermon by Muhammad Ali in the great mosque of Delhi convinced him that he had a God-given mission to renovate the Muslim community of India. He became famous, as already mentioned, in 1927 by his book on jihad. He then acquired a religious journal, *Tarjuman al-Quran*, where he expressed up to his death his religious and political thought and published in installments his commentary on the Qur'an. At the end of the 1930s he had framed his theory of the Islamic state; he began to pose as a kind of *mujaddid* or even *mahdi*, engaged in a millenarian crusade. He started gathering around him a group of devout followers who formed the kernel of his organization, the Jama'at-i Islami, founded in 1941 and turned into a political party in Pakistan in 1956. In 1947 he chose to join Pakistan to make it an Islamic state; he was the main theorist to influence the debate about the Islamic constitution (Binder 1961; Gaborieau 2000a). Although he had to make many compromises and obtained very few substantive constitutional clauses, he succeeded in having Pakistan proclaimed an Islamic Republic. He spent the rest of his life fighting with his party for a more substantial Islamization of the State of Pakistan. Although he is often considered as a cold rationalist and activist, a recent biography has shown that he remained throughout his life faithful to the inspiration of his youth, and always considered himself as divinely inspired, with no authority above himself. He is still venerated by his close disciples as a charismatic figure (Nasr 1999, pp. 127–40).

We must now emphasize a very important fact: these lay charismatic leaders had more influence on the course of the events than the *ulama*. Two instances may illustrate this statement. The first one was the partition of the subcontinent in 1947; the Indian *ulama* had by a large majority opposed this step and stood for a united multi-religious India; those who joined the Muslim League and Jinnah in their demand for Pakistan were a tiny minority led mainly by two famous Deobandi scholars, Ashraf 'Ali Thanawi and Muhammad Shafi'. Nevertheless, almost all the Muslim voters in the elections of 1945–46 opted for Pakistan. As a leading historian has stressed long ago (Hardy 1969), the Muslim community ignored the traditional authority of the *ulama*, to follow in a more archaic way a charismatic leader, who had built on the plans of Iqbal for a separate Muslim state; this was none other than Muhammad Ali Jinnah (1876–1948): in spite of his proverbial coldness, he had know from the beginning of his career how to mobilize the crowds in the name of Islam; he devised the strategy to obtain a massive vote in favour of Pakistan, bypassing the apparently well established authority of the *ulama*. The second instance is the debate in Pakistan for framing a constitution (Binder 1961; Gaborieau 2000a) between 1948 and 1956. It would seem that the *ulama*, who had organized in two rival (Deobandi and Barelwi) national associations, should have come forward as the most efficient proponents of a demand for an Islamic constitution. They proved to be unprepared, having nothing more in mind than the outmoded model of the medieval caliphate; they had to give way to Maududi. He had come forward with a more modern theory of the Islamic state, which he had framed as early as 1938. He was, following Binder's phrase, the real leader and "catalyst" of the debate (Binder 1961, p. 70). He imposed that Pakistan be declared, at least in name, an "Islamic Republic".

CONCLUSION

We have now to draw the lessons from our analysis: has religious authority changed during these four decades? There is clearly a double change. First in the identity of the holders of this authority. They are neither the Sufis nor the *ulama*. It is remarkable that the most important decisions for the future of the South Asian Muslim community — namely partition of the subcontinent in 1947, and the transformation of Pakistan into an Islamic state in 1956 — have been taken following the lead of laymen Iqbal, Jinnah and Maududi. The second change is in the nature of the authority: eschewing both mystical inspiration and rational argumentation, these leaders, imbued with their own mission, built on messianic aspirations of the Muslim community and played on their own charisma.

The importance of religious charisma among political laymen has endured. The most spectacular evolution in Pakistan was again triggered by another charismatic leader, a populist orator who invoked religious authority to thrill his audience: Zulfiqar Ali Bhutto (1928–79) is wrongly viewed as a secular democratic leader: in fact he consciously and systematically used Islam to legitimize his internal and external politics. He did more than anybody else — even his successor Zia-ul-Haq who is usually blamed for that — to promote the Islamic identity of Pakistan, and to Islamize its institutions (Jaffrelot 2000, pp. 241 and 415–17 [English translation 137 and 245–46]; see Gaborieau 2000a).

To come back to the question we asked in the introduction, Professor Nasr was right in pointing out that charismatic millenarian religious authority, embodied in lay politicians, was the real innovation since the third decade of the twentieth century. It supplanted the more legal-rational form of authority, in Weberian terms, which was promoted by the British colonization, and adopted in varying measures by the modernists and by traditionalist *ulama* like the Deobandis. It revived in a way a type of leadership which had been illustrated in the early nineteenth century by Sayyid Ahmad Barelwi. But while the later was the last avatar of medieval modes of leadership (Gaborieau 2000b), the new millenarism, as exemplified by Azad and Maududi, was a prefiguration of Islamism as promoted later for instance in Egypt (Carré 1984). This recent epilogue should read as a caution against the dangers of charismatic leadership; it also illustrates the limits of the authority of the *ulama*, which can be easily bypassed.

References

Adams, Charles J. "The Ideology of Mawlana Mawdudi". In *South Asian Politics and Religion*, edited by Donald E. Smith. Princeton: Princeton University Press, 1966, pp. 371–97.

———. "Mawdudi and the Islamic State". In *Voices of Resurgent Islam*, edited by John L. Esposito. New York: Oxford University Press, 1983, pp. 99–133.

Ahmad, Mumtaz. "Islamic Fundamentalism in South Asia: The Jama'at-i-Islami and the Tablighi Jama'at". In *Fundamentalism Observed*, edited by Martin E. Marty & Scott Appleby, vol. I. Chicago: University of Chicago Press, 1991, pp. 457–530.

Ahmed, Ishtiaq. *The Concept of an Islamic State: An Analysis of the Ideological Controversy in Pakistan.* London: Frances Pinter, 1987.

Binder, Leonard. *Religion and Politics in Pakistan.* Berkeley: University of California Press, 1961.

Bozdemir, Michel. "La question du califat". *Les Annales de l'autre Islam*, no. 2 (special issue 1994).

Buehler, Arthur F. *Sufi Heirs of the Prophet: The Indian Naqshbandiyya and the Rise of the Mediating Shaykh.* Columbia: University of South Carolina Press, 1998.

Carré, Olivier. *Mystique et Politique. Lecture révolutionnaire du Coran par Sayyid Qutb, frère musulman radical*, Paris, Presses de la FNSP/Le Cerf, 1984, 1984.

Clementin-Ojha, Catherine & Marc Gaborieau. "La montée du prosélytisme dans le sous-continent Indien", *Archives de Sciences Sociales des Religions*, no. 87 (1994): 13–33.

Cragg, Kenneth. *Counsels in Contemporary Islam.* Islamic Surveys No. 3. Edinburgh: Edinburgh University Press, 1965.

Dedebant, Christèle. *Le voile et la bannière. L'avant-garde féministe au Pakistan.* Paris: CNRS-Éditions, 2003.

Digby, Simon. "The Sufi Shaikh as a Source of Authority in Mediaeval India". In *Islam et Société en Asie du Sud/Islam and Society in South Asia*, edited by Marc Gaborieau. Paris: EHESS, 1986, pp. 57–77.

Douglas, Ian Henderson, *Abul Kalam Azad: An Intellectual and Religious Biography*, edited by Gail Minault & Christian W. Troll. Delhi: Oxford University Press, 1988.

Dupont, Anne-Laure & Catherine Mayeur-Jaouen. "Débats intellectuels au Moyen-Orient dans l'entre-deux-guerres". *Revue des Mondes Musulmans et de la Méditerranée*, no. 95-98/1 (special issue 2002).

Ernst, Carl W. & Bruce B. Lawrence. *Sufi Martyrs of Love: The Chisti Martyrs of Love.* New York: Palgrave Macmillan, 2002.

Friedmann, Yohanan. "The Attitude of the *Jam'iyyat-i 'Ulama'-i Hind* to the Indian National Movement". *Asian and African Studies* (Haïffa), vol. 7, 1971, pp. 157–80. [Reprint in Mushirul Hasan. *Inventing Boundaries: Gender, Politics and the Partition of India.* New Delhi: Oxford University Press, 2000, pp. 157–79.]

———. 1986, "Islamic Thought in relation to the Indian Context". In *Islam et*

Société en Asie du Sud/Islam and Society in South Asia, edited by Marc Gaborieau. Paris: EHESS, 1986, pp. 79-91.

Gaborieau, Marc, ed. *Islam et Société en Asie du Sud/Islam and Society in South Asia*, Collection Purushârtha, no. 9. Paris, EHESS, 1986.

———. 1989, "Les oulémas/soufis dans l'Inde moghole: Anthropologie historique de religieux musulmans". *Annales ESC*, no. 5 (1989): 1185–204.

———. "Les musulmans de l'Inde: Une minorité de 100 millions d'âmes". In *L'Inde contemporaine de 1950 à nos jours*, edited by Christopher Jaffrelot. Paris: Fayard, 1996, pp. 466–93.

———. "Renouveau de l'Islam ou stratégie politique occulte? La Tablîghî Jamâ`at dans le sous-continent indien et dans le monde", in *Renouveaux religieux en Asie*, edited by Catherine Clementin-Ojha. Paris: Ecole Française d'Extrême Orient, 1997, pp. 211–29.

———. "Criticizing the Sufis: The Debate in Early-Nineteenth-Century India". In *Islamic Mysticism Contested: Thirteen Centuries of Controversies and Polemics*, edited by Frederick De Jong & Bernd Radtke. Leiden: Brill, 1999, pp. 452–67.

———. "Islam et Politique au Pakistan". In *Le Pakistan*. Paris: Fayard, 2000a, pp. 393–416. (English translation, *A History of Pakistan and Its Origins*, edited by Christophe Jaffrelot. London: Anthem Press, 2002*a*, pp. 235–49).

———. 2000b, "Le mahdî oublié de l'Inde Britannique: Sayyid Ahmad Barelwî (1786–1831), ses disciples et ses adversaires". *Revue des mondes musulmans et de la Méditerranée*, no. 91–94 (2000): 257–73. Special issue *Mahdisme et millénarisme*, edited by Mercedes Garcia-Arenal.

———. "L'Inde de 1919 à 1941: Nationalismes, 'Communalisme', Prosélytisme et Fondamentalisme". *Revue des mondes musulmans et de la Méditerranée* , no. 95–98/1 (2002): 111–25. Special issue *Débats intellectuels au Moyen-Orient dans l'entre-deux-guerres*, edited by Anne-Laure Dupont & Catherine Mayeur-Jaouen.

———. " 'Wahhabisme' et modernisme: Généalogie du réformisme religieux en Inde". In *Le Courant réformiste musulman et sa réception dans les sociétés arabes*, edited by Maher Al-Charif, & Salam Kawakibi. Damas: Institut Français du Proche-Orient, 2003, pp. 115–38.

Gaborieau, Marc & Christophe Jaffrelot. "Réformes religieuses et nationalisme". In *Histoire de l'Inde moderne, 1480–1950*, edited by Claude Markovits. Paris: Fayard, chap XXIV, 1994, pp. 540–60. (English translation, *A History of Modern India, 1480–1950*. London: Anthem Press, 2002, pp. 450–67.)

Gaborieau, Marc & Malika Zeghal. "Autorités Religieuses en Islam". *Archives de sciences sociales des religions*, no. 125 (2004): 5–21.

Gardet, Louis. *L'islam: Religion et communauté*. 2nd edition (first published 1967). Paris: Desclée de Brouwer, 2002.

Grandin, Nicole & Marc Gaborieau. *Madrasa: La transmission du Savoir dans le Monde Musulman*. Paris: Editions Arguments, 1997.

Hardy, Peter. "The `*Ulamâ* of British India". Conference paper (reprinted in *Journal of Indian History*, Jubelee volume, 1973). London: SOAS, 1969.

———. *Partners in Freedom — and True Muslims: The Political Thought of Some Muslim Scholars in British India, 1912–1947.* Stockholm: Scandinavian Institute of Asian Studies, 1971.

———. *The Muslims of British India.* Cambridge: Cambridge University Press, 1972. Reprinted in Delhi, India: Cambridge University Press, 1998.

———. "The Authority of Muslim Kings in Mediaeval India". In *Islam et société en Asie du Sud/Islam and Society in South Asia,* edited by Marc Gaborieau. Paris: EHESS, 1986, pp. 37–55.

Hasan, Mushirul, *Mohamed Ali: Ideology and Politics.* New Delhi: Manohar, 1981.

———. *Nationalism and Communal Politics in India.* New Delhi: Manohar, 1991.

———, ed. *Islam and Indian Nationalism: Reflections on Abul Kalam Azad.* New Delhi: Manohar, 1992.

Heymann, Florence. *Un Juif pour l'islam.* Paris: Stock, 2005.

Jaffrelot, Christophe. *Les nationalistes hindous: Idéologie, implantation et mobilisation des années 1920 aux années 1980.* Paris: Presses de la FNSP, 1993. (Revised English translation: *The Hindu Nationalist Movement and Indian Politics, 1925 to 1990.* Londres: Hurst & Co, 1996).

———, ed. *Le Pakistan.* Paris: Fayard, 2000 (English translation, *A History of Pakistan and Its Origins.* London: Anthem Press, 2002).

Jalal, Ayesha. *The Sole Spokesman: Jinnah, the Muslim League and the Demand for Pakistan.* Cambridge: Cambridge University Press, 1985.

Lelyveld, David. *Aligarh's First Generation: Muslim Solidarity in British India.* Princeton: Princeton University Press, 1978. (2nd edition, New Delhi: Oxford University Press, 1996).

Long, Roger D. *The Founding of Pakistan: An Annotated Bibliography.* Lanham, Maryland: The Scarecrow Press, 1998.

Markovits, Claude. *Histoire de l'Inde moderne, 1480–1950.* Paris: Fayard, 1994. (English translation, *A History of Modern India, 1480–1950.* London: Anthem Press, 2002.)

Masud, Khalid. *Travellers in Faith: Studies of the Tablîghî Jamâ'at as a Transnational Islamic Movement for Faith Renewal,* Leyde: E.J. Brill, 2000.

Matringe, Denis. *Un islam non arabe: Horizons indiens et pakistanais.* Paris: Téraèdre, 2005.

Metcalf, Barbara Daly. *Islamic Revival in British India: Deoband, 1860–1900.* Princeton: Princeton University Press, 1982.

———. *Moral Conduct and Authority: The Place of Adab in South Asian Islam.* Berkeley: University of California Press, 1984.

Minault, Gail. *The Khilafat Movement: Religious Symbolism and Political Mobilisation in India.* Delhi: Oxford University Press, 1982.

———. *Secluded Scholars: Women's Education and Social Reform in Colonial India.* Delhi: Oxford University Press, 1998.

Nasr, Seyyed Vali Reza. *The Vanguard of Islamic Revolution: The Jama'at-i Islami of Pakistan.* Londres: I.B. Tauris, 1994.

———. *Mawdudi and the Making of Islamic Revivalism.* New York: Oxford University Press, 1996.

Popovic, Alexandre & Gilles Veinstein. *Les Voies d'Allah: Les ordres mystiques dans le Monde musulman des origines à aujourd'hui.* Paris: Fayard, 1996.

Richards, John F., ed. "The Formulation of Imperial Authority under Akbar and Jahangir". In *Kingship and Authority in South Asia.* Madison: University of Wisconsin Publication Series, 1978, pp. 252–85.

———. "Norms of Comportment among Mughal Imperial Officers". In *Moral Conduct and Authority: The Place of Adab in South Asian Islam,* by Barbara D. Metcalf. Berkeley: University of California Press, 1984, pp. 255–89.

Robinson, Francis, Art. "'Abd al-Bari". In *Encyclopaedia of Islam.* 2nd edition. Leiden: E.J. Brill, 1980. Supplement, fasc. 1–2, pp. 4–5.

———. *The 'Ulama of Farangi Mahall and Islamic Culture in South Asia.* London and Delhi: C. Hurst & Co, and Permanent Black, 2001.

Sanyal, Usha. *Devotional Islam & Politics in British India: Ahmad Riza Khan Barelwi and his Movement, 1870–1920.* New Delhi: Oxford University Press, 1996.

———. *Ahmad Riza Khan Barelwi: In the Path of the Prophet.* Oxford: Oneworld Publications, 2005.

Shaikh, Farzana. *Community and Consensus in Islam: Muslim Representation in Colonial India, 1860–1947.* Cambridge: Cambridge University Press, 1989.

Smith, W. Cantwell. "The *'ulamâ'* in Indian Politics". In *Politics and Society in India,* edited by C.H. Philips. London: George Allen & Unwin Ltd, 1963, pp. 39–51.

Troll, Christian W. *Muslim Shrines in India.* 2nd edition with a "Preface" by Marc Gaborieau, 2003. Delhi: Oxford university Press, 1989.

———. "Two Conceptions of Da'wa in India: Jamâ'at-i Islâmî and Tablîghî Jamâ'at".*'Archives de sciences sociales des religions,* no. 87 (1994): 115–33.

———. "Sharing Islamically in the Pluralistic Nation-State of India: The Views of Some Contemporary Indian Muslim Leaders and Thinkers". In *Christian-Muslim Encounters,* edited by Y.Y. Haddad & W.Z. Haddad. Gainesville: University Press of California, 1995, pp. 245–62.

2

UNDERSTANDING *AL-IMAM'S* CRITIQUE OF *TARIQA* SUFISM

Michael Laffan

The dissemination of Islam in Indonesia in the twentieth century has been a process inextricably bound up with the active engagement of Southeast Asians with their emerging national communities. As Benedict Anderson has argued, such communities were increasingly "imagined" from the nineteenth century through the crucial engine of "print capitalism", both regionally and in the world at large, and in ways that superseded older faith-based identities (Anderson 1991). For the Indonesian case though, I have argued that this process of imagining was more complicated, and that it drew upon, and was reinforced by, the communal experiences of Muslim pilgrims as they crossed the well-worn paths of their home isles or were carried by steamers across the sea-lanes of the Indian Ocean (Laffan 2003).

Over time, many such sojourners would return to their home ports or hinterland communities with thoughts about their faith, their place in the world, and how the practice of the former might impact on the rank of the latter. Certainly the debates that were set in motion — most often concerning modernity, independence and reform — suffused the growing public sphere. Indeed they had their after-effects well into the end of the twentieth century, although the present state of doctrinal alignments — between "modernists", "traditionalists" and (more recently) "Salafists", tends to obscure the instabilities and shifting nature of the positions taken by their forerunners.

In this chapter I therefore wish to revisit an early stage in the process of "modern" religious change in Southeast Asia by a close textual analysis of passages in the seminal Malay journal *al-Imam* (The Leader). I shall do so mainly in order to ascertain the extent to which its programme aligned with that imputed to the Cairo-based Muslim reformers Muhammad 'Abduh (1849–1905) and Rashid Rida (1865–1935). More specifically, I will examine the arguments that were voiced in respect of the acceptable role of Sufism in the modern world. Here I shall argue that just as Muslim national imaginings in Southeast Asia had to draw on earlier, religiously-based, modalities of exchange, the editors of *al-Imam* should be seen as transitional figures emerging from an internal learned critique rather than presenting an absolute break with the past. It is also my contention that by opting more clearly, and indeed condescendingly, for this abrasive in mid-1908, the editors of this journal may well have sowed the seeds for its failure by alienating what may well have been a large part of their readership.

In any case, they sowed the seeds for both the exacerbation of arguments between so-called Kaum Muda ("young pople") and Kaum Tua ("old people") in the region, and perhaps even between Arabs and Malays. In regard to this last point, I suggest that, well before the political alliance of the Cairene Salafiyya movement and the Wahhabiyya crystallized in the 1920s, a key group of Sayyids, so-called by virtue of their genealogical claims to descent from the Prophet, would find it increasingly hard to remain at the helm of *al-Imam* and sustain their self-proclaimed position as leaders of the Islamic community. This was because as they were reaching out to other Muslims above the winds, the style of reformism that they were drawing on, while valorising the early, Arab, days of Islam, was nonetheless denying their own claims to authority.[1] As I will suggest, it was the very instability and, ultimately, the perceived incompatibility of Sayyid and Malay objectives that saw each pursue their own, increasingly nationalized, paths to the Islamic modern (either with or without the *tariqa*s or mystical "orders").

BUILDING A BRIDGE TO MECCA AND THE NINETEENTH CENTURY

Lately, Martin van Bruinessen has reprised some of his earlier work on the Naqshbandiyya *tariqa* and its impact in Southeast Asia from the latter part of the nineteenth century (Van Bruinessen, 2008). Drawing on both collective memory in Indonesia in the 1980s and 1990s and the work of Snouck Hurgronje (1857–1936) a century before that, he has traced the trajectories of the competing lines of the Khalidiyya branch, whose centre was located on the hill of Abu Qubays in Mecca.[2] In so doing, Van Bruinessen casts much light on the subsequent developments (and indeed discontinuities) of the Khalidiyya in Sumatra and Java before and after the deaths of the rival shaykhs, and the suppression of open *tariqa* activities by the Saudi regime.

In this article too, Van Bruinessen draws on the literature connected to the works briefly promulgated from Singapore by the Mecca-based Isma'il al-Minankabawi (a.k.a. Minangkabawi) in the 1850s, who was heavily criticized by a local Hadrami shaykh, Salim bin Sumayr, and then the anti-*tariqa* epistles launched from the Mecca, and released in print in Cairo and Padang between 1906 and 1908, by Ahmad Khatib al-Minankabawi (1860–1915). Broadly based as this article is though, its Indonesian focus — by which I mean that the actors are linkable to debates among Indonesians-in-the-making in the Hijaz, and the future Indonesian locales of West Sumatra and Java — has the unintended effect of occluding the wider discourse about Sufism and its discontents marshalled at the time Ahmad Khatib was writing, and by an imagined community that one can link just as readily to the post-colonial entities of Malaysia and Thailand. Indeed, before I turn to look at the presentation of Sufism in a journal often claimed from the northern side of the Straits of Malacca, but seldom by Indonesians, I wish to briefly highlight the opinions of one Mecca-based scholar from Patani, Ahmad bin Muhammad Zayn al-Fatani (1856–1906/7), who was appointed to run the Malay subsection of the official Ottoman printing press in Mecca shortly before Snouck's visit there in 1885.

My reasons for so doing will become clearer below. Yet before I proceed I should note that Werner Kraus (1999) has already linked al-Fatani and *al-Imam* as contemporary authorities for questions on Sufism arising at Kelantan, postulating that each dealt with the same issue, and perhaps even the exact same question. Where I would differ from Kraus is in the use of sources, and most especially for *al-Imam*, as his interpretation of the latter rested on translations provided in the work of Abu Bakar Hamzah (1991), whose reading of that journal is in my view too much informed by his own reformist position.[3] Still, to understand the atmosphere in which *al-Imam* was promulgated, we should certainly follow Kraus's lead and link these discussions.

Ahmad bin Muhammad Zayn al-Fatani was just one member of a distinguished family that had long played a role in linking Meccan scholarship to the Malayo-Muslim "Jawi" tradition in mainland Southeast Asia (Matheson and Hooker 1988, pp. 28–30). What made him stand out though was his seminal role in printing that scholarship from Mecca, at a time when Cairo was coming to play a major role in the production of such texts for the Jawi market. According to his descendant, Wan Mohd. Shaghir Abdullah, al-Fatani ventured to Cairo around 1880, and worked for a time checking Jawi (i.e., Arabic script Malay) books in production there, either in the famous bookshop established by Mustafa al-Babi al-Halabi, or perhaps at the office of the Government Printing Office.[4] The latter is more likely, I suspect, and seems to have formed the connections that saw him promoted to the director of that press when its Meccan office was opened in 1884.

Clearly al-Fatani visualized a market for Jawi books, but it was one for traditional fare. Hence he saw to it that a significant proportion of the offerings of the Meccan press (some twelve books) were the printed versions of *fiqh* written by former and contemporary generations of Jawi scholars, including himself. As far as the question of Sufism goes, these works were by and large restrained glosses of extant works, and not the aggressively polemical critiques of Sayyid 'Uthman (1822–1914), who recycled Bin Sumayr's attacks on Isma'il al-Minankabawi, and was then commencing his assaults on the mystics of West Java from his redoubt in Batavia.

This is not to say though that Sayyid 'Uthman was not an upholder of Sufi-tinted ideals, for he certainly was, and in his polemical tracts, such as his often cited (and still printed) *Manhaj al-istiqama fi al-din bi al-salama* (Programme for the safe practice of religion), published in the wake of the Ciligon uprising of 1888, he drew regularly on the works of al-Ghazali (1058–1111) and Ibn Hajar al-'Asqalani (1372–1449), not to mention Muhammad Arshad al-Banjari (1710–1812) and the Mecca-based Nawawi of Banten (1813–97), who had already staked a claim to be the ultimate authority for many Javanese in the 1880s and 1890s.[5] This was certainly apparent to Snouck Hurgronje on his visit to Mecca, holding Nawawi up thereafter in his *magnum opus* as an exemplar — if a self-effacing one — of what he chose to call "ethical" or yet "scientific" Sufism (Snouck Hurgronje 1931, pp. 268–72, 284).

Over time, al-Fatani, who also attracted Snouck Hurgronje's attention as "a savant of merit" (Snouck Hurgronje 1931, pp. 286–87), would make his name much like Nawawi, but as the primary authority for the Malays of the Peninsula and what is now Thailand and Cambodia, rather than Java or yet Indonesia. It was most likely for this reason that he was the authority sought at some time around 1905 by Raja Muhammad IV of Kelantan (a Malay state that would remain under Siamese suzerainty until 1909), who wrote to Mecca for an opinion on the purported practices of a Sufi order whose teacher, named as "Haji Encik 'Id bin Haji Encik Din Linggi, a student (*anak murid*) of Shaykh Muhammad Dandarawi", had arrived in the area in the year of writing and had gathered some *murid* of his own (al-Fatani 1957, pp. 179–80).

According to Kraus (1999, pp. 741–42), the group in question was a branch of the Ahmadiyya-Rashidiyya led at Kota Bharu by a Minangkabau born in Negeri Sembilan called Muhammad Said bin Jamal al-Din al-Linggi (1875–1926). Kraus also states that al-Linggi had returned to the Peninsula in 1900, and that he represented one of four branches of the Ahmadiyya to find a home on the Malay Peninsula at the end of the nineteenth century.

In his request, the Raja of Kelantan asked about the implications of assemblies where men and women, both young and old, came together. More especially, he was concerned about the ecstatic visions reported by those participants who had become *majdhub* or "attracted" (from the verbal noun *jadhba*):[6]

> There are some who believe in affirming that the *tariqa* of Haji Enjik Id is correct, and some do not. Thus, could your Excellency clarify [the matter] here? For I want to know about the matter of *majdhub* that has occurred. And in what way shall I actually indicate the situation in which *majdhub* might properly occur? This is because, in the space of two to three days, immature youngsters become excessively *majdhub*; even more so than fully responsible and mature adults. It is not that I do not believe that this course [could be valid], but that I have not yet heard [whether it is], for there has not been as yet anyone in Kelantan who has carried out such worship. Hopefully we can get a text or indubitable proof that can be discussed at length in answer to the aforementioned words, such as they are.[7]

In his preamble to the *fatwa*, written in 1324 (1906–07),[8] al-Fatani cites references to the need for the mutual consideration of law (*fiqh*) and Sufism (*tasawwuf*) before he writes of having once been "received" into the Ahmadiyya by its people, it being "a *tariqa* the like of the one mentioned in this question", but that his experiences in relation to the matter of "attraction" (*jadhba*) differed (al-Fatani 1957, pp. 180–81). Hence he had consulted with the local *ulama* of the day who served as a bridge between the "two seas" of juridical and mystical knowledge (*mengangkatkan sual ini kepada ahli masa ini daripada ulama yang menghimpunkan antara dua laut yang tersebut*) (al-Fatani 1957, p. 181). That said, no answer was immediately forthcoming, and what followed was therefore derived from his extensive reading of the words of the Sufis (*kalam al-sufiyya*; p. 181).

The resultant *fatwa* was certainly exhaustive. In essence it did not condemn the order in question outright, but gave an extensive explanation, based on the writings of various past greats, such as Muhammad Abi l-Wahhab al-Shadhili and Sidi 'Ali al-Khawass, of the sorts of *majdhub*, ranging from those entailing a state of no benefit and error when contrasted with the righteous and active engagement of the "strider" (*salik*) to the moments of slipping away experienced by just such a true seeker of gnosis (pp. 182–83). That said, al-Fatani's sources and images were not just "classical" but modern. At one point he even likened *jadhba* to being akin to a train journey of three days over a distance more usually traveled in thirty (p. 181).

On the whole, al-Fatani laid out the essential principles by which mystical instruction could be given. The primary criterion was an elitist and circumscribed knowledge of the *Shariah*, and most especially that of the *shaykh*, whose behaviour had to be assessed in total. He also wrote that while *jadhba* could be satanically-inspired delusion, there were also occasions in which the common people (*'awamm*) falsely claimed that they had had visions thereby attempting to assert of superiority over the elite (*khawass*). Clearly al-Fatani wanted true esoteric experiences to be restricted. This is also affirmed by his citing Sidi 'Ali al-Khawass to affirm that *jadhba*-inspired visions, if indeed genuine, were never to be communicated to the common or ignorant people (pp. 188–89).

In his response, al-Fatani also made reference to the question of *tariqa* practices being quite widespread, having already fielded (private) requests for *fatwa*s on the issue from other parts of Siam and from Perak, and that in those cases it seems that pre-Islamic practices had been introduced into *tariqa* rituals by the ignorant (p. 191). He also likened the agitated comportment of less-learned *tariqa* practitioners to the behaviour of devotees at gatherings to recite rhyming poems as led by certain Hadrami shaykhs, suggesting in any event that the "shifting about" and "hand waving" were "due to the rapture resulting from when such things are taught to the ignorant commoners among the Javanese and Malays" (*sebeb lezat yang hasil daripada demikian itu kepada juhal al-awam daripada orang Jawa dan Melayu*, p. 192).

On the other hand though, al-Fatani conceded that truly pious commoners might experience sound visions with the aid of Muslim *jinn* rather than the devil (p. 195), and at the end of the day he implied that the order in question could be sound given that its teacher claimed a lineage from one of the two main *khalifa*s appointed by founder Ahmad ibn Idris (1760–1837). The first mentioned was a Sidi Muhammad Salih, while the second, Sidi Ahmad al-Dandarawi — the father to the man who had taught the Kelantan shaykh — was noted as already being famous for his prior connection to the Shadhiliyya (p. 204).

Clearly al-Fatani was immersed in a world of learning in which the *tariqa*s and their practices could intersect and be accepted as conforming to orthodoxy. Hence he made a plea that not all *tariqa*s were to be blackened by the behaviour of some:

> And so the people of the *tariqa*, whether shaykhs or murids, should not be abused; especially those who have been known for their prior pursuit of the knowledge of the Sharia before entering the *tariqa*. And if a few of them should fall into abeyance of the Sharia — even for a moment — due to their human failings (lit. because of their lack of infallibility), ... as long as they have not fallen into obvious sin, or any unbelief sanctioned by them that cannot be explained clearly in one way or another, or if it prove necessary to stand against their transgression, then they should ... [be allowed] to seek [to renew] their affiliation with God (*mencarikkan intisab Allah*) (al-Fatani 1957, p. 205)

In sum then, al-Fatani affirmed that the practices of the order could be deemed sound if the prerequisites of knowledge and *Sharia* were answered and as long as all esoteric knowledge was confined to the learned or gifted elite. In this he was utterly consistent with the Ghazalid tradition, which emphasizes the twinned importance of both the external, normative, and internal, ethical, aspects of Islam. Moreover, the remaining pages of the *fatwa* were given over to the mutually reinforcing role of the *ulama* of *fiqh* and *tasawwuf* respectively with frequent quotations from works in Malay and Arabic. Al-Fatani affirmed that not only were a knowledge of both the inner and outer sciences of Islam crucial, they were to be learned in addition to the (modern) knowledge of the world, with which all Muslims "can defend and elevate the sovereignty of Islam against all others" (*belajar ilmu sharia zahir dan batin dan segala ilmu dunia dan kepandaian yang dapat memelihara dengan dia akan kerajaan islam dan meninggikan dia atas segala yang lainnya*; p. 209).

By comparison with al-Fatani though, another Malayo-Meccan voice was far more scathing of the activities of certain ecstatic Sufis of Southeast Asia, and of those in his home region of West Sumatra in particular. Between 1906 and 1908, Ahmad Khatib of Padang issued a series of vitriolic polemics against the Naqshbandiyya Khalidiyya, the tone of which, as Van Bruinessen has observed, might be adduced from his titles, such as his "Exposition of the adulteration of the liars in their posing as sincere believers" (*Izhar zaghl al-kadhibin fi tashabbuhihim bi al-sadiqin*), "Clear signs to the righteous ones to eliminate the superstitions of certain fanatics" (*al-Ayat al-bayinnat li al-munsifin fi izalat khurafat ba'd al-muta'assibin*) and "The sharp sword that eradicates the words of certain deluded people" (*al-Sayf al-battar fi mahq kalimat ba'd ahl al-ightirar*).[9]

That said, it is interesting to observe that, much as Ahmad Khatib is claimed by scholars like Noer as a sort of proto-modernist, or yet by Hamka as a proto-nationalist, others have even tried to claim that he was, in fact, an initiated member of the Naqshbandiyya himself (Sanusi and Edwar 1981, p. 27). If this were the case then this could well make him somewhat like al-Fatani, though of a much more disaffected than disconnected order. Indeed, one even wonders whether al-Fatani was so mild in his *fatwa* because he remained connected to the Ahmadiyya, or yet because he suspected that the subject of criticism was Muhammad Said al-Linggi, who had reportedly studied under him, Ahmad Khatib, and Nawawi Banten in Mecca in the early 1890s (Kraus 1999, pp. 742–43).

In any event, the point I want to make here is that the Mecca-based Jawi teachers and Sayyid 'Uthman in Batavia were all linked to a long history of internal criticism of ecstatic Sufism within the discursive framework of "traditional" Islam, and one well summarized by Elizabeth Sirriyeh (1999). The watershed for the transition from this mode to a more aggressively "modern" form is the opening of the twentieth century, where indigenously-owned religious newspapers finally took their place in an already crowded market of lithographic and typographic offerings. This moment is also seen as the opening salvo in a war on tradition, backwardness and, indeed, "Sufism" to be consigned to an allegedly dwindling coterie of aging *tariqa* shaykhs. To look at this moment then we shall turn our attention from Mecca to Singapore.

THE APPEARANCE AND SIGNIFICANCE OF *AL-IMAM*

While Ahmad Khatib is understood to have allowed his Meccan students to read the work of Muhammad 'Abduh[10] — and his "slashing blade" certainly gouged great gashes in the communities of the *nagaris* of West Sumatra — the real debut of 'Abduh's ideas is held to have come in the form of a monthly paper which appeared in Singapore from July 1906 to December 1908.

The appearance and influence of *al-Imam* has been discussed in numerous works, commencing with William Roff's landmark *The Origins of Malay Nationalism,* which placed the Singaporean journal in relation to its Riau backers and the wider Muslim world.[11] Certainly it arrived with a relatively loud thump. Its reported print-run of 5000 copies (or even the 2000 mentioned by Straits Settlements statistics) would dwarf that of most Malay periodicals — or at least those with Malayo-Muslim, rather than Chinese or Indo-European editors — for some time; leading one to wonder in fact who its readers were.[12] While there have been differing analyses of the political importance of the journal, each study after Roff has largely accepted his core, and indeed logical, suggestion that the journal followed the line developed by 'Abduh and Rida to the letter. To this end, the editors are often portrayed as absolute opponents of Sufism per se by virtue of their opposition to the practices of local Sufi fraternities, and most especially the Naqshbandiyya (see below), although this is an over-reading of the attitude of the Cairene reformers based more on the attitude adopted by Rashid Rida in later life.[13] Indeed, writers like Abu Bakar Hamzah (1991), characterize the journal in such terms, even if the evidence in *al-Imam*'s case is drawn not from the whole life of the journal, but from the last year of publication.[14]

Furthermore, much of the way that the view of *al-Imam* has been shaped reflects Malay and Indonesian views of Islam in the 1960s and later. For example, Roff's linking of the views on Sufism of the first nominated editor, Shaykh Tahir Jalal al-Din (1869–1956), to those of his protector and relative in Mecca, Ahmad Khatib, are based upon interviews with the son of the former, and from the polemical writings of Hamka, whose own father had been a student of Khatib (Roff 1967, p. 61). And while this is not to say that the suggestion is wrong, i.e., that Khatib and Tahir were opposed to the *tariqas*, this chapter will hopefully propose a more nuanced reading of their attitudes to *tasawwuf* as a whole.

The other matter on which all accounts seem to agree is the changing nature of the editorial board in 1908. As far as the initial line-up was concerned, this was clearly a joint venture perhaps made at a time and place where ethnic distinctions were still a little fuzzy. The nominated editor, Shaykh Tahir, was a Minangkabau graduate of Cairo's al-Azhar, whilst the director, Shaykh Muhammad Salim al-Kalali, was a Hadrami born in Cirebon with extensive links to Aceh.[15] Also of note were Sayyid Shaykh al-Hadi (c. 1867–1934) and Haji Abas bin Muhamad Taha (his contemporary Haji Abas etc.). The former was connected to the Riau royal family, the latter was born in Singapore of Minangkabau parentage, and spent much of his youth in Mecca.

Of all the editors, it may well be that Taha's voice would prove crucial in regard to questions of Sufism, but there is one other figure to consider first. This was Muhammad bin 'Aqil bin Yahya, about whom Roff once had little to report, but who has since occupied his attention (Roff 2002). Indeed the person of Bin 'Aqil gives us a hint as to the complex relationship that some members of *al-Imam* had with Sufism, Sayyid privilege and even colonialism.[16] This particular Hadrami was in fact the widely travelled son-in-law of Sayyid 'Uthman, and is also said to have been an active correspondent with the presses of the Middle East, sending in attacks on Dutch misrule in the Archipelago in the 1890s under the pen-name of "Sayf al-Din al-Yamani" (Andaya 1977, p. 138).

Even if Bin 'Aqil was Sayf al-Din, such matters seem largely forgotten when one reads *al-Imam*. There is little extreme antagonism for the Dutch (or even the British) but a resignation to colonial rule for those unable to practise their faith properly. The journal itself was adjudged a sound enterprise by Sayyid 'Uthman himself on a visit to Singapore soon after its inauguration.[17] And after some concerns raised by the Dutch consul in Singapore, Snouck Hurgronje's successor at the Office for Native (and previously Arab) Affairs, G.A.J. Hazeu, reported that, after reading some of its articles on plans for a new school, complaints about Dutch misuse of Java's "simple" people, and hope expressed that the Japanese might liberate them one day, he still found that "the issues appearing up to the present [were] of very little interest" and that there was little cause to ban its circulation.[18] Such may well have been the case for Hazeu, who was apparently little interested in Islam or Islamic activism that did not directly threaten colonial rule (Van Dijk 2002, p. 80). And even if there would never be a direct threat during his tenure, had Hazeu perused the journal some four months later he might well have noticed a new debate that was taking shape in its question and answer pages.

On the whole it would be fair to characterize *al-Imam* as a journal that took its sources from a variety of Egyptian papers (not least of which was *al-Manar*) and therefore appeared to some outside observers as a propaganda organ for Istanbul, especially given that Cairo was — technically — Ottoman territory. The central theme of *al-Imam* though was less of waving the Caliphal banner (which it did do) than activating Muslims to use their own intellect to reach a proper understanding of their faith, to improve themselves and compete with other peoples on the road to progress and, ultimately, independence. To that end the journal presented the exemplary history of the struggles of the Prophet and regularly lambasted "the Malays" or "the people of our side here" for falling into indolence and irreligion (and under foreign government). Religion was advanced as "the proven cure for the ills of our community" (*al-Imam* 1, no. 1 (23 July 1906); see also Roff 1967, p. 56) while all Malays (and Southeast Asians in general) were urged to abandon allegedly useless superstitions that held them back.

But while *al-Imam* was never short on rhetorical links to global Islam, defining superstition, and indeed all the various causes of a putative local backwardness, required an active engagement with local affairs. To this end *al-Imam* replicated *al-Manar*'s question-and-answer column (which itself replicated the form of the *fatwa*), though as will become clear below, it was Abas bin Muhamad Taha, rather than Shaykh Tahir, who seems ex post facto to have been the one supplying the answers. Apparently it was much to the chagrin of the editors that the subject that would dominate these pages over the course of 1908 was a theme often cast as the major bugbear of the Cairo-oriented modernists, Sufism (*al-tasawwuf*). However, as we shall see, it is too easy to simply lump all the variant parts of the debate as being about Sufism per se. Rather it is necessary to unpack the debate with specific reference to its milieu, being the emergent public sphere in a region that linked communities of readers in urban centres from Sumatra to Southern Siam and Borneo, and the more lexically precise points of reference with regard to *tariqa* practice, namely the elements of *suluk*, *tawajjuh* and *rabita*.

The Problematics of *Suluk* and *Tawajjuh*

For a journal now perceived to have been distinctly opposed to "Sufism", it is striking that there was no discussion of any *tariqa* matter, let alone *tasawwuf*, for its first eighteen issues, which might lead one to conclude that, perhaps mirroring colonial views of the "Qur'an schools" as being out of step with modern times at best, and as hotbeds of ignorant fanaticism at worst, the journal held a similar attitude to *tasawwuf* as having no practical role to play in the betterment of the physical state of local Muslims. As such it deserved little attention. However, this aversion ended on 3 January 1908, when *al-Imam* published a series of questions on the matter of *suluk* sent in by Haji Abas bin Abd al-Rahman Rawa of Penang.

Before we turn to his questions, we should note that use of the word *suluk*, from the Arabic form meaning "strider" (*salik*), implies following the Sufi path in an active manner. As we have seen in the *fatwa* of al-Fatani, it is often paired with (and differentiated from) the concept of *jadhba*. In Javanese literature too, *suluk* is an alternative term for Islamic mysticism as a field of knowledge. However, in the Malay world it was also a term used in a more limited sense to describe the practice of isolation (*khalwa*; Mal. *khalwat*) whereby a Shaykh would take his students aside for a period to instruct them, either individually or in small groups, in the initial stage of their candidacy as his adepts.

It was clearly this aspect of withdrawal from society that most concerned Haji Abas of Penang, who outlined a series of inter-related problems as follows:

> (1) A person undergoing *suluk* asks permission from his guru for permission to visit his sick mother, yet permission is not given and the mother dies. (2) A woman becomes sick during *suluk* and asks for permission from her guru to meet with her husband, but permission is not given and the wife dies.[19] (3) Two parents wish to meet with their child undergoing *suluk*, but

> permission is not given by the guru for the child to meet with the parents. (3) A person who does not understand the principles of prayer and the rules regarding their correct or incorrect practice enters *suluk*. Can such be called for in Islam? (*al-Imam* 2, no. 7 (3 January 1908): 222)

The answer printed immediately below was relatively brief:

> To prevent someone from meeting their parents, partner or family member by reason of their undergoing *suluk* is most certainly not something called for in the Most Holy Islamic Sharia as against those things that are obvious poppycock (*karut-karut*) — and most especially if the persons who carry out *suluk* are lazy and vagrants without any knowledge. True *suluk* and true *tariqa* is to teach such people that they should not abstain from participating actively in life, and to demonstrate to them that the dictates of religion will bring them to happiness in this life and that to come. Indeed the *suluk* described above should [really] be called *tarika* [تاريك] not *tariqa* [طريقة]. As a matter of fact, the questions here have been addressed many times before, to the extent that they may be found in the smallest books available in Malay, namely those dealing with matter of prayers etc. One might ask any knowledgeable person in any town. Still, if there is something that is too difficult, then the question can be sent to *al-Imam*. (*al-Imam* 2, no. 7 (3 January 1908): 222)

And with that it would seem that the matter is resolved. The tone of the answer makes it plain that there is either a lack of interest on the part of the respondent, or at least an unwillingness to tackle questions felt to be obvious and indeed treatable by the extant elementary literature. Further, the lack of a long response seems to discount the possibility that the question was manufactured as an excuse to launch into a discursive point. Rather the sense communicated is that *Sharia*-oriented piety is an implicit part of true *suluk* in the wider meaning of the term, while the deliberate mis-spelling of the word *tariqa* is calculated to demonstrate the textual ignorance of local practitioners, given that Malay does not differentiate between a palatal /ṯ/ and a normal /t/, between /k/ and /q/, or between long and short vowels. In fact it could even be read as an affirmation that this sort of behaviour had nothing to do with (proper) *tariqa* Sufism. Most certainly this is not a radical critique of the orders as "the greatest hindrance to the development of Malayo-Islamic culture" ascribed to Shaykh Tahir in January 1908.[20]

Apparently though, and probably beyond the wildest dreams of the editors, this was not the end to questions revolving around localized Sufi practices that would increasingly dominate the pages of *al-Imam* over the course of the year and that would draw in reaction from the length and breadth of the Malay World. Indeed the next salvo came in the following issue, with a much longer question purportedly sent from a Malay territory under Siamese rule (*Sual dari tanah Malayu jajahan Siam*; *al-Imam* 2, no. 8 (4 February 1908): 255–58).

Even if this may not necessarily have come from Kelantan, it seems to resonate, in spirit if not in detail, with the royal letter sent to al-Fatani only three years previously. In this particular letter, an anonymous plaintiff wrote questioning the activities of an unnamed teacher of the Ahmadiyya-Rashidiyya. This particular guru was allegedly teaching the practice termed here as *tawajjuh* — being described as the active visualization of the Divine through the mediation of the Shaykh.[21] More scandalously, and like the Kelantan case, it would appear that instruction was being given to mixed assemblies of men and women, young and old, the educated and the ignorant. Some of these aspirant Sufis were also apparently linked to the royal family and believed that by joining the order they were guaranteed a place in paradise. An account was then given (missing from the 1957 version of the Kelantan *fatwa*) of raucous dancing with incense-filled braziers which caused the floor and walls to shake, frightening the neighbours.[22] At the conclusion to such raptures the *shaykh* would bring the assembly to a close by calling out "shush". Those still spellbound were then struck by the shaykh with a cane and would relate their ecstatic visions in loud voices — claiming to have seen the Prophet and all his descendents, or all those in the grave, or Heaven and Hell. Some purportedly claimed to have seen God enthroned, whilst a child could even declare that He was seated in nearby coconut palms. Such visions were either disclosed in the presence of the Shaykh or concealed, but in any event the Shaykh himself would confirm that they were luminous experiences sent from God (*tajalli*), and most certainly not Satanically-inspired delusion; which the questioner implies they are, based on the obvious ignorance and inexperience of those students concerned.

The letter made several further charges — including that of disturbing (decent) fellow mosque-goers — before asking several questions:

> So what is the ruling on such a *tariqa*? Was the Prophet's *tariqa* like this or not? And if the Prophet's *tariqa* was like that, then we ask which *hadith* explains it so that we might refer to it in order to know. And if it was not like that, then is it an innovation (*bid'a*)? And if it is, then what sort of innovation is it? Is it a positive innovation (*bid'a hasana*), or one which is reprehensible and misguided (*bid'a qabiha dan dalala*)? And if it is a positive innovation, then what is the form of such? But if it is a misguided innovation,

> then is it obligatory for the ruler and those in authority to censure (*menta'zirkan*) its practitioners? And what should be the ruling as regards the *shaykh*? Should the ruler expel him from the land so that he may no longer lead the ignorant astray or teach then that which is not incumbent? Please give us a ruling on all these questions in detail because the matter has already afflicted our *negeri*, and divided it religiously. (*al-Imam* 2, no. 8 (4 February 1908): 257–58)

Clearly the members of this *tariqa* were set up for a grilling. The response was made formally after boiling down the questions thus:

(1) did such a *tariqa* exist at the time of the Prophet?
(2) if it is innovation (*bid'a*) then what sort is it?
(3) if it is a misguided innovation (*bid'a dalala*) then what should the ruler do?
(4) what is the punishment for the shaykh?
(5) should the ruler issue censure against this?

The answer to the first point commenced by stating that there was no such *tariqa* in existence at the time of the Prophet, and went into questions of the basic principles of the categories of legality in the *Sharia* and the relevant rewards or punishments awaiting one in the afterlife (pp. 258–59). The Prophet had called upon mankind to stress true belief (*'aqida*) against false belief, and emphasize the five gradients, including whether something is obligatory (*wajib*), normative (*sunna*), disliked (*makruh*) or forbidden (*haram*), in the proper expectation of Divine reward or punishment. The *ulama* of the *Sharia* have put all such information in the books of *fiqh*; accepting these rules is called Islam, belief in the Qur'anic verses is *iman*, while enacting the rules of the *Sharia* (both in its *usul* and *furu'*) is called following the *tariqa* of the Prophet. Following further explanation of the imperative to cling to the rope of God (p. 260), the respondent then promised to complete his answer in a forthcoming issue.

A SAYYID REVOLUTION? — *TARIQA* PURSUED

The rest of the answer certainly came, but it is worth noting that the issue in question antedated what seems to have been a revolution of one group of Sayyids at the expense of Shaykh Tahir (who was then in Egypt) and Salim al-Kalali. As the colophon makes clear, in February 1908 the journal passed into the control of *Sayyid* Muhammad bin 'Aqil, *Sayyid* Shaykh al-Hadi and *Sayyid*

Hasan bin Shahab, who now registered themselves as the "Al-Imam Company Ltd". (*al-Imam* 2, no. 9 (5 March 1908): 291–93). Now too editorial control was exercised by Abas bin Muhamad Taha.

Although Roff (2002, p. 105) has remarked that the content of the journal was not noticeably altered, there is to my mind a striking upsurge in the intensity and prominence of the attention given to questions of *tariqa*, starting with the promised conclusion to the Siam-*fatwa*. In this section, the unidentified respondent claimed that the editors had heard various local reports from people who had joined a *tariqa*, and that these dwelt upon all manner of indecent behaviour (*munkar-munkar*). Some involved scandalously mixed assemblies, including while washing themselves, and even the exposure of the women's bodies. Worse still, some women claimed that the students suckled at the breast of God, while others alleged that the gurus performed *khalwa* with beautiful young women. "Clearly", intoned the voice of *al-Imam*:

> this *tariqa* is playing with religion, is the way of the lost, and deviates from the *tariqa* of our Prophet as brought down [to us] by the ulama of *sharia* and *tasawwuf*. [It even] insults the Sharia because the ignorant surmise that this is the Sharia of the Prophet and that his *tariqa* is like this. As a matter of fact the *tariqa* of our Prophet is to work with the pure Book of God against all things that are blameworthy (*tercela*), and to adorn all work and praiseworthy actions for all mankind so that even unbelievers of sound mind can see that they represent purity. (*al-Imam* 2, no. 9 (5 March 1908): 271–72)

If read quickly, and without knowledge of the first exchange on *suluk*, it would be relatively easy to interpret this passage as a call for the return to the Qur'an and as a damning indictment of all things connected with contemporary Sufism in the Malay world in 1908. However we are once more struck by the need to give the common conceptual equation of Sufism with *tariqa* more nuance. After all, the explicit and equal reference here to "the ulama of Sharia and *tasawwuf*" declares that, like the *Jawi ulama* of Mecca, the editors saw themselves as inheritors to a lineage of *both* the legists and mystics of the past rather than any desire to abrogate the epistemological structures that they had established.

That said, *al-Imam* was still about reconfiguring the (Malay) present in radical ways to conform to a particular vision of the *tariqa* of the Prophet. In this project the traditional Malay rulers would be assigned a role; that of patron and policeman. Hence in responding to the third part of the question, the practices in question were declared to be misguided innovation (*bid'a dalala*) and it was therefore incumbent upon the ruler and men of power to forbid the *tariqa* in question, in addition to any gurus who associated such actions with the *Sharia*.[23]

As a practical solution, *al-Imam* advised that all rulers build madrasahs to inculcate proper knowledge in every place, and with an eye to their rank on the world stage:

> so that there will be a guru to teach that they might know what qualities have a bearing on their lives, and that they will be enriched above the unbelievers in the business of the world ... Have we not seen the example of the people of Japan, whose king established good schools [inculcating] all the knowledge of the world such that they excelled and bettered the nations of Europe in matters pertaining to the world, of livelihood and of the manufacture of armaments? In the end they bettered them and belittled the greatest king of Europe [i.e the Tsar] and preserved themselves from the domination of foreign lords. (*al-Imam* 2, no. 9 (5 March 1908): 273)

The remainder of this section then treats the reader to a discourse on the *ulama* as the blessing (*baraka*) of the earthly life, which is itself the seedbed of the afterlife (*al-dunya mazra'at al-akhira*), and further lecturing to local kings to follow the *Sharia* to make trade possible, to open possibilities for people, to protect the country from those who threaten it, and to make justice between near and far, rich and poor.

Indeed there is a none-too subtle call made for rulers to work for the entire community rather than their own families. The best investment that they could make is to defend the root (*asal*) and branches (*furu'*) of religion by supporting the *ulama* financially; by compelling all to study what is right and to enter into a relationship with the *ulama* who *really* travel the path of the hereafter by the *tariqa* of the Prophet, so that modern students could be sent to appropriate schools so that their hearts might experience (real) *tawajjuh*:

> Let students be taught that the legal status (*hukum*) of whatever business they carry out rests on conditions (*shart*) and that it is forbidden to inflict upon them the fraud of the deceivers (*dajjal-dajjal*) of our time who make them commit to innovations as a *tariqa*, or those of their acts which contravene the actions of the Companions [of the Prophet] and the Successors [who came after them] who link us to the religion of our Prophet, for it is a threat to their religion, and their world, as is the case with *the tariqa in this question*. ... For all who enter into *this tariqa* must be ignorant of religion and their task in their world, which they have left by reason of it being a *tariqa* that contravenes the Sharia, and in order to study the skills of *their* world. For they have moved away [from this world] with their *dhikr* dances

> and their twirling (*bertariq*) and their killing of the self with their jumping and stamping and such things that are nothing other than a danger to this life and that to come. (*al-Imam* 2, no. 9 (5 March 1908): 277; emphasis mine)

From here on the answers come quickly: it is declared necessary for the raja to expel the guru from the country so that he cannot lead ignorant people astray, for such a teacher is "more evil that 1,000 unbelievers" (p. 277); while the fifth response affirms that such teachings are to be censured, for they work against the raja by leading his people to ignorance (p. 278). As the Prophet was reputed to have said: "Every innovation is error and all error is consigned to Hell" (p. 279).

Brevity was never an element of *al-Imam's* rhetorical arsenal and from here on the articles were increasingly wordy, though after a brief pause, given that the next salvo was launched in May. Herein mention was made that dedicated *ulama* teach all the instructions of their religion, such as cleanliness, prayer, fasting, zakat and the like, "so that all people may be cured of the disease of ignorance", and convinced that all such teachings as these are "the true *tariqa* and correct *suluk*" emphasized by the Prophet (*al-Imam* 2, no. 11 (May 1908): 336).

The engagement proper was once more within the question and answer pages, and the editor(s) referred to the great many letters received in relation to the question on *tariqa* and *suluk* "as taken by some whose eyes God has closed to other doors of income (*rizq*)" by trading in their religion, and in accumulating goods from the poor (*al-Imam* 2, no. 11 (May 1908): 347). One such letter was sent by the *penghulu* of Ampang Kuala Lumpur, dated 3 Rabi' al-awwal 1326 (5 April 1908), which *al-Imam* abridged in the form of three questions:

> A teacher teaches *tariqa suluk* as described below:
> (1) The teacher teaches about various *latifas* [energy points in the body], one of which is the *laylat al-qalb* manifested in the form of the teacher which is conjoined with the heart of the student, so that, when present, it commences *dhikr*. [He teaches that] if this is not the case, then the *dhikr* is not valid. What is the ruling [on this]?
> (2) A student enters into *suluk*, and then a letter comes from his mother in Perak saying that his father is sick and calls him home. The student asks permission, which is refused, and his father dies. What is the ruling?
> (3) A husband and wife enter *suluk* together in different places, they then become ill, asking permission of the guru to meet with their [respective] partners, but it is not granted and the husband dies. What is the ruling? (*al-Imam* 2, no. 11 (May 1908): 347–48)

In response, *al-Imam* referred to its previous pronouncement in vol. 2 no. 7, but conceded that as the answer was apparently not clear enough it would be reiterated. The still anonymous mufti also noted that when that issue had been discussed it had pertained to matters in Penang, but that since that time many such questions had come to the attention of the journal in relation to the practice of *suluk* in whatever negeri in question. The stage was thus set for an authoritative statement of relevance for an imagined audience of *ulama* spanning all the Malay negeris, and "thus", declared *al-Imam*, "we hope that all the respected shaykhs who shall read this answer, which we have made so clear, will do so carefully and receive what ever clarification or censure [they are due]." (*al-Imam* 2, no. 11 (May 1908): 348)

Reflecting the question, the first answer was not about the practice of *suluk* per se, but rather asserted that it was a field of knowledge taught by the *tariqa* and *suluk* shaykhs. It was also phrased in a way that established the writer's familiarity with those terminologies, commencing with an outline of "the *latifa* of the heart" (*latifat al-qalb*), explained as being one of the ten such points identified by the *tariqa* shaykhs as constituting the body (*al-Imam* 2, no. 11 (May 1908): 349). Of these, five were subsumed within "the world of command" (*'alam al-amr*) — the heart (*qalb*), spirit (*ruh*), secret (*sirr*), the hidden (*khafi*) and the most secret (*akhfa*); the other five, meanwhile, included the soul/breath (*nafs*) and the four elements (*'anasir*), or those names of God Almighty never enunciated by the Prophet, nor by the Companions nor the Righteous Generation.

This last point in particular, or at least its phrasing, lead the response to conclude, or at least add, that:

> Those who invoke these names throw something in (*menoko'*) to religion which is not a part of religion. Among such [practices] is the invocation of the form of the guru in the heart or between the two eyes. This is called *rabita*, and is an innovation that is absolutely forbidden due to its greater propensity to lead to polytheism than monotheism. (*al-Imam* 2, no. 11 (May 1908): 349)

From here the answer reaffirmed, and in terms far stronger than the first response to Haji Abas of Penang, that any guru preventing his students from maintaining his or her familial or marital obligations had in fact led them to commit an act of betrayal (*derhaka*). The response then went on to lecture the community — and assumedly the many shaykh readers that *al-Imam* was imagined to have — on the nature of Islam and ecstatic Sufism; having already widened the scope of its lexical attack to now include the knowledge of *latifas* and the practice of *rabita*. The final phrases of this passage are of particular interest here:

> Islam is the religion of nature (*din al-fitra*), cleansed by God Almighty of any monasticism (*ruhbaniyya*) that troubles it or makes heavy demands that are not part of it. Yet, as was foretold by our Prophet, God's peace and blessings be upon him and his companions, the sickness of people of past times (*penyakit orang yang dahulu-dahulu*) has grown among us. Hence some followings have arisen and new signs (*isharat*) have been manifested subsequent to the original time and the excellent centuries (*kemudian daripada sadr al-awwal dan qurun yang fadila*). Indeed: the true *tasawwuf* that is most praiseworthy is the proper path of the Prophet ... and all his companions and the leaders of learning, for there is no rim (*bingkai*) and no spur (*serong*) [i.e., no extraneous adornment], as is said in the *Ihya 'ulum al-din* [of al-Ghazali] and the *Risala* of [Abu l-Qasim] al-Qushayri (986–1072), and other such works. The greats among the people of *tasawwuf* of former days were the pick of all men, such as the men of erudition, the greats of the 'Alawite Sayyids (*al-sadat al-'alawiyyin*), and those who followed in their path by following the words of the Book and the Sunna of the Prophet. Yet [now there are] those who have made a god of their selfish passions and have corrupted their religion by adding to it and misrepresenting it, composing all sorts of works of deviation ... So what do you gentlemen think of people who have been led astray by God ... from knowledge, whose hearts and eyes have been befuddled, and whose visions have become hazy? Indeed those of this ilk are mostly peddlers of religion (*saudagar-saudagar agama*) who drink the blood of all the poor and destitute. They are to humanity like a tick on the human body, only making one sick and filthy and sticking in [their spike] (*memantakan*), giving not a single benefit. Let all people guard themselves against them if they are God-fearing and hope for His mercy in the Afterlife! Otherwise they should run from them and advise others to do the same for God, His Prophet and Islam. This is because one of these people is more dangerous to all Muslims together than a multitude of devils! (*al-Imam* 2, no. 11 (May 1908): 349–51)

THE *UTUSAN MELAYU* EXCHANGES: EXPOSING THE SAYYID FOUNDATIONS OF *AL-IMAM*

The gauntlet had been thrown down, and such forceful statements as these would clearly have upset any readers (and their auditors) that may have been of more *tariqa*-minded bent. Indeed we need here to consider the argument made by Muhsin Mahdi that print capitalism in some parts of the Muslim world may have depended on the pre-existence of the sorts of interlinked readerships maintained by the Sufi brotherhoods (Mahdi 1995, pp. 6–7; see also Eickelman and Salvatore 2005, pp. 12–13; and Ernst, forthcoming). Certainly Ian Proudfoot's (1997) argument about the importance of lithography in the mid-nineteenth century, and its paving the way for the acceptance by the twentieth century of the sorts of typographic offerings that *al-Imam* offered, provides us with a view of how actively Sufis were involved in early print capitalism, and most especially in its vernacular forms. With this in mind, it seems highly probably that certain Sufis were well aware of the content *al-Imam* may well have chosen to answer the challenge, though not in *its* question and answer pages. Rather they turned to other papers, including another Singaporean paper that was making its mark in the region. Edited by Mohd Eunos Abdullah (b.1876), this was the *Utusan Melayu* (The Malay Messenger).

Perhaps the most successful Malay periodical of the early twentieth century, the *Utusan Melayu* is a paper declared by Anthony Milner to have fostered the debut of a "bourgeois public sphere" in the region that would invite an "unwitting" Islamic response from *al-Imam* (see Milner 1995, pp. 89–136 and 137–92). Apart from creating a false chronology of western intervention and Muslim reaction in the story of Malay politics, Milner's focussing on the *Utusan Melayu*'s claim that it was not a religious paper (p. 133), and indeed his overplaying of some supposedly primordial Islamic opposition to liberalism (or yet kingship), misrepresents the relationship between the two as one of rivalry for Malay minds, and ultimately Malay politics.

Yet while both were avowedly different in emphasis and set in two competing type-faces — one (mainly) Roman and the other Jawi — they were never really competitors. For a start, *al-Imam* was a monthly magazine, while the *Utusan Melayu* appeared every two days. I would furthermore argue that their respective proprietors saw the other as complimentary voices for modernization in the region. The *Utusan Melayu* was not at all opposed to religion, and a weekly jolt of politics and science sat quite well against *al-Imam*'s prescriptions for a religiously-informed solution to the ills of the community. Indeed the editors of *al-Imam* were unabashed in welcoming the *Utusan Melayu* on the scene when it was launched in 1907, and regularly quoted from its pages, or used them to advertise their own projects. One such endeavour was the al-Iqbal school, the first modernist school established in Singapore with a hybrid curiculum of Islamic and Western subjects, including English, history and bookkeeping.[24]

Be that as it may, certain disgruntled voices chose the *Utusan Melayu* as a vehicle of complaint in May 1908 — knowing full well that both the editors and readers of *al-Imam* would most likely see these complaints as well. The first flash appeared in the Jawi pages, when a (badly spelt) letter from a certain "S.A." (Sayyid A.?) of Penang appeared in the issue of 23 May 1908.

> I saw in *al-Imam* issue 11 of 3 May 1908 that the response of *al-Imam* [to a question] stated that to summon up the form of the guru in the heart or between the eyes is called *rabita*, and that such an act is an innovation sternly condemned by virtue of its propensity to lead to polytheism being stronger than monotheism. So where is this answer derived from? Is there a proof in the Qur'an or Hadith (or a text)? Where is such a thing mentioned in a book [such as] the *Sirr al-salikin* (sic, read: *Sayr al-salikin*) of Shaykh Abd al-Samad Palembang or in any of the Malay and Arabic books with Qur'anic proofs or those based on Hadith and the acts of the Companions? Why not go and pay a visit to the respected Sayyid 'Abd Allah Zawawi who is in Singapore in order to understand, and how such baseness (*nafsu*) should be answered! (*Utusan Melayu*, 23 May 1908)

The reaction was soon in coming, but was tucked in at the end of the correspondence pages of the next issue. Here, under the Arabic rubric "the *rabita* of the people of the *tariqa*", the still anonymous mufti treated a question sent in by Tengku Muhamad Jamil of Serdang, East Sumatra, as to whether two Qur'anic verses (3: 200 and 5: 35) were evidence for the practice of *rabita*. Predictably the answer, drawing on the exegetical works of al-Khazin (d.1340) and "the two Jalals" (al-Mahalli [d.1459] and al-Suyuti [d.1505]), was in the negative, and argued instead that the *ayats* in question referred to *jihad* and obedience.[25] The emphasis on patience (*al-sabr*) and union (*al-rabita*) in the first was not to be construed as the practice of summoning the form of the guru while performing the *dhikr*, nor yet should the term *wasila* (i.e., connection) mentioned in the second, be taken as proof for the *tariqa* practice of seeking the mediation of the shaykh. Rather, as the response went on to emphasize, "there are no verses at all that give justification to the *tariqa* gurus, rather there are those that actually forbid them" (*al-Imam* 2, no. 12 (1 June 1908): 381). These are then cited, following excerpts from the Qur'anic commentary of al-Khazin, and al-Qushayri, who is quoted as the final proof that such an interpretation of the two verses brought forward as evidence by the shaykhs was negated with respect to the question of the sincerity (*ikhlas*) of one's devotions.

> By performing *ikhlas* one protects one's heart from seeing or observing creatures. Even the form of the guru, if seen at the moment of *dhikr*, is to look at a creature. And this is a great wrong, for to place a newly-created being in the place of the Everlasting God is like putting a lowly coolie in the place of the raja. (*al-Imam* 2, no. 12 (1 June 1908): 381–82)

And it was at this juncture that the reaction came:

> We were amazed to read what was written in the *Utusan Melayu* on 21 Rabi' al-akhir in regard to the request made under the cover of the initials S.A. of Penang. He wanted proof from us given our rejection of *rabita* in number 11, not knowing that it is a matter of principle (*qa'ida*) for the person bringing something forward [to prove its authenticity]! … Thus our answer to S.A. is: Kindly show us that the *rabita* was known to the Prophet or was taught by him to any of his companions or that one of the companions enacted it. Furthermore, demonstrate to us what meaning may be assigned to this *rabita* and what proof (*dalil*) applies to those who carry it out, for how could it not be proven by the Qur'an?, given that God Almighty has said: "We did not leave anything out of it" [Q 6: 38]. So, if such a true proof is found in line with our request, rather than going to the bother of sending it to other papers, just send it straight to us to headline it in *al-Imam* with stars and with big letters. Just leave out this talk of Shaykh Abd al-Samad Palembang (may God have mercy on him) and his Excellency Professor Sayyid 'Abd Allah al-Zawawi (may God protect him) for these two are accounted ulama whose work states and elucidates matters brought down from God and His Prophet without either of them [taking the] the right to fiddle with or add anything to religion that is not of it. However, as we believe that S.A. will prove unable to bring forth any such proof, could [we ask] kindly that Habib [al-Zawawi] help him? Still, we suspect that he will rather keep things to himself, for al-Sayyid Abd Allah al-Zawawi is one of the foundations of *al-Imam* (*rukn min arkan al-imam*) … and we have absorbed in our breasts his teachings and directions; *being the general guidance not to stir the lost and the hypocrites.* (*al-Imam* 2, no. 12 (1 June 1908): 382–83; emphasis mine)

Even so, the stirring had begun, and now the journal had entered a new, decidedly more antagonistic phase. And so it was too that the name of 'Abd Allah al-Zawawi was summoned up by both apparent defenders and detractors of *tariqa* Sufism in the region. So who was 'Abd Allah al-Zawawi?

Born in Mecca in 1850 to a distinguished teacher and Sufi master, Muhammad Salih al-Zawawi, the precocious 'Abd Allah had been educated at home and his excellence had been acknowledged begrudgingly in the 1870s by the Meccan establishment which awarded him a teaching post in the sacred Mosque (Snouck Hurgronje 1931, p. 184; 1941, p. 14). Snouck Hurgronje claims to have met him in the Hijaz through a member of the royal family of Pontianak, whose colony in Mecca he wrote as being under the control of the Zawawis — the younger would train the students to the requisite level of "the Holy Science" before the senior would accept them as his adepts in the Naqshbandiyya — though it is possible that another link came through the mediation of his Bantenese informant in Jeddah, Aboe Bakar Djajadiningrat (Laffan 2003, p. 59).

'Abd Allah also seems to have maintained connections, again via his father, with the royal house of Riau. Either way, these connections served him well — as did his personal relationship with Snouck Hurgronje — when political changes in the Hijaz forced him into exile in 1893. He then spent the next fifteen years travelling in India and Southeast Asia, being granted permission by the Dutch government to reside unhindered in the Netherlands Indies. In fact he visited Riau in 1894 while en route for Pontianak, and it is no coincidence that the local press there soon published works by both him and his father the following year (Van der Putten 1997, p. 732).

What is especially interesting here is that the text by his father was a work of Sufi instruction, and more specifically for the *dhikr* of the Mujaddadiyya branch of the Naqshbandiyya, written at Riau in 1883. This text, the *Kayfiyat al-dhikr 'ala al-tariqa al-naqshbandiyya al-mujaddadiyya al-ahmadiyya* (The Means of Dhikr as practised by the Naqshbandiyya Mujaddadiyya Ahmadiyya, (Riau, 1895–96)), may well have been the first text of any sort published with the name al-Zawawi. As Snouck Hurgronje had observed in Mecca, the learning and piety of father and son had apparently not engendered a need at that time to produce any "literary activity" (Snouck Hurgronje 1931, p. 185). The reference here though to his *dhikr* being of the Ahmadiyya version of the Mujaddadiyya is also curious, and one wonders if this is also an oblique reference to Muhammad Salih al-Zawawi as master of more than one order, much as Sidi Ahmad al-Dandarwawi was described by al-Fatani as a known Shadhili. Was the elder Zawawi even identical with the Sidi Muhammad Salih praised by al-Fatani as al-Dandarawi's other true khalifa (cf al-Fatani 1957, p. 204)? In any event, this was not the last Sufi text produced in Riau, and at least two other Naqshbandi manuals (neither penned by a Zawawi) appeared in 1904 and 1905 respectively (Van der Putten 1997, p. 728, n. 20).

Meanwhile, al-Zawawi's personal connection with the editors of *al-Imam*, if it was not founded already in the Riau linkage, was made all the stronger by his friendship with Bin 'Aqil. According to one British official, Bin'Aqil — who was seen as a valuable local ally by the British — had even toured Japan with al-Zawawi at the close of the century (Roff 2002, p. 100). Retrospectively it is easy to see the influence of al-Zawawi permeating the pages of *al-Imam*. In November 1907, he was painted as "the great opponent of *bid'a* and champion of the Sunna", while the following month he was cited as the senior authority for a *fatwa* (on eating crabs). He was also mentioned regularly in relation to Singapore's al-Iqbal school while a later issue would describe his activities in Malaya, Sumatra and Java, and mentioned his trips to China, Japan, India and Syria (see especially *al-Imam* 3, no. 6 (25 November 1908)). Indeed much of the impetus for *al-Imam* to describe the wonders of Japan — which it regularly compared to degradation of the Malays — may well come at his urging, if not from Bin 'Aqil.

But while al-Zawawi might be held up as a paragon of virtue by each side — with all involved recognizing his authority as a Meccan sayyid — we might also ponder the implications of his relationship with Snouck Hurgronje. For just as he appears to have helped clear the way for the latter's visit to Mecca in 1885, Snouck Hurgronje returned the favour vis-à-vis his period of Southeast Asian exile. In fact he may well have looked with a kindly eye on the activities of al-Zawawi's Singaporean friends, so we might not find it so surprising that Sayyid 'Uthman pronounced the journal sound, or that Hazeu felt so little concern at alarmist reports of its pro-Ottoman content. Such a favour was returned it seemed, with no real invective launched against the Dutch as was promulgated by often anonymous Hadramis in the journals of Beirut and Cairo. Indeed, whereas one Cairene paper had published just such a letter and warned of the plots of "Duktur Snuk" in November 1902 (*Misbah al-sharq*, 28 Sha'ban 1320), it is somewhat remarkable that a response in *al-Imam* to Guru Ahmad Mustafa of Ampenan's question about the names of the westerners who had entered Mecca and Medina in secret (printed immediately before the question of Haji Abas Rawa on Suluk) mentioned Niebuhr, Burckhardt and Burton, but made no reference to Snouck Hurgronje or his alter ego 'Abd al-Ghaffar (*al-Imam* 2, no. 7 (3 January 1908): 219–22).

There is much indeed that 'Abd Allah al-Zawawi would rather "keep to himself", for it is also curious to find he often addressed Snouck Hurgronje in his letters as "al-Hajj 'Abd al-Ghaffar", knowing full well that Snouck had been expelled from the Hijaz before being able to undertake that ritual and thus claim the title.[26] Even if it was an address dispensed tongue in cheek, could it have been that he meant this in an entirely different way, given that Sufis often speak of the real Hajj as a journey to the inner truth? And should we therefore wonder if Snouck Hurgronje's path — his "inner path" (*sayra dakhiliyya*) to Mecca, as al-Zawawi's former student, Aboe Bakar Djajadiningrat, termed it[27] — was in fact an ethical, or yet "scientific" Ghazalid Sufism of the elite whose company he seems to have shared, both in Mecca and the Indies, concealed behind a shared programme advocating a practical (apolitical) Islam for the masses?[28]

But to return to *al-Imam* ... Having dispensed with the letter of 'S.A.' and declared a personal allegiance to al-Zawawi, the last issue of volume 2 went on to detail an answer on the buying and selling of shares (quoting *al-Manar*) and discussing the Iqbal School and Hijaz Railway, before issuing an apology that the poems of Raja Hasan could not be included due to the sheer volume of letters received. Abas bin Muhamad Taha would then conclude with a retrospective, now signing himself off as "the author (*pengarang*) of *al-Imam*", wherein he affirmed that in keeping with its original mission, the journal was:

> the fiercest enemy of all innovation, superstition, obvious poppycock, followings, and condemned practices that have been absorbed by their practitioners. It calls upon all Muslims to unite and erect what it required for the life of this world and the next, such as building schools and developing all living people in their work of the world through knowledge (*ilmu*) and skills (*kepandaian*) that lead to their strengthening to make triumphant their people and religion. (*al-Imam* 2, no. 12 (1 June 1908): 390)

The matter was by no means resolved though for the alleged partisans of innovation and poppycock, and the Jawi letters to the *Utusan Melayu*, and indeed other Malay papers, now came in greater numbers, though it should be noted that not all were against *al-Imam*. On 4 June 1908, a letter signed H.A.B.'. of Palembang was published in the *Utusan Melayu* in reaction to a call posted in the *Taman Pengetahuan* (The Garden of Knowledge) of 23 Rabi' al-akhir 1326 (24 May 1908). Apparently this call, posted under the name "al-Ma'mum", i.e., "The Led", an obvious play on the pretensions of *al-Imam*, had urged *al-Imam* to ask forgiveness and recant. This then led the Palembang author to go back and check *al-Imam*, where he found the article of vol. 2 no. 12 that had rejected the *rabita* of the people of the *tariqa* by way of Qur'anic proofs:

> So I compared the words of al-Ma'mum and *al-Imam* and found that the difference between them was as between night and day (lit. "between earth and sky"), for *al-Imam* had adduced the word of God while al-Ma'mum had used words that could by no means trump (*menindeh*) those of *al-Imam*, or which could not invalidate at all those in the afore-mentioned issue. This is because the words of Shaykh Junayd Baghdadi and those of the *tariqa* shaykhs, even if they are all saints (*walaupun mereka itu awliya' sekalipun*), cannot refute the proof of the Qur'an ... for we follow the Qur'an and the Prophet ... So it is incumbent upon Shaykh Junayd and the *tariqa* shaykhs to follow the Qur'an and the Prophet. In any event, the statement of al-Ma'mum proves that he is not learned enough and should study *al-Imam*.

> Indeed he should ask forgiveness of *al-Imam*, not *vice versa*. I hope that the "manager" (*manajer*) or author of *al-Imam* will, should time and space allow, answer again, in addition to including [the answer] in this *Utusan Melayu*, so that we do not have to wait a long time for *al-Imam* to respond, and also because not everybody reads *al-Imam*, especially here at Palembang. (*Utusan Melayu*, 4 June 1908)

A few days later an anonymous correspondent wrote in to attack the Palembang author for his misreading of the chain of events and argument — noting that al-Ma'mum had been responding to an earlier issue of *al-Imam* (vol. 2, no. 11), and counselling that Mr H.A.B.'. of Palembang — whose understanding of things seemed as far removed "as the East is from the West" — should not be so eager to leap in between the two and act as some sort of "mufti" himself (*Utusan Melayu*, 9 June 1908). Another reaction came on the 11 June, signed by "a Friday preacher" (*khatib*), who similarly condemned the Palembangese for his eagerness to take sides or for "trying to be the (trickster) mousedeer and stand between two fighting elephants" as he would obviously get squashed, which tells us that some locals at least knew who al-Ma'mum was, and that he may well have been a shaykh of influence. As the worldly-wise *khatib* advised:

> What's the use of intervening in a matter we don't understand? Know well, H.A.B.'.P., that the press (*akhbar-akhbar*) should not to be turned into a battle-ground for such obvious poppycock (*karut karut*) as this provocation (*usutan*)! We believe that neither al-Ma'mum nor *al-Imam* are innocent (*suci*) in this "question and answer". We reckon that it will only be a dozen months or so before this, and especially this false referee (*hakim palsu*) H.A.B.'.P., will all fall silent. That would be for the best. (*Utusan Melayu*, 11 June 1908)

The message was thus to leave it to the big boys, who, after all, only came out to fire their salvos once a month. Perhaps with that in mind, another correspondent signing himself as Masbuq commended another authoritative source, namely the *Izhar zaghl al-kadhibin* of Ahmad Khatib, in which was cited a *fatwa* given by the then Imam of the Shafi'i *madhhab* in Mecca, Muhammad Sa'id bin Muhammad Babusayl, along with affirmations given by 'Abd al-Karim Daghistani and Shu'ayb bin 'Abd al-Karim al-Maghribi (*Utusan Melayu*, 13 June 1908). In its barely-expounded particulars, the *fatwa* was in answer to the question of the *suluk* and *rabita* of "the Naqshbandiyya and other [orders] of our day":

> For many [of] them contravene our Sharia, for not a single jot of [such techniques] was obtained at the time of the Companions and the Successors.

> Hence it is obligatory for every person in authority to do away with whatever is overturned by the Sharia ... for the best *tariqa* and the closest to God Almighty is to study religion and work with that knowledge truly and genuinely. (*Utusan Melayu*, 13 June 1908)

And with that, the editors of the *Utusan* rather hoped that the matter, and the mud-slinging, was at an end for them.

For *al-Imam* though the question of the *tariqa*s was by no means resolved. In fact, its tone and rhetoric became increasingly strident. On rejoining the fray, Abas Taha of *al-Imam* would emphasize that his journal had never claimed to be bringing new teachings to the Malays, and bemoaned the fact that "so much ink had been spilt on the words of those who claim to be the people of *tariqa* (lies and calumny [*bohong dan dusta*]!)" (*al-Imam* 3, no. 1 (1 July 1908): 8). Even so, ever more space was devoted to debating the question of *tariqa* practice, though it should be said that the vast bulk of attention was focused on the Khalidiyya, with occasional cross-reference to the hybrid Qadiriyya wa-Naqshbandiyya offshoot founded by Ahmad Khatib Sambas (d. ca. 1875) (see Van Bruinessen 2000, pp. 376–84). Sufi masters were urged to come out in public and defend their teachings. And though no shaykhs emerged, advocates and naysayers alike wrote to engage in debate. 'Abd Allah al-Zawawi also continued to be a name of contention, and *al-Imam* consistently emphasized a linkage with him, translated his lectures, and decried the claims allegedly made by *tariqa* members who also claimed his sainted person as a source of authority.

Throughout though one must credit the editors with giving space (and often the front page) to all. One (reformed or merely fictional?) Naqshbandi adept, Murid al-Haq (Student of the Truth) of Hulu Kampar, Perak, even sent in a letter laying out the entire genealogy (*silsila*) of the order and the entrance procedures deriving from Shaykh Sulayman Zuhdi at Abu Qubays. Apparently all had been well until he was about to commence with the *rabita* and *tawajjuh*, but just as he affirmed to his teacher that he had prepared for these, "suddenly, like a bat out of hell (*seperti 'afrit min al-jinn*), in came someone with a copy of *al-Imam*, which I read with great disappointment, for therein were published my doubts and wonderings about *this tariqa*" (*al-Imam*, vol. 3 no. 3, 30 July 1908, pp. 41–45). And so, fearing the rage of his guru lest he confront the latter with his doubts, he had written to *al-Imam* ...

By comparison, and after suggesting that *al-Imam* had been sold a lie by certain people who were interested in misrepresenting the *tariqa*s, Murid al-Yaqin (Student of Conviction) of Pulau Tawur, Kuala Lapis, Pahang, defended the learning and authority of the Khalidiyya as compared with "some of the *tariqa*s of today", and urged Murid al-Haq to examine the writings of Khatib

Sambas, not to mention the works of Isma'il al-Minankabawi, and 'Abd al-Majid ibn Muhammad al-Khani's (1846/7–1900/01) *Bahja al-saniyya fi al-tariqa al-naqshbandiyya* — which he noted could be found listed as item number 13 in the catalogue of Haji Muhamad Siraj.[29]

Meanwhile the voice of *al-Imam* — whilst looking on and sometimes commenting in a critical vein (and it was certainly critical of the purported beliefs of Khatib Sambas)— could still quote approvingly (or selectively at least) from a very mixed bag, including Sayyid 'Uthman, *al-Manar*, Mahmud Shukri al-Alusi (1857–1924) *and* indeed such Sufi luminaries as al-Junayd al-Baghdadi (d. 910), 'Abd al-Qadir al-Jilani (1077–1166), al-Busiri (d. 1296) — author of the famous *Burda* recited in the poetry gatherings mentioned by al-Fatani; though never, it seems, from Ahmad Khatib.

Al-Imam's quoting of al-Jilani apparently led one *tariqa* shaykh in Sambas, Borneo (assumedly a student of the late Khatib Sambas himself), to declare that the journal had associated the saint with polytheism (*shirk*), though *al-Imam* pointed to a letter from Sumatra signed by '.A (Abdullah Ahmad?) and urged the community at Sambas to judge for themselves who best understood the Sufi master's words — them, or the likes of al-Ma'mum (*al-Imam* 3, no. 3 (29 August 1908): 84–85). By November the journal was running extensive quotes on the matter from *al-Manar*, which had joined in the Southeast Asian debate on *tariqa* itself in August following questions repeated to it by correspondents on the Malay peninsula (Abaza 1998, pp. 109–10). Hence, to observers newly drawn in to the debates, and certainly to local *tariqa* shaykhs, the transformation to Cairene mouthpiece would appear to have been complete. Meanwhile, political conditions had at last changed in the Hijaz itself, to allow Sayyid 'Abd Allah to cease his peregrinations, and to return to Mecca where he would replace the late Sayyid Babusayl and assume the rank of the foremost authority on questions of Shafi'i law in the Holy City.

CONCLUSION

> Once a native prince asked him whether the insurance of buildings, merchandise etc. against damage of any kind were not to be declared allowable according to the Moslim law. Abdallah [al-Zawawi] showed me the letter of that prince as well as his answer, which he wrote down immediately after receiving it. The latter contained a condemnation in the strongest terms of all insurance contracts as being so many kinds of gambling. On my remark that I remembered having witnessed Sayyid Abdallah himself insuring cases of tea which he dispatched to Mecca, he freely conceded the truth of my statement. But, he added, if now and then I give in to the

> seduction of transgressing the Divine Law in my own worldly interest, I do not want to increase the weight of my sins by teaching others that such actions are lawful. The prince has not asked, what Sayyid Abdallah does, but what Allah prescribes to a Moslim to do. (Snouck Hurgronje 1941, pp. 15–16).

Seeing beyond the rhetoric of clinging to the book of God, the nobleness of the *Sharia* and the *tariqa* of action, the implication to be drawn from the exchanges in *al-Imam* (and the *Utusan Melayu*), I would suggest, is that it was the alleged pseudo-Sufism of local *tariqa* shaykhs of modern, fallen, times, rather than Sufism (or perhaps even the *tariqas*) per se, that was to be abandoned as it impeded one's progress in the life of the world. Such a message was by no means new and had been advanced by the *ulama* of previous centuries who were responsible for communicating trends in Islamic discourse linking Southeast Asia and the Middle East (see Azra 2004). These included *ulama* like Abd al-Samad of Palembang (1704–89), who was (like al-Zawawi) praised by both *al-Imam* and its detractors.

The difference now, I would suggest, was that with the advent of heightened relations with Mecca and a greater (and certainly lucrative) Jawi presence there, the once exclusivist Southeast Asian Sufi market had become overcrowded. Sometimes there were even several competing variants of the same order, or at least competing shaykhs claiming the sole rights to the silsila of the master(s) of Abu Qubays. Hence I would suggest that the intellectual trajectory of *al-Imam* is best understood as an outgrowth of an earlier, elitist Sufism that was linked to royal coteries now on the back-foot to rampant colonialism. Moreover, it was a Sufism that was finding its leadership challenged in Mecca, where far too many adepts seemed to be enrolling in the *tariqas* with far too little training, and locally, where the field being swamped by a tsunami of minor shaykhs who could readily make use of printed texts (and perhaps even some that they were responsible for printing) rather than demonstrating individual mastery of materials handed down after hard hours of study at the feet of the master, and beyond the gaze of the common folk.

At the end of the day, what we may well have in *al-Imam*, at least initially, is a rather standard *Sharia*-oriented facade. After all, the journal regularly claimed to be defending the ignorant and the helpless from charlatan *tariqa* shaykhs, but nowhere are the learned said to be at risk. As such, it still maintained the principle that there was an elect, who as we have seen above, intersected to a large degree with the elect of 'Alawi lineage. Hence the riddle of underlying affiliation is, I suspect, solved by closer attention to the personal relationships of the Sayyid editors. And when 'Abd Allah al-Zawawi appears in the printed pages of contention in Singapore, being the chosen locus for a conflict taking place from Siam to Sumatra, one must raise the question as to whether he may have represented the Mazhariyya order.

Even if 'Abd Allah al-Zawawi was not a practising *tariqa* shaykh, and had come, with the passing of his father, to prefer the "scientific Sufism" advocated by the scholarly elite (as well as Muhammad 'Abduh and Snouck Hurgronje for that matter), this avowedly modern friend to Dutch orientalists and accomplished exile in Asian waters would ultimately return to his birthplace to preside as Imam of the Shafi'i *madhhab*. There, and in partnership with the increasingly tradition-minded Sharif Husayn, he would both continue to send articles to the Malay presses of Sumatra (Laffan 2003, p. 199), to adjudicate in disputes between Kaum Muda and Kaum Tua (Kaptein 2008), and to preside over a world in which the *tariqa*s remained, for that moment, and until his death in the assault on Ta'if in October 1924, full participants.

But what of the largely Malay readers of *al-Imam* and the non-Sayyid authors still associated with it? I have already noted above that the scholarship in the evolution of the archipelago-wide dichotomy based around the all too-clear fault-line of modernity is often backdated to *al-Imam* — and my own previous work has been no exception to this. But while there is still good reason to see the emergence of the journal and its actors at a pivotal moment in Malay history, the complex positions of the editors at the time are obscured when looking back from the perspective of a Salafizing Malaysia; a perspective that has the Sufis thrown onto the camp of Kaum Tua, "traditionalist", opposition and thus out of its pages (or at least its editorial board).

I hope that what I have shown here is that, just as Mahdi and Hourani have implied for West Asia, this is a problematic splitting at best and that, for the time, those later claimed as Kaum Muda modernists or Kaum Tua traditionalists were actively debating their space together. Indeed, if we heed suggestion of a linkage between Sufi markets and print capitalism, shedding in the process the absolute distinction between print-savvy modernists and print-blind traditionalists, then we might well conceive, after mid-1908, that a great many *tariqa* members might well have lined up behind "al-Ma'mum", "Murid al-Yaqin" and the followers of "old" Khatib Sambas, and ceased paying subscription fees for a journal that was now so clearly targeting their beloved masters in the name of the "young" Cairene upstarts. In fact, it is just this scenario which was invoked by S.T. of Singapore and S.S. of Kuala Lumpur, who brought the entire matter before *al-Manar* in August of 1908, claiming that after *al-Imam*'s explanations had been issued, the local Sufi shaykhs instructed the common people (*al-'amma*) to cease reading the journal.[30]

Meanwhile, for those Malays who did agree with the anti-Sufi message that undermined the "traditionalist" Sufi elite, there were also implications to be taken from other aspects of the teachings of 'Abduh and Rida. Most especially, they had to deal with the notion that Sayyids had no privileged right to a superior position in Islamic societies. And so, looking beyond the Arab-centric reading of Islamic history still presented by Rida (and in turn by *al-Imam*), some reformers would increasingly emphasise the local needs of their communities vis-à-vis Middle Eastern comparisons, and sought equal representation as Muslims — regardless of their prestige or lack thereof.

A sign of this may be seen in the fact that several new Islamic journals arose in Singapore in the months after *al-Imam* collapsed, though none attempted to capture the same market, or yet to devote large space to the issue of the *tariqas*. Of these, three had clear connections with Hadrami, or Sayyid, concerns while one alone, *Neracha* (The Scales), announced an explicitly Malay constituency.[31] And whereas *al-Imam* had commenced in 1906 with its editors announcing that they were "not of the same lineage as the people of this place" but felt "indebted to its country and people" by virtue of their residence there (*al-Imam* 1, no. 1 (23 July 1906)); by 1912 an editorial in *Neracha* — also edited by Abas Taha of *al-Imam* — declared that to be Malay (or Jawi) was to have different aims from others, and that the Malays, having read "the newspapers of the world", were to meditate on their relatively backward status, and to activate themselves "to obtain the honour and progress demanded of our people" ("Kaum Melayu", *Neracha* 2, no. 42 (2 Sha'ban 1330/17 July 1912): 1). Even so, this was explicitly declared to be a struggle separate from the things "demanded by the Turks and Egyptians". Where the Sayyid and the (*tariqa*) Sufi fitted in the future was then anybody's guess, though neither were by any means out of the race for the leadership of the Muslims of Southeast Asia yet.

Notes

I wish to thank the KNAW, IIAS, ISIM and our colleagues within the Indonesian Academy for facilitating such an exciting project over the last four years. I would also like to express my gratitude here to all my Dutch and Indonesian colleagues, particularly Nico Kaptein, Kees van Dijk, Noorhaidi Hasan, Martin van Bruinessen, Moch. Nur Ichwan, and Jajat Burhanudin.

1. The first hint of this came in 1905, when Rida issued his *fatwa* on marital parity (*kafa'a*) in response to a question from Singapore; asserting that the daughter of a Sayyid could marry outside Sayyid circles, in this case to an Indian Muslim. For recent discussion of this *fatwa* and of *kafa'a* in general, see Ho (2000), pp. 203ff.

2. On the founder of the Khalidiyya and its impact in the Middle East, see Hourani (1981*a*).
3. In Hamzah's work, and that of Milner after him, many of the terms used in the journal have been glossed in line with the rhetoric of the 1980s, whereby the notion of *umma* can only refer to the entire community of believers (rather than "the nation") while the *ulama* of *sharia* could be referred to as "theologians".
4. See Shaghir Abdullah (1990), pp. 201–06. Until the mid-twentieth century the bookshop of al-Halabi was the primary Cairene imprinter for Jawi works and retains today a certain magical aura among Southeast Asians, despite its dilapidated interior and diminished stocks.
5. For the text itself, with its numerous attributions to the words of Ibn Hajar al-'Asqalani, Abd al-Qadir al-Jilani, Muhammad Arshad al-Banjari and Nawawi al-Bantini, see 'Uthman n.d., passim. For a preliminary biography and assessment of 'Uthman's works, including the *Manhaj al-istiqama*, see Azra (1999).
6. See al-Fatani (1957), pp. 179–210. On *majdhub*, see Gramlich (1985), p. 1029.
7. Al-Fatani (1957), p. 180. It is noteworthy that in this version of the text there is no exact description of the activities of the *tariqa* — including stamping feet and men and women coming together when the lights are extinguished — as attributed to the question by Kraus (1999), p. 745 based on three subsequent variants of the *fatwa*.
8. Cf. Kraus (1999), p. 744, who gives the date as 1321 or 1323.
9. For discussion of this literature, based in part on the work of Schrieke, and a fuller treatment of the place of Ahmad Khatib in the history of ant-Sufi polemics in Indonesia, see Van Bruinessen (1999), whose title translations I have modified slightly here.
10. See Noer (1973), p. 32, who half-heartedly repeated oral claims that copies of an anti-colonial paper produced by 'Abduh and Jamal al-Din al-Afghani, *al-'Urwa al-wuthqa* (The Indissoluble Bond), were smuggled into the Javanese port of Tuban after the Dutch had banned it, although it seems from the contemporary observations of Van den Berg (1886), p. 174 that copies were in free circulation among the Arabs of the Netherlands Indies.
11. See Roff (1967) and also Andaya (1977), Hamzah (1991), Milner (1995), Mat Ton (2000), and Laffan (2003). On the Riau genesis see also Van der Putten (1997), p. 730, who draws on Andaya's comments about the journal's importance as a vehicle for the Riau nobility to voice their grievances, and points out the connection between *al-Imam*'s financial backer, Raja Ali Kelana, who had returned from an unsuccessful trip to the Middle East in 1904–05 to gain support for the fading sultanate.
12. On the official figures, see Proudfoot (1985), p. 26. It is also worth noting that *al-Manar*, which admittedly faced more competition, only had an initial print-run of 300–400 copies in its first three years. See Shahin (1993), p. 12.
13. Indeed, questions have long been raised regarding 'Abduh's own Sufi past, and even that of Rashid Rida, who had himself been a member of the Khalidiyya. See

Hourani (1981*b*), p. 96 and Asad (2001), pp. 5–6. As Shahin has implied, even in later life Rida's criticism was more of the alleged political quiesence of the orders than their doctrinal deviation. See Shahin (1993), p. 47.

14. In his own discussion, Hamzah (1991), pp. 22, 37–49 concentrated almost entirely on one question from Siamese territory (which I shall also examine here) and made passing reference to (seemingly earlier) criticisms of "sellers of talismans". A too speedy reading of Roff will also lead one with the impression that *al-Imam* was consistently anti-Sufi, or at least anti-*tariqa*, though again his evidential base is clearly derived from 1908 as opposed to 1906–08, and Roff was always more careful to state that the target was the *tariqa* and not *tasawwuf* per se.
15. Roff, on the other hand, states that he was an Arab of Acehnese background. According to a worried Dutch Consul in Singapore, al-Kalali had played some sort of unspecified role in the early years of the Aceh War. See Spakler to Snouck Hurgronje, Singapore, 9 August 1906; *Nationaal Archief*, A.190 box 451.
16. Othman (2002), pp. 45–46 also observes that he was a trusted confidante of the British, and most especially of Colonial Secretary R.J. Wilkinson.
17. See Spakler to Snouck Hurgronje, Singapore, 9 August 1906, *Nationaal Archief*, A.190 box 451.
18. See G.A.J. Hazeu to GG, Weltevreden, 16 March 1908, *Nationaal Archief*, Vb 29 September 1908, no. 9.
19. The text states that the husband dies, but this seems to make little sense.
20. This assertion was made by Mustajab in 1977 and was repeated by Kraus (1999), p. 750. In any case Shaykh Tahir seems to have been in Egypt at the time.
21. By its consistent spelling as *tawajjuh*, this refers to the Naqshbandi practice of intense concentration, as opposed to the short interview (*tawâjuh*) held between the shaykh and the adept during the early stages of training. Cf. Hourani (1981), p. 92; Snouck Hurgronje (1931), p. 240.
22. In the versions cited by Kraus such details are included, though it seems possible that they may well have been infused into the *fatwa* from the question to *al-Imam* rather than vice versa as he suggested.
23. The text makes reference to prophetic traditions calling on Islam to be defended in accordance with one's capability and an affirmation is made that it is incumbent on all *ulama* to challenge such with the proof of their intellect (*'aql*) and to say to those in power that it is incumbent on kings to encourage every good thing for their people and to use their rank to work for both the hereafter and this life. Moreover it is declared incumbent upon rulers to look after their people with their goods based on the prophetic tradition that "every shepherd is responsible for his flock" (*kull ra' mas'ul 'an ra'iyyatihi*; p. 273).
24. In the latter respect though there was a moment of sadness when, after its failure in Singapore and removal to Riau, the defunct school's master was forced to sell

its stock of books — including "Istanbul printings of the Qur'an" and works of *fiqh*, *tafsir* and geography. See *Utusan Melayu*, 2 June 1908.

25. For a discussion of the historical importance of these particular exegetical texts in Southeast Asia, see Riddell (2001), pp. 139–67.
26. See the various letter of 'Abd Allah al-Zawawi to Snouck Hurgronje now held at Leiden University: L.Or. 8952.
27. Aboe Bakar to Snouck Hurgronje, 19 March 1897, LOr. 8952.
28. Drewes (1957), pp. 13–14 once noted Snouck Hurgronje's evolving interest in the Sufi orders and their importance to Islam, their state of "degeneration" in Aceh, and indeed the fact that a great many of the theses that he supervised at Leiden University were on the subject of mysticism or the orders in the archipelago. Steenbrink (1999), pp. 703–04, meanwhile, points out how Snouck Hurgronje defended the member of the orders as "unorthodox" but generally more tolerant subjects in his official advice for the colonial government.
29. *Al-Imam* 3, no. 3 (29 August 1908): 77–83. More correctly, the work was entitled *al-Bahja al-saniyya fi adab al-tariqa al-'aliyya al-khalidiyya al-naqshbandiyya* (The Gleaming Splendor: Concerning the manners of the lofty *tariqa* of the Naqshbandiyya Khalidiyya). Most likely it was that published posthumously at the Maymuniyya press of Cairo at the instigation of the Cairene publisher, and fellow Syrian, Mustafa al-Babi al-Halabi in AH 1319/ 1901–02 CE.
30. See "al-Rabita 'ind al-naqshbandiyya wa ta'at al-murid li shaykhih", *al-Manar* 11 no. 7 (30 Rajab 1326 (28 August 1908)): 504–14, and especially pp. 506–07, where Taha is described as being behind the campaign against the shaykhs, who were scrambling to limit the journal's influence. See also Abaza (1998), pp. 109–10.
31. It also seems likely that other *al-Imam* veterans were feeling increasingly uncomfortable with Rashid Rida. In later years Bin 'Aqil, by then a staunch defender of the 'Alawite Sayyids, wrote against the latter (Roff 2002), p. 103.

References

Abaza, Mona. "Southeast Asia and the Middle East: *Al-Manar* and Islamic Modernity". In *Mediterranean to the China Sea: Miscellaneous Notes*, edited by Claude Guillot, Denys Lombard, and Roderich Ptak. Wiesbaden: Harrassowitz Verlag, 1998, pp. 93–111.

al-Fatani, Ahmad bin Muhammad Zayn bin Mustafa. *Al-Fatawa al-fataniyya*. "Siam": Al-Matba'a al-Fataniyya, 1957.

Anderson, Benedict. *Imagined Communities: Reflections on the Origin and Spread of Nationalism*. Revised edition. London: Verso, 1991 [1983].

Andaya, Barbara Watson. "From Rum to Tokyo: The Search for Anticolonial Allies by the Rulers of Riau, 1899–1914". *Indonesia*, no. 24 (1977): 123–56.

Asad, Talal. *Thinking about Secularism and Law in Egypt*. Leiden: ISIM, 2001.

Azra, Azyumardi. "A Hadrami Religious Scholar in Indonesia: Sayyid 'Uthman' ". In *Hadrami Traders, Scholars and Statesmen in the Indian Ocean, 1750s–1960s*, edited by Ulrike Freitag and William G. Clarence-Smith. Leiden, New York and Köln: Brill, 1997, pp. 249–63.

———. *The Origins of Islamic Reformism in Southeast Asia: Networks of Malay-Indonesian 'Ulama' in the Seventeenth and Eighteenth Centuries.* Leiden: KITLV/ Asian Studies Association of Australia, 2004.

Bayly, C.A. *Empire and Information: Intelligence Gathering and Social Communication in India, c.1780–1870.* New York: Cambridge University Press, 1996.

Berg, L.W.C. van den. *Le Hadhramout et les Colonies Arabes dans l'archipel Indien.* Batavia: Imprimerie du Gouvernement, 1886.

Bruinessen, Martin van. "Controversies and Polemics Involving the Sufi Orders in Twentieth-century Indonesia'. In *Islamic Mysticism Contested: Thirteen Centuries of Controversies and Polemics*, edited by Frederick De Jong and Bernd Radtke. Leiden: Brill, 1999, pp. 705–28.

Bruinessen, Martin van. "Shaykh 'Abd al-Qâdir al-Jîlânî and the Qâdiriyya Order in Indonesia". *Journal of the History of Sufism*, no. 1–2 (2000): 361–95.

Bruinessen, Martin van. "After the Days of Abû Qubays: Indonesian Transformations of the Naqshbandiyya Khâlidiyya". *Journal of the History of Sufism*, 5 (2008): 225–51.

Dijk, C. van. "Colonial fears, 1890–1918: Pan-Islamism and the Germano-Indian plot". In *Transcending Borders: Arabs, Politics, Trade and Islam in Southeast Asia*, edited by Huub de Jonge and Nico Kaptein. Leiden: KITLV Press, 2002.

Eickelman, Dale F. and Armando Salvatore. "Muslim Publics". In *Public Islam and the Common Good*, edited by Dale F. Eickelman. Leiden: Brill, 2004, pp. 3–27.

Ernst, Carl. "Sufism, Islam, and Globalization in the Contemporary World: Methodological Reflections on a Changing field of Study". In *Islamic Spirituality and the Contemporary World*, edited by Azizan Baharuddin. Kuala Lumpur: Centre for Civilisational Dialogue, University of Malaya, forthcoming.

Gramlich, R. "Madjdhûb". In *The Encyclopaedia of Islam.* Second edition, vol. 5, p. 1029. Leiden: Brill, 1991.

Hamzah, Abu Bakar. *Al-Imam: Its role in Malay Society 1906–1908.* Kuala Lumpur: Media Cendekiawan, 1991.

Ho Engseng. "Genealogical figures in an Arabian Indian Ocean diaspora". Doctoral dissertation, University of Chicago, 2000.

Hourani, Albert. "Sufism and Modern Islam: Mawlana Khald and the Naqshbandi Order". In *The Emergence of the Modern Middle East*, by Albert Hourani. Oxford: Macmillan, 1981*a*, pp. 75–89.

Hourani, Albert. "Sufism and Modern Islam: Rashid Rida". In *The Emergence of the Modern Middle East*, by Albert Hourani. Oxford: Macmillan, 1981*b*, pp. 90–102.

Kaptein, Nico. "Southeast Asian Debates and Middle Eastern Inspiration: European Dress in Minangkabau at the Beginning of the Twentieth Century". In *Southeast*

Asia and the Middle East: Islam, Movement, and the Longue Duree, edited by E. Togliocozzo. Stanford: Stanford University Press, 2008, pp. 176–98.

Kraus, Werner. "Sufis und Ihre Widersacher in Kelantan/Malaysia: Die Polemik Gegen de Ahmadiyya zu Beginn des 20. Jahrhunderts". In *Islamic Mysticism Contested: Thirteen Centuries of Controversies and Polemics*, edited by Frederick De Jong and Bernd Radtke. Leiden: Brill, 1999, pp. 729–56.

Laffan, Michael F. *Islamic Nationhood and Colonial Indonesia: The Umma below the Winds.* London and New York: RoutledgeCurzon, 2003.

Mahdi, Muhsin. "From the Manuscript Age to the Age of Printed Books". In *The Book in the Islamic World: The Written Word and Communication in the Middle East*, edited by George N. Atiyeh. Albany: State University of New York Press/ Library of Congress, 1995.

Mandal, Sumit K. "Natural Leaders of Native Muslims: Arab Ethnicity and Politics in Java under Dutch Rule". In *Hadhrami Traders, Scholars and Statesmen in the Indian Ocean, 1750s–1960s*, edited by Ulrike Freitag and William G. Clarence-Smith. Leiden, New York and Köln: Brill, 1997, pp. 185–98.

Mat Ton, Abdul Aziz. *Politik al-Imam*. Kuala Lumpur: Dewan Bahasa dan Pustaka, 2000.

Matheson, V. and M.B. Hooker. "Jawi Literature in Patani: The Maintenance of an Islamic Tradition". *JMBRAS* 61-1 (1988): 1–86.

Milner, Anthony. *The Invention of Politics in Colonial Malaya: Contesting Nationalism and the Expansion of the Public Sphere.* Cambridge: Cambridge University Press, 1994.

Noer, Deliar. *The Modernist Muslim Movement in Indonesia 1900–1942.* Kuala Lumpur: Oxford University Press, 1973.

Othman, Mohammad Redzuan. "Conflicting Political Loyalties if the Arabs in Malaya before World War II". In *Transcending Borders: Arabs, Politics, Trade and Islam in Southeast Asia*, edited by Huub de Jonge and Nico Kaptein. Leiden: KITLV Press, 2002, pp. 25–40.

Proudfoot, Ian. "Pre-war Malay Periodicals: Notes to Roff's Bibliography Drawn from Government Gazettes". *Kekal Abadi* 4, no. 4 (December 1985): 1–28.

Proudfoot, Ian. "Mass Producing Houri's Moles or Aesthetics and Choice of Technology in Early Muslim Book Printing". In *Islam: Essays on Scripture, Thought and Society: A Festschrift in Honour of Anthony Johns*, edited by P.G. Riddell and A.D. Street. Leiden: Brill, 1997, pp. 161–84.

Putten, Jan van der. "Printing in Riau: Two Steps toward Modernity". *BKI* 153, no. 4 (1997): 717–36.

Riddell, Peter. *Islam and the Malay-Indonesian World.* Honolulu: University of Hawai'i Press, 2001.

Roff, William R. *The Origins of Malay Nationalism.* New Haven and London: Yale University Press, 1967.

Roff, William R. "Murder as an Aid to Social History: The Arabs of Singapore in the Early Twentieth Century". In *Transcending Borders: Arabs, Politics, Trade and*

Islam in Southeast Asia, edited by Huub de Jonge and Nico Kaptein. Leiden: KITLV Press, 2002, pp. 79–95.

Sanusi, Latief M., and Edwar et al. *Riwayat Hidup dan Perjuangan 20 Ulama Besar Sumatera Barat.* Padang: Islamic Centre Sumatera Barat, 1981.

Shaghir Abdullah, Hj. Wan Mohd. "Bahasa Melayu Bahasa Ilmu: Mininjau Pemikiran Syeikh Ahmad bin Muhammad Zain al-Fattani". *Jurnal Dewan Bahasa*, no. 34 (March 1990): 201–206.

Shahin, Emad Eldin. *Through Muslim Eyes: M. Rashid Rida and the West.* Herndon: International Institute of Islamic Thought, 1993.

Sirriyeh, Elizabeth. *Sufis and Anti-sufis: The Defence, Rethinking and Rejection of Sufism in the Modern World.* London: Curzon, 1999.

Snouck Hurgronje, C. *Mekka in the Latter Part of the 19th Century: Daily Life, Customs and Learning of the Moslems of the East-Indian-Archipelago*, translated by J.H. Monahan. Leyden: Brill, 1931.

Snouck Hurgronje, C. "Some of My Experiences with the Muftis of Mecca". *Jaarverslagen van het Oostersch Instituut te Leiden 1934–40*, no. 4 (1941): 2–16.

Steenbrink, Karel. "Opposition to Islamic Mysticism in Nineteenth-century Indonesia". In *Islamic Mysticism Contested: Thirteen Centuries of Controversies and Polemics*, edited by Frederick De Jong and Bernd Radtke. Leiden: Brill, 1999, pp. 687–704.

Trimmingham, J. Spencer. *The Sufi Orders in Islam.* Oxford: The Clarendon Press, 1971.

'Uthman bin 'Abd Allah bin 'Aqil bin Yahya. *Manhaj al-istiqama fi al-din bi al-salama.* Jakarta: Maktabat al-Madaniyya, n.d.

Archival Sources

Nationaal Archief, The Hague; A. 190 box 451.

Snouck Hurgronje Papers, Leiden University; Cod. Or. 8952

Periodicals

al-Imam, Singapore

al-Manar, Cairo

Misbah al-sharq, Cairo

Neracha, Singapore

Utusan Melayu, Singapore

3

TRADITIONAL ISLAM AND MODERNITY

Some Notes on the Changing Role of the *Ulama* in Early Twentieth Indonesia

Jajat Burhanudin

> But, ironically, while print enabled *ulama* to greatly extend their influence in public affairs, it was also doing serious damage to the roots of their authority. By printing the Islamic classics, and the print run for a major text could be as many as ten thousand copies, and by translating them into the vernaculars they undermined their authority; they were no longer necessarily around when the book was read to make up for the absence of the author in the text; … Books, which they literally possessed, which they carried in the hearts, and which they transmitted with a whole series of mnemic aids to memory, could now be consulted by any Ahmad, Mahmud or Muhammad, who could make what they will of them. Increasingly from now on any Ahmad, Mahmud, and Muhammad could claim to speak for Islam (Robinson 1993, p. 245).

The printing press exerted great influence on the way religious authority was created and shaped. The cited quotation confirms what happened during the printing era in the Muslim community in the Netherlands Indies, in which the rise of various voices of Islam by various Muslim leaders — not merely the traditional *ulama* — became a leading feature.

They engaged in a contest of interpreting and discoursing Islam. In Indonesia, the increase in the number of Muslims "who could claim to speak for Islam" began to occur in the early twentieth century. This proceeded alongside the rise and the development of Islamic reformism in an increasingly modernized colony as the consequence of the Dutch Ethical Policy of the period. And one of the most prominent features of reformism was the advance of the products of printing presses (journals, newspapers, and books) in social and intellectual live.

The use of the printing press meant that Muslims no longer had to turn to a recognized *mufti* only. In one issue of *Islam Bergerak* (10 June 1917), one of the newspapers published by Hadji Misbach (a leading leftist Muslim activist of the Sarekat Islam), there was a question from a reader about eating pork when one was starving and could not find any other food to eat. This is only one example of the way contemporary Muslims in the Netherlands Indies asked for religious opinions (*istifta'*). Journals and newspapers published in that period had a special column for giving *fatwas* — commonly referred to as *tanja djawab* (question and answer) — which offered readers the opportunity to send questions to the editors to get an explanation on issues ranging from religious practices to sophisticated subjects of theology and philosophy. Indeed, one salient feature to emerge with the printing press is the changing mode of presenting Islam. In the past, Muslims would have a submitted a problem like the one dealt with in *Islam Bergerak* directly to the *ulama* of pesantrens. This had formed part of Muslim religious practice. The difference here is that the question was sent to a newspaper. The *fatwa* seeker (*mustafti*) invited an editor, not an *ulama*, to give a religious explanation.

The role journals and newspapers assume, presented a radical departure in the tradition of *kitab* writing. In the past *kitabs* (religious books) had been the single source of Islamic learning in pesantrens and at the same time in the issuing of *fatwa* (Van Bruinessen 1990; Kaptein 1997). The *kitab*, therefore, had emerged as one of the basic pillars of *ulama*'s existence. In the early twentieth century, this position of *kitab* in the making of Islamic discourse began to be challenged. The printing press emerged as a new source of Islamic learning and a new medium for issuing *fatwa*. In this regard, the journal *al-Imam* published in Singapore and *al-Munir* published in Padang in West Sumatra were pioneers. Appearing from 1906 to 1908, *al-Imam* was the first journal to introduce the ideas of Islamic reformism to Southeast Asia. And the spirit of *al-Imam* then became the inspiration for publishing *al-Munir* (1911–16) which is acknowledged as sowing the seed for the development of Islamic reformism in Indonesia.

Much has already been written about these two journals. What is the main concern here is that both *al-Imam* and *al-Munir* contributed to the introduction of a new mode of Islamic intellectual tradition, in which print media emerged as a medium alongside the *kitabs* of the pesantrens (Burhanudin 2004, pp. 27–62). In addition to discoursing Islamic reformism, print media also presented Islam in a new language, Malay, and in a new script, the Latin script (*Rumi*). The journal and newspapers published after *al-Imam* and *al-Munir* used Latin script. The use of Latin script had a specific meaning. The spread of *Rumi* is to be partly attributed to the colonial project of replacing the Arabo-Islamic influence on the Muslims in the Netherlands Indies by Western culture, as J. Pijnappel (1822–1901) did in 1860 (Mandal 1994, pp. 112–14) and then found its expression in Holle's policy of urging the Sundanese *penghulus* in West Java to use Latin script (Laffan 2003, p. 145; Moriyama 2003). Even so, the use of *Rumi* in the journals and newspapers of the early twentieth century is also to be explained as the reformist project of presenting Islam to the newly-emerging Muslims audiences, in which the Western attributes of modernity — including Latin script — were already there.

In this regard, the growth of a vernacular press, those published by Eurasians, Chinese and Indonesians (Adam 1995), can be viewed as a model for the reformist journals. Coming from urban centres in the Netherlands Indies, the advocates of the Islamic reform movement had to cope with, and belonged to, the growing urban communities. In such a situation, the use of *Rumi* became the most plausible choice reformist Muslims could make, to ensure that the reform message would reach a wider readership. Close contact with the growing elite of people who had followed modern education contributed to having reformist Muslims decide in favour of employing *Rumi* for their journals and newspapers. In addition, the relaxed attitudes of the Javanese, which formed a major segment of the readership, to the *Jawi* script (Adam 1995, p. 40) was another factor that led the editors and publishers to use *Rumi* instead of *Jawi*. All this resulted in the decreased use of *Jawi* to the extent that it became economically irrelevant in the growing printing industry.

Thus, partly due to the emergence of the printing press, Islamic reformism succeeded in the creation of a space within which Muslims, with different outlooks and orientations, contested to define Islam in Indonesia. Muslims began to engage in debates about religious issues, contested opinions and interpretations of Islam, which were entrenched in their different backgrounds of religious education and world view. Polemical debates, discussions, and contests constituted a major feature in the development of Islam during the early twentieth century. The issues which emerged in the debates and contests covered many important aspects of Islamic teachings. Legal reasoning (*ijtihad*), the attributes of God, blind obedience to the Islamic schools of thought (*taqlid*), prompting at graves (*talqin*), and visiting graveyards (*ziyara*) were among the most disputed and discussed matters (Federspiel 2001, pp. 53–66; Noer 1973). Moreover, the contested issues widened in scope and substance. They began to be not only concerned with religious but also with social and political matters. The debates on the relationship between Islam and nationalism and even communism can be taken as examples (Federspiel 1970, pp. 38–39; Shirasihi 1990).

This development can be explained from the fact that the print media provided the Muslims with easy access to Islamic teachings. Muslims began to study Islam without going to and staying in pesantrens, which in the past had been the most authoritative centre for Islamic learning (Dhofier 1982). They instead could find religious books, journals, and newspaper in bookshops, libraries, and other places that formerly had hardly been associated, from a traditional point of view, with Islamic learning. Moreover, Islam was delivered in a more vernacular and mundane manner. The sacredness of Islamic classical texts began to erode with the acceptance of the modern printing press (Robinson 1993, pp. 229–351). This process was enhanced by the publication of translations of Islamic classical texts which had previously been consulted by relatively few people and had circulated exclusively among the religious elites. Thus, Hadith literature and manual practices of Islamic rituals now could be found not only in the pesantren where they were studied in the presence of *ulama*, but also in schools and at home.

With this development, the Islamic reform movement contributed to the growth of a new mode of religious thinking that was based on printed media. Among Muslims in mainly urban centres, oral tradition — which had been firmly established in the transmission of Islamic knowledge — began to be challenged by the reading of printed books and articles. Books, journals, newspapers, and pamphlets contributed to the production of religious meaning, and hence created a significant change in the making of religious authority among Muslims in the Netherlands Indies. The *ulama* were no longer the only single authoritative body in the formation of Islamic knowledge and discourse. New sources of religious knowledge and authority started to emerge on the basis of reading the products of the printing press. With this, Islamic reformism contributed to forming an important foundation for the rise of religious plurality, in which new voices of Islam began to emerge in the intellectual landscape in the Netherlands Indies.

NEW ISLAMIC VOICES AND LEADERSHIP: ONE EXAMPLE

A leader whose voice represents the rise of a new configuration of Islam was the Sarekat Islam (SI) leader H.O.S. Tjokroaminoto. His rise to prominence in the SI is an obvious mark of the changing leadership in Islam in the Netherlands Indies. Tjokroaminoto had no experience of studying *kitabs* in pesantrens. Nor had he joined the *Jawi* community of people from the Netherlands Indies studying Islam in Mecca or Cairo. Nevertheless, he significantly engaged in the making of Islamic discourses in early twentieth century Indonesia.

Born on 16 August 1882 in Bakur, a small town in Madiun in East Java, Tjokroaminoto came from a Javanese aristocratic family (*ningrat*). This background can be traced back to Kasan Basari, a leading *'alim* of eighteenth century Java and the leader of Pesantren Tegalsari of Ponorogo, who after marrying the daughter of the Ruler of Surakarta had joined a Javanese aristocratic family. His grandfather, Mas Adipati Tjokronegoro, had been *bupati* (regent) of Ponorogo, while his father, Raden Mas Tjokroamiseno, had been *wedana* (chief district officer) of Madiun.

Like other *ningrat* families of that period, the young Tjokroaminoto had a Western education. In 1902 he graduated from a Dutch school, the OSVIA (the Training School for Native Civil Servants), in Magelang, having completed a seven-year course that opened the way for a *priyayi* career. Thus, at the age of twenty, Tjokroaminoto began his career as a *pangreh praja* He became a clerk at the regency of Ngawi. In 1905, after three years, he left the office and began a new career in the urban centre of Surabaya in East Java. Here, he was employed at the Cooy & Coy firm while completing evening classes from 1907 to 1910. Then he worked as an engineer at the Rogjampi sugar factory in Surabaya.

It was while being employed at the sugar factory that Tjokroaminoto was approached to join the Sarekat Islam. In May 1912, he officially became a member and then led the Surabaya branch of the Sarekat Islam. This was his debut as a politician. In December 1912 Tjokoaminoto also became the manager of the commercial company of the SI, the *Setia Oesaha*, that backed the SI activities including the publishing of *Oetoesan Hindia* one of SI's leading organs. His political role continued to grow in importance when he was entrusted with the crucial task of converting the SI branches into local SIs. This move had become necessary after the colonial authorities — due in part to the involvement of SI members in anti-Chinese riots (Azra 1994, pp. 27–53) — had refused to grant legal recognition to a newly-proposed statute of a nationwide SI, drafted by Tjokroaminoto in 1913. Batavia only recognized the legal status of SI branches. Therefore, the conversion of SI branches into local SIs was the most strategic option to take.

Thus, with the support of D.A. Rinkes, the Advisor for Native Affairs, Tjokroaminoto — who Rinkes described as being "gifted with a fine political instinct that can be useful in every sense" (Shiraishi 1990, p. 72) — entered the political arena. Not only did he succeed in converting the SI branches into local SIs, but this mission also paved the way for him to become the supreme leader of the organization. On 18 February 1914, at a meeting in Yogyakarta, Tjokroaminoto was appointed the chairman of the newly-established Surakarta-based Central Sarekat Islam (CSI), founded as a forum for establishing cooperation among the local SIs (Noer 1973, p. 106; Shiraishi 1990, p. 73). Hence, Tjokroaminoto appeared as the leader of the SI movement, reflecting his wish to be a "Muslim patriot", who dedicated his energy to the Islamic movement (Amelz 1952, I, p. 64). Tjokroaminoto's political activities in the SI are beyond this study. What is to be emphasized here is the fact that he represented the rise of newly-demanded leadership within the Muslim community of the Netherlands Indies that "could claim to speak for Islam".

Much more importantly, Tjokroaminoto's speaking for Islam also emerges from his publications. Two of his books are particularly important: *Islam dan Socialisme* (*Islam and Socialism*), 1924 and *Tarich Agama Islam, Riwajat dan Pemandangan atas Kehidupan dan Perdjalanan Nabi Muhammad S.A.W.* (*The History of Islam, Biography of Muhammad and Notes on His Life and Journey*) 1950. In the first, Tjokroaminoto countered the assertion of a group of socialists in the SI that Islam and the tackling of economic, political and social problems were incompatible. By concluding that this was not the case, Tjokroaminoto defended Islam against socialism (Melayu 2002, p. 43). His *Tarich Agama Islam* discusses the history of Arab people during the time of the Prophet Muhammad. Tjokroaminoto hoped that Muslims in the Netherlands Indies could learn from the way the Prophet and his companions had built up the Islamic community (*umma*), on the grounds of which Muslims of that period achieved their pride and triumph (Tjokroaminoto 1950, p. 8).

Turning to the new Islamic leadership, these two books are illustrative of the way Tjokroaminoto spoke for Islam. In addition to presenting Islam in a new mode of writing format, Tjokroaminoto demonstrated that his formation of Islamic knowledge was based upon what Eickleman (1992, p. 652) asserts as "persuasion and the interpretation of accessible texts", not upon the often inaccessible Arabic *kitabs* which had to be studied under the authority of *ulama*. Reading his *Tarich Agama Islam*, for instance, it is clear that

Tjokroaminoto stated that the content of this book was based on the works of such leading Indian Muslim scholars of the period as Sayyid Amr 'Ali's *The Spirit of Islam* (1922), Muhammad Mawlana 'Ali's *Muhammad and the Prophet* (1924), and Khwaja Kamal al-Din's *The Ideal Prophet* (1925) (Tjokroaminoto 1950, p. 7).

With Tjokroaminoto, a new picture of leadership emerged in the Islamic community in the Netherlands Indies. His political and intellectual careers confirmed the conditions under which such Muslim activists could acquire the authority to speak for Islam to Muslim audiences. This phenomenon should be attributed to the development of Islamic reformism which, aided by the Dutch modernization efforts, contributed to creating the climate which provided Muslims like Tjokroaminoto with the opportunity to emerge as leaders who engaged in defining Islam for Indonesian Muslims. As such, Tjokroaminoto is only one example. Many other "Tjokroaminotos" can be found in the Netherlands Indies at that time, including the *ulama* of pesantrens who participated — in a negotiated way — in the modernization process in the early twentieth century.

NEGOTIATING MODERNITY: THE *ULAMA* IN THE CHANGING NETHERLANDS INDIES

While the Islamic reformism gained its stronghold among a mainly urban Muslim community the *ulama* of the pesantrens had been consolidating their position. Driven by intensifying contacts with the Middle East, and enhanced by the Dutch colonial policy which aimed at creating new religious elites and knowledge (*penghulu*), the *ulama* emerged as a distinct social group. They became the heart of what came to be known as traditionalist *kaum santri* whose ideas and modes of conduct differed from those of the modernist kaum santri in the urbanized areas of the Netherlands Indies.

During the nineteenth century, the *ulama* of the pesantrens evolved into a self-confident community that identified itself in distinct religious terms and social behaviour (Sutherland 1979, pp. 27–28; Kuntowijoyo 1991, pp. 123–37), laying the foundations for the well-known socio-religious division of *santri*, *priyayi* and *abangan* as was observed by Clifford Geertz (1960) in Java in the 1950s. This process continued to develop, to the extent that the *santri* represented a specific cultural system in which the Islamic doctrine emerged profoundly — more than in the cases of both *abangan* and *priyayi* — "to serve, for an individual or for a group, as a source of general, yet distinctive, conception of the world, the self, and the relations between them" (Geertz 1973, p. 123; 1960). Although not always exclusive, the *santris* cultivated their own mode of religious knowledge and ritual practices different from those associated with both *abangan* and *priyayi.*

In the early twentieth century, as the Islamic public sphere came into existence, the socio-religious divisions of the Javanese Muslims into *santri*, *abangan*, and *priyayi* were no longer that simple. Leaving aside developments in the *abangan* and *priyayi* groups, there emerged a division within the santri community between the traditionalist group which was closely associated with the *ulama* of the pesantrens, and the modernist or reformist faction which was more urban-based and was represented by the Muhammadiyah. Beyond that, the early twentieth century also saw a growing involvement of *ulama* in the newly-created atmosphere in the Netherlands Indies — following the advent of Islamic reformism — in a contest to define Islam for Indonesian Muslims.

In such a situation, the encounter with and the adoption of modernity appeared to be a leading feature in the social and intellectual lives of the *ulama* in that period. The *ulama* of the pesantrens began to adopt modern devices and facilities, including the printing press, in order to revive and adapt traditional Islamic knowledge to the new demands of modernity in a changing society. In this regard, the socio-intellectual experiences of two leading *ulama*, Hasjim Asj'ari and Wahab Chasbullah, should be paid attention to. They represented a growing trend amongst contemporary *ulama* in the Netherlands Indies who increasingly embraced modern ways in their efforts to reformulate a long-established traditional Islam amidst the new demand for modernity.

HASJIM ASJ'ARI AND WAHAB CHASBULLAH: CONNECTING *ULAMA* TO MODERNITY

Hasjim Asj'ari (Muhammad Hashim Ash'ari) was born on 14 February 1871 in Jombang in East Java. Hasjim Asj'ari came from a leading family of *bongso poetihan* (devout Muslim communty or *santri*). His father, Kyai Asj'ari, was an *'alim* of Pesantren Keras, an area near Jombang. Also his grandfather and great-grandfather, Kyai Uthman and Kyai Sihah, were leaders of pesantrens, in Gedang and Tambakberas respectively, both also in the vicinity of Jombang. With such a family background, it is no surprise that Hasjim Asj'ari grew up in a pesantren learning environment, with his father as the teacher responsible for his basic Islamic knowledge. Then, like other students of pesantrens, he continued to study with a variety of East Javanese and Madurese *ulama*, including the highly-respected Sufi *'alim*, Khalil Bangkalan and a leading Surabayan *kyai*, Kyai Ya'qub. The latter chose him as a son-in-law and financed his travel to Mecca in 1891 to perform the hajj and for further study. After a stay of one year in Mecca, Hasjim Asj'ari returned to Java, just after his wife and newly-born child had died. Three months later he returned to Mecca and rejoined the *Jawi* students living there. He was to stay in Mecca for seven years (Aboebakar 1957, pp. 55–63; Dhofier 1982, pp. 93–94; Khuluq 2001, pp. 14–21).

During his second stay in Mecca (1893–99), Hasjim Asj'ari continued studying Islam. Mahfud Termas, one of the leading *Jawi ulama* of the time, was his most important teacher who contributed greatly to the formation of his Islamic knowledge. From Mahfudz Termas, Hasjim Asj'ari learned primarily the standard *kitab* of Hadith of Imam Bukhari (*Sahih Bukhari*), which led him to be recognized as an authoritative expert on this subject (Dhofier 1982, p. 93). Also from Mahfudz Termas, Hasjim Asj'ari studied Sufism, especially the Shari'ah-oriented Sufism of al-Ghazali as Nawawi Banten had already espoused (Snouck Hurgronje 1931, pp. 271–72). Through Mahfudz Termas, therefore, Hasjim Asj'ari became linked up with a long-lasting tradition of Sufism that can be traced back to Nawawi Banten and before him Akhmad Khatib Sambas (d.1875), a leading Sufi *'alim* of Java who was intimately connected with the founding of the Qadiriyah-Naqsabandiyah, the most widespread Sufi order in Java (Zulkifli 2002, pp. 15–21; Van Bruinessen 1992, pp. 89–92).

Beyond this, the education he received in Mecca strengthened Hasjim Asj'ari's socio-intellectual background, and hence contributed to him becoming a great *'alim*. In 1899 Hasjim Asj'ari returned to East Java. Shortly after assisting his grandfather at Pesantren Gadang, he established his own pesantren in Tebuireng. Here in Tebuireng, Hasjim Asj'ari established his career as an *'alim*, following in the footsteps of Saleh Darat and Khalil Bangkalan (Arifin 1993, pp. 74–78; Dhofier 1982, pp. 103–10). More importantly, his career confirmed his intellectual standing of belonging to the pesantren milieu as well as his social commitment to the Javanese *ulama* community. It should be noted that when Hasjim Asj'ari joined the *Jawi* students the intellectual circumstances in Mecca were changing. The reformist discourse in Cairo started to gain influence among the *Jawi* in Mecca. Yet, unlike Thaher Djalaluddin of Sumatra and Ahmad Dahlan of Yogyakarta, Hasjim Asj'ari had no scholarly interest in the debate in Cairo. He instead continued to operate within the intellectual domain of his *ulama* family in the pesantrens of East Java.

It is not surprising that Hasjim Asj'ari's close relationship with Mahfudz Termas was more important in the formation of his Islamic knowledge than the ideas of the rising prominent *Jawi 'alim*, Ahmad Khatib of Minangkabau.

Besides his moving mostly in the Javanese community in Mecca — while the majority of Ahmad Khatib's *Jawi* students came from Sumatra and the Malay Peninsula (Snouck Hurgronje 1931, pp. 264–67; Dhofier 1982, p. 94) — Hasjim Asj'ari's intellectual contact with Ahmad Khatib was also minimized by their different opinions about Sufi orders. Ahmad Khatib strongly rejected these, especially the Naqshabandiyah, departing from a moderate stance of Nawawi Banten and Khatib Sambas to whom Hasjim Asj'ari traced — through Mahfudz Termas — his Islamic intellectual genealogy (Dhofier 1982, p. 95). Thus, for Hasjim Asj'ari, the long-established pesantren milieu appeared to be a cultural foundation that directed his learning experiences as well as the future line of his social and intellectual life after returning to Java.

Indeed, Hasjim Asj'ari's fame as a great *'alim* of Java was established in his Pesantren Tebuireng. Here, not only did he provide his students with Islamic learning, as the *ulama* commonly did (and do) in their pesantrens, but he also contributed greatly to the making of a well-established *ulama* community. This role can be explained by the fact that he was one of the higher-ranking *ulama* within the Javanese *ulama* network, which made him into a doyen who had authority to be a leader of the *ulama* community. In his Pesantren Tebuireng, many *ulama* were educated later became leaders in their Muslim communities. More importantly, Hasjim Asj'ari's Islamic opinions voiced in his Pesantren attracted other leading *ulama* — including Khalil Bangkalan — to come to listen to his injunctions and advice. As a result, he emerged as the next great *'alim* after Khalil Bangkalan of Madura whose name was included in the intellectual genealogy of pesantren tradition (Dhofier 1982, p. 92). Beyond this, he became one of Indonesia's most revered *'alim* of the early twentieth century, to whom the *ulama* of Java and Madura paid high respect, honouring him with the title of "Hadratus Shaykh" (the Grand Shaykh) (Arifin 1993, pp. 74–75; Dhofier 1982, pp. 95–96).

In addition to the role played by the pesantren culture of the student-teacher relationship, Hasjim Asj'ari's acquiring the status of Hadratus Shaykh is also important in showing that he represented the idealized *ulama* leadership of the time. He lived at a time when the *ulama* and the Indonesian Muslims encountered socio-cultural changes subsequent to the modernization promoted by the Dutch. In this regard, Hasjim Asj'ari pioneered the establishment of a self-confident community of *ulama*, enabling them to enter the social and intellectual stage of a modernized Netherlands Indies. This found its expression in the moral backing he gave to one of his leading students, Wahab Chasbullah, whose social and religious activities brought him in close contact with the reformist Muslims in the urban centre of Surabaya. It was Wahab Chasbullah who continued with and carried out the spirit of Hasjim Asj'ari to lead the *ulama* of the pesantrens to participate in the condition of modernity of early twentieth century Indonesia.

Born on March 1883 or 1884, Wahab Chasbullah came from an *ulama* family. His father, Kyai Chasbullah, was an *'alim* of Pesantren Tambakberas in Jombang in East Java. His great-grandfather, Kyai Sihah, had established this pesantren (Fealy 1996, pp. 2–3). With such a family background, it is no wonder that Wahab gained his education in pesantrens. He is even known as a "true wandering *santri*" (*santri kelana sejati*), who spent fifteen years learning Islam in seven different pesantrens, including those of Khalil Bangkalan in Madura and of Hasjim Asj'ari in Jombang (Dhofier 1982, pp. 25–27; Zuhril 1983a). The experience of being educated by these two great *ulama* was of special significance for Wahab Chasbullah. Especially in the pesantren of Hasjim Asj'ari. Wahab Chasbullah had contact with many future prominent *ulama*, with whom he would lead the awakening (*nahda*) of the *ulama* community in Indonesia. Among them were Kyai Bisri Syansuri of Pesantren Denanyar in Jombang, Kyai Abdul Karim of Pesantren Lirboyo in Kediri, Kyai Abbas from Pesantren Buntet, Cirebon, and Kyai As'ad Syamsul Arifin of Situbondo (Fealy 1996, p. 4; Aboebakar 1957, pp. 122–23).

As was common in those days for a *santri* who had completed their pesantren education, Wahab continued his studies in Mecca. In 1911, he left East Java for the Hejaz, joining the *Jawi* students. He is said to have studied many fields of Islamic knowledge from the leading *ulama*. To mention some of them: Mahfudz Termas, Muchtarom Banyumas, Ahmad Khatib, Kyai Bakir Yogya, Kyai Asy'ari Bawean, Sayyid Shaykh al-Yamani, Sayyid Shaykh Bakr Satta, and Shaykh Akhmad al-Daghestani (Aboebakar 1957, p. 123). In addition to gaining more in-depth knowledge of Islam, this Meccan period — like his stay in Tebuireng — provided Wahab Chasbullah with the opportunity to expand his social network, which led him to be involved in the emerging political activities of the *Jawi* community in Mecca. Together with Bisri Syansuri (1886–1980), another future leading *'alim* who was studying in Mecca, Abbas of Jember, Raden Asnawi of Kudus, and Dahlan of Kertosono, Wahab Chasbullah founded the Meccan branch of the Sarekat Islam (Wahid 1995, p. 74; Fealy 1996, p. 6). By doing so, Wahab Chasbullah began to enter public life, his involvement becoming the deeper after he returned to East Java in 1914 or 1915.

East Java was the region where Wahab Chasbullah's religious and political career started. Instead of returning to his hometown in Tambakberas in Jombang, he settled in Surabaya. In 1916 he married a daughter of Kyai Musa, an *'alim* and prosperous trader in Kertopaten, a neighbourhood in

Surabaya, and became a teacher at his father-in-law's pesantren (Fealy 1996, p. 7; Anam 1985, p. 24). Living in Kertopaten, while maintaining his connection with the pesantren of Jombang, Wahab Chasbullah experienced from nearby the hectic political life of the metropolitan city of Surabaya. His broad network that he had established in Mecca, going beyond *ulama* circles, intensified. He regularly met such leading figures of the Indonesian nationalist movement as Mas Mansoer, the future leader of Muhammadiyah, Tjokroaminoto of the SI, Wahidin Soediro Hoesodo of Budi Utomo, and Dokter Soeatomo of the Surabaya Study Club (Zuhri 1983b, p. 24).

Surabaya in those days was one of the largest cities of the Netherlands Indies, where the sugar, *kretek* (rolled clove cigarettes), and batik industry and trade thrived and in which Indonesians and the Arabs and later the Chinese had an important share (Clarense-Smith 2002, p. 148; Mandal 2002, pp. 176–77). In socio-political terms Surabaya also experienced the growth of its population which contributed to the development of the city in the 1920s and 1930s as "the home of a large selection of *pergerakan* groups" (Frederick 1989, p. 40). It was Surabaya that provided Wahab Chasbullah with the opportunitiy to engage with important figures. His contact with the above-mentioned future leaders of the Indonesian nationalist movement was of significance. Not only did it mark the establishment of links between the traditional Islam of the pesantrens and the reformist-nationalist movement, but it also sparked the revival of the *ulama* community, with Wahab Chasbullah emerging as the principal figure. Under the spiritual guidance of the doyen of the pesantren *ulama*, Hasjim Asj'ari, Wahab Chasbullah encouraged and directed the *ulama* to participate in the drive for modernity.

Thus, in 1916, Wahab Chasbullah together with Mas Mansoer founded the Madrasah Nahdatul Watan, a modern-styled Islamic educational institution following the path laid by the Islamic schools of *kaum muda ulama* of West Sumatra (Laffan 2003, pp. 227–28). With the financial backing of a businessman, Abdul Kahar, and the support of the emerging leader Tjokroaminoto, a new building was erected for Nahdlatul Wathan (Anam 1985, p. 25). It was here that the leadership of Wahab Chasbullah really took shape. The Madrasah served not only as an educational institution, but also as the meeting place for a number of young *ulama* whom Wahab invited to teach: Bisri Syansuri of Jombang, Abdul Halim Leuwimunding of Cirebon, Alwi Abdul Aziz, Maksum and Kholil of Lasem-Rembang, East Java (Zuhri 1983a, pp. 25–26; Fealy 1996, p. 7). As a result, it was through this madrasah that Wahab Chasbullah laid the foundation for a strong network among the future leaders of pesantren *ulama*.

Contributing to Wahab Chasbullah's prominence was the fact that he had a significant amount of economic capital. As has been noted (Fealy 1996, pp. 7–8; Noer 1973, pp. 229–30), besides being a religious teacher, Wahab also engaged in the trading of mainly agricultural products from Tambakberas, rice and wheat. Later, he extended his commercial activities to include sugar and precious stones. One of his most successful business ventures was his hajj agency. He started working as a pilgrim shaykh for his father-in-law. Later, after his father-in-law had died, he successfully managed the firm and then became a major agent for the Kongsi Tiga Shipping line. Yet at the same time, Wahab Chasbullah used his economic skills to empower the *ulama* network. In 1918, he helped establish Nahdlatul Tujar (*Nahdat al-Tujar*, or the Awakening of the Traders), an association for commercial networking among Muslim traders of Jombang and Surabaya with Hasjim Asj'ari as its chairman and Wahab Chasbullah as its treasurer and legal adviser (Fealy 1996, p. 7).

It was this Wahab Chasbullah, with his leadership skills, broad network and thriving business, who played a major role in voicing the *ulama*'s interests in the changing landscape of the Netherlands Indies. With the spiritual support of Hasjim Asj'ari, Wahab Chasbullah greatly contributed to connecting the world of *ulama* of the pesantrens with the modern world. The importance of Wahab Chasbullah's efforts are none the more evident than in the formation of an *ulama* association in 1926, Nahdlatul Ulama (NU). With the NU, the engagement of the *ulama* in defining Islam for Indonesian Muslims intensified, and their creating their religious authority enhanced. In addition, one other important point that should be paid attention to here is the transformation of the *ulama*'s intellectual life, as will be revealed in the short biographies of two other *ulama*, Ihsan Jampes and Ahmad Sanusi.

IHSAN JAMPES AND AHMAD SANUSI: MAINTAINING *KITAB* WRITING

Kitab writing was one of the main concerns of the *ulama* of the pesantren. They wrote many *kitabs* in various fields of Islamic knowledge which continued to be a source of pesantren learning. In the beginning of the twentieth century, *kitab* writing constituted one leading feature of the *ulama* reformulating tradition and hence their engagement in the modernized Netherlands Indies. Turning to the issue of the printing press, the *ulama* benefited from the technology of printing. Indeed, the printing press — which had been rejected by the Muslims due to its secularizing impact in the sacred transmission of Islamic learning — became an inherent part of the intellectual life of the Muslims in the modern era. Moreover, instead of undermining *ulama*'s authority, as some scholars assert (Robinson 1993, pp. 229–51; Eickelman and Anderson 1997, pp. 43–62; 1999), the technology of printing provided them with possibilities to preserve, enhance and even develop their authority in new but still distinctive ways.

In this regard, two leading *ulama* of early twentieth century Indonesia can be taken here as representing the above-mentioned trend. Ihsan Jampes of Kediri in East Java is one of them. Born in 1901, Ihsan Jampes (Ihsan bin Muhammad Dahlan bin Salih) grew up in a pesantren milieu. His father, Muhammad Dahlan, was an *'alim* of a pesantren he had established in his home town. Ihsan Jampes gained his education in pesantens. He is reported to have studied Islam with several *ulama*: Kyai Khazin of Kediri, Kyai Maksum of Magelang, and the celebrated *'alim*, Kyai Khalil Bangkalan of Madura. In 1926, he went to Mecca for the hajj. But he did not take up residence in Mecca to study Islam. He returned to Java and took over the leadership of his father's pesantren. It was the start of Ihsan's career as an *'alim* with his Pesantren Jampes in Kediri (Barizi 2004, pp. 548–54).

It was from his pesantren that an intellectual portrait of Ihsan Jempas emerged. In addition to providing his students with Islamic learning, as other *ulama* of pesantrens, Ihsan wrote several *kitabs*. Three important ones have to be mentioned here: *Siraj al-talibin* (*The Guidance for the Seekers* [*of Islamic Knowledge*]) on Sufism (two volumes written in the 1930s), *Ta'rih al-'ibarat* (*The Explanation on Allegorism*, 1930s) on astronomy, and *Manahij al-'Imdad* (*The Method of Explanation*, 1940s) on *fiqh* and Sufism. With these publications Ihsan Jampes put the pesantren tradition of writing *kitabs* into the heart of the emerging print culture of Indonesian Islam. Looking at his works, it is clear that they were made in the traditional format of *kitab* writing. They were commentaries (*sharh*) on well known *kitabs* by leading *ulama*. *Siraj al-talibin* was a commentary on *Minhaj al-'Abidin* of al-Ghazali (d.1111), *Manahij al-'Imdad* was on *Irshad al-'Ibad* by Shaykh Zayn al-'Abidin al-Malibari (d.982 H), while *Ta'rih al-'ibarat* was on *Natija al-Miqat* by the *Jawi 'alim* of Semarang, Central Java, Kyai Dahlan of Semarang.

Due to print technology, the above kitabs of Ihsan Jampes reached a wider audience. *Siraj al-talibin* has been reprinted several times by publishing houses in Southeast Asia and the Middle East. At present, two editions of this *kitab* are available, one published in Singapore and the other by Dar al-Fikr of Beirut. As a result, this *kitab* can still be bought in bookshops in Indonesia. Much more importantly, this kitab contributed to making the intellectual ideas of Ihsan Jampes remain an important source of pesantren learning and Islamic discourse in contemporary Indonesia. This printed *kitab* made Ihsan Jampes gain a leading position in the *ulama* network of

Indonesia. He was (and is) regarded as an outstanding *'alim*, highly respected by the leading *ulama* of Java (Barizi 2004, pp. 557–59). Thus, print technology provided Ihsan Jampes with facilities to achieve an important intellectual standing. The same can be said of the second *'alim* of the period, Ahmad Sanusi of West Java.

Born in Sukabumi on 18 September 1889, Ahmad Sanusi came from an *ulama* family of the Priangan (*ajengan*). Just like Ihsan Jampes, Ahmad Sanusi grew up in a pesantren milieu. His father, Hadji Abdoerrahman, was an *'alim* who led a pesantren in the area. Ahmad Sanusi gained his basic education in a number of pesantrens in West Java. The Pesantren of Cisaat in Sukabumi, and those of Cianjur and Garut in the eastern Priangan are reported as the places where he studied. From these pesantrens he continued his study in Mecca. In 1909 he departed from Sukabumi for the Hejaz where he joined the *Jawi* students circle (*halaqah*) (Basri 2003, pp. 226–27). As Ihsan Jampes, Ahmad Sanusi made pesantren the arena of his career. After about eleven years of study in Mecca, he returned to Sukabumi, to assist his father in managing his pesantren in Cantayan (Basri 2003, p. 228). And, as Ihsan Jampes did in Kediri, Ahmad Sanusi also established his career as an author of religious works, in addition to giving Islamic instructions to his students.

Ahmad Sanusi's publications differ from those of Ihsan Jampes. He was more in favour of writing short treaties rather than devoting his energy to scholastic works like Ihsan Jampes' *Siraj al-talibin*. His subjects mainly concerned issues controversial in Muslim circles. Among his around 100 publications, in Arabic and Sundanese, are: *al-Silah al-mahiyah li tur°q al-firaq al-mubtadi'ah* on the Muslim groups that he identified as the followers of Mu'tazila, Shi'a and *bid'a* practice; *Manz°mat al-rijal* on *tawassul* (one of the debated issues of the period); *al-Mufhima fi daf'l al-khayat* on his criticism of reformist discourse, arguing the significance of following one particular school of Islamic thought (*taqlid*); and *al-Qaul al-mufid fi bayan al-ijtihad wa al-taqlid* on *ijtihad* and *taqlid*. With his works, Ahmad Sanusi dealt with a variety of issues which very much occupied the minds of contemporary Indonesian Muslims, showing himself to be a defender of traditional Islam to which he culturally and religiously belonged.

Therefore, Ahmad Sanusi added a new element to the picture of Indonesian *ulama* of the period. He was a debater and writer, besides being a teacher of students in his pesantren. Indeed, he was well known from his debates with the Dutch-appointed religious penghulu elite — locally termed *Pakauman* — and the reformists of the Persatuan Islam (Persis). His debates with the penghulus concerned the legal status of transliterating the Qur'an into Latin script. In Ahmad Sanusi's view this transliteration was allowed, while the *Pakauman* considered it forbidden. Facilitated by the newly-founded "Comite Permoesjawaratan Menoelis al-Qur'an dengan Hoeroep Latijn" (Committee of deliberation concerning the writing of the Qur'an with Latin script), a debate was held in Sukabumi on 25 October 1936. The main debaters were Ahmad Sanusi and Uyek Abdoellah, representing two different and conflicting views of the transliteration dispute (Iskandar 2001, pp. 192–206; Basri 2003, pp. 237–40). Other issues of debate with reformists concerned for instances *ijtihad*, *taqlid*, *talqin* (prompting at the grave), and *ziyara* (visiting the graveyard) (Iskandar 2001, pp. 206–66).

CONCLUDING REMARKS

The experiences of the leading *ulama* I have presented demonstrate the way the *ulama* adapted to the condition of modernity of the Netherlands Indies in the early twentieth century. Their experiences confirm the acknowledged capabilities of *ulama* to negotiate changing circumstances.

Print technology provided them with facilities to not only participate in a modern way of life which the reformist faction had already began to embrace, but also to strengthen the emerging *ulama* network. Here, I would argue that the rise of the printing press contributed to the creation of an "imagined" *ulama* community in Indonesia. This *ulama* community continued to develop, to the extent that they formed a leading faction in the continuous effort even until today in defining Islam for Indonesian Muslims.

Of course, with the rising use of print and then electronic media as well as the advance of mass higher education, the *ulama* of the pesantrens today are not the single makers of Indonesian Islam. Many new Muslim leaders, coming from different socio-intellectual backgrounds, have emerged in contemporary Indonesia. The new Muslim leaders are mostly graduates from universities, in addition to the pesantrens. Some of them have even studied in Western countries. Such Muslim leaders present new Islamic ideas which are different, albeit not always, from those of the *ulama* of the pesantrens. Nevertheless, it does not mean that the *ulama* have ceased to present the Islamic voices. Using ways and methods adapted to modernity, the *ulama* significantly participate in the making of contemporary Islamic discourses.

The Indonesian experience provides us with ample evidence of the continued pivotal role of the *ulama*. Modernity appears to have contributed to enabling the *ulama* to use a more effective way to define Islam and in turn enhance their authority. Nowadays, the *ulama* participate in diverse roles, going beyond their traditional domain in the religious institution in the villages. In addition to their role as the leaders of the pesantrens, some Indonesian *ulama* are now also engaging in presenting Islam through print and electronic media, which in the past has been associated exclusively with reformist Muslims in the cities. Moreover, the *ulama* also participate in such big national political events as the general election, showing their continued influence and role within the Islamic community.

To be mentioned in this regard is the continued increase in the number of Islamic learning centres, the pesantrens, which have been regarded as one of the basic pillars of *ulama*'s existence. Data at the Ministry of Religious Affairs show that in 1977 there were about 4,195 pesantrens with a total number of students (*santris*) of 677,384. In 1981, there were 5,661 pesantrens with 938,397 students. In 1985, the number of pesantrens reached 6,239 with 1,084,801 students. In 1997, the Ministry of Religious Affairs counted 9,388 pesantrens with a total number of students of 1,770,768.

It is clear that the *ulama* have been able to maintain their existence in the changing Indonesian Muslim society. They can no longer be understood as representing the old-fashioned Islam of the past, the so-called traditional Islam, as the early modernization theories assumed. Instead, the *ulama* serve the tradition by responding to the new demands of modernity.

References

Aboebakar, H. *Riwayat Hidup K.H.A. Wahid Hasjim dan Karangan Tersiar*. Jakarta: Panitia Buku Peringatan Al-marhum K.H.A. Wahid Hasjim, 1957.

Adam, Ahmat bin. *The Vernacular Press and the Emergence of Modern Indonesian Consciousness (1855–1913)*. Ithaca: SEAP, Cornell University, 1995.

Amelz. *H.O.S. Tjokroaminoto: Hidup dan Perjuangannya*. Jakarta: Bulan Bintang, 2 vols., 1952.

Anam, Choirul. *Pertumbuhan dan Perkembangan Nahdlatul Ulama*. Solo: Jatayu, 1985.

Arifin, Imron. *Kepemimpinan Kiyai: Kasus Pondok Pesantren Tebuireng*. Malang: Kalimasahada Press, 1993.

Azra, Azyumardi. "The Indies Chinese and the Sarekat Islam: An Account of the Anti-Chinese Riots in Colonial Indonesia". *Studia Islamika* 1, no. 1 (1994): 25–53.

Barizi, Akhmad. "Al-Harakah al-Fikriyyah wa al-turath 'inda al-Shaikh Ihsan Jampes Kediri: Mulahazah Tamhidiyyah". *Studia Islamika* 11, no. 3 (2004): 541–71.

Basri, Husen Hasan. "K.H. Ahmad Sanusi: Membangun Format Ideal Relasi Agama dan Politik". In *Transformasi Otoritas Keagamaan: Pengalaman Islam Indonesia,* edited by Jajat Burhanudin and A. Baedawi. Jakarta: Gramedia-PPIM UIN Jakarta, 2003, pp. 225–62.

Burhanudin, Jajat. "The Fragmentation of Religious Authority: Islamic Print Media in the Early 20th Century Indonesia". *Studia Islamika* 11, no. 1 (2004): 23–62.

Bruinessen, Martin van. "Kitab Kuning: Books in Arabic Script Used in the Pesantren Milieu". *BKI* 146 (1990): 226–69.

Clarense-Smith, W. Gervase. "Horse Trading: The Economic Role of Arabs in the Lesser Sunda Islands, c. 1800 to c. 1940". In *Transcending Borders: Arabs, Politics, Trade, and Islam in Southeast Asia*, edited by Huub de Jonge and Nico Kaptein. Leiden: KITLV Press, 2002, pp. 143–62.

Dhofier, Zamakhsyari. *Tradisi Pesantren: Studi tentang Pandangan Hidup Kyai*. Jakarta: LP3ES, 1982.

Eickelman, Dale F. "Mass Higher Education and the Religious Imagination in Contemporary Arab Society". *American Ethnologist* 19, no. 4 (1992): 643–55.

Eickelman, Dale F. and Jon W. Anderson, eds. "Redefining Muslim Publics". In *New Media in the Muslim World: The Emerging Public Sphere*. Bloomington: Indiana University, 1999, pp. 1–18.

———. "Print, Islam, and the Prospects for Civic Pluralism: New Religious Writing and Their Audiences". *Journal of Islamic Studies* 8, no. 1 (1997): 43–62.

Fealy, G. "Wahab Chasbullah". In *Nahdlatul Ulama: Traditional Islam and Modernity in Indonesia*, edited by G. Barton and G. Fealy. Clayton: Monash Asia Institute, 1996, pp. 1–41.

Federspiel, Howard M. *Islam and Ideology in the Emerging Indonesian State: The Persatuan Islam (Persis), 1923 to 1957*. Leiden: E.J. Brill, 2001.

———. "Islam and Nationalism: An Annotated Translation of and Commentary on *Islam dan Kebangsaan*, a Religious-political Pamphlet Published by *Al-Lisaan* in the Netherlands East Indies in 1941". *Indonesia*, no. 24 (1977): 39–85.

Frederick, William H. *Vision and Heat: The Making of the Indonesian Revolution*. Ohio: Ohio University Press, 1989.

Geertz, Clifford. *The Religion of Java*. New York: The Free Press, 1960.

———. *The Interpretation of Culture*. New York: Basic Books, 1973.

Iskandar, Mohamad. *Para Pengemban Amanah: Pergulatan Pemikiran Kiai dan Ulama di Jawa Barat 1900–1950*. Jakarta: Mata Bangsa, 2001.

Islam Bergerak, 10 June 1917.

Kaptein, N.J.G. *The Muhimmat al-Nafa'is: A Bilinguan Mecan Fatwa Collection for Indonesian Muslims from the End of the Nineteenth Century*. Jakarta: INIS, 1997.

Khuluq, Latiful. *Fajar Kebangunan Ulama: Biografi K.H. Hasyim Asy'ari*. Yogyakarta: LKIS, 1999.

Kuntowijoyo. "Serat Cabolek dan Mitos Pembangkangan Islam". In *Paradigma Islam: Interpretasi untuk Aksi*, edited by A.E. Priyono. Bandung: Mizan, 1991.

Laffan, Michael F. *Islamic Nationhood and Colonial Indonesia: The Umma Below the Winds*. London and New York: Routledge and Curzon, 2003.

Mandal, Sumit K. "Finding Their Place: A History of Arabs in Java under the Dutch Rule 1800–1924". Ph.D. Thesis. New York: Colombia University, 1994.

———. "Forging a Modern Arab Identity in Java in the Early Twentieth Century".

In *Transcending Borders: Arabs, Politics, Trade, and Islam in Southeast Asia*, edited by Huub de Jonge and Nico Kaptein. Leiden: KITLV Press, 2002, pp. 163–84.

Melayu, Hasnul Arifin. "Islam as an Ideology: The Political Thought of Tjokroaminoto". *Studia Islamika* 9, no. 3 (2002): 35–81.

Moriyama, Mikihiro. "A New Spirit: Sundanese Publishing and the Changing Configuration of Writing in Nineteenth Century West Java". Ph.D. Thesis. Leiden: Leiden University, 2003.

Noer, Deliar. *The Rise of the Modernist Muslim Movement in Indonesia*. Singapore: Oxford University Press, 1973.

Robinson, Francis. "Technology and Religious Change: Islam and the Impact of Print". *Modern Asian Studies* 27, no. 1 (1993): 229–351.

Shiraishi, Takashi. *An Age in Motion: Popular Radicalism in Java*. Ithaca and London: Cornell University Press, 1990.

Snouck Hurgronje, C. *Mekka in the Latter Part of the 19th Century*. Leiden: E.J. Brill, 1931.

Sutherland, Heather. *The Making of a Bureaucratic Elite: The Colonial Transformation of the Javanese Priyayi*. Singapore: Heinemann Educational Book, 1979.

Tjokroaminoto, H.O.S. *Islam dan Socialisme*. Jakarta: Bulan Bintang, 1950 [1924].

———. *Tarich Agama Islam, Riwajat dan Pemandangan atas Kehidupan dan Perdjalanan Nabi Muhammad S.A.W.* Jakarta: Bulan Bintang, 1950.

Wahid, Abdurrahman. "Pesantren sebagai Subkultur". In *Pesantren dan Pembaharuan*, edited by M. Dawam Rahardjo. Jakarta: LP3ES, 1974.

Zuhri, K.H. Saifuddin. *Kyai Haji Abdulwahab Khasbullah: Bapak dan Pendiri Nahdlatul Ulama*. Jakarta: Bulan Bintang, 1983*a*.

———. *Guruku Orang-Orang dari Pesantren*. Bandung: Al-Ma'arif, 1983*b*.

Zulkifli. *Sufism in Java: The Role of the Pesantren in the Maintenance of Sufism in Java*. Jakarta: INIS, 2002.

4

THE ROLE AND IDENTITY OF RELIGIOUS AUTHORITIES IN THE NATION STATE

Egypt, Indonesia, and South Africa Compared

Abdulkader Tayob

The transformation of Muslim societies has created new opportunities for Islam's religious scholars. *Ulama* have proved more resilient than earlier predictions that they would sooner or later be replaced by new elites. They have shown that the technocrats and bureaucrats of modernization and progress could not so easily marginalize them. They have also proved wrong many observers who thought that modern forms of communication and dissemination would threaten their monopoly of religious texts and authority in society. This essay contains a plea to look more carefully at the organization, role and instruments of the *ulama* in modern states and societies. It presents a review of *ulama* authority in modern South Africa, Egypt and Indonesia with a particular emphasis on their institutional formation, the limits and power of their *fatwas*, and their relation within and/or dependence on states. Within this framework, it is argued that the *ulama* play a crucial role in creating, delineating and negotiating a "religious" space in modern Muslim societies.

THE *ULAMA* IN CONTEMPORARY SCHOLARSHIP

With the re-emergence of religions in public life in the last few decades of the twentieth century, assessments of religious scholars have correspondingly changed. Earlier studies were focussed on the progressively subservient role that the *ulama* were forced to occupy in the different stages of modernization from the nineteenth century. The modernist experiments seemed set to undermine the influence of the religious classes. The nationalist and socialist trends in the period leading up to de-colonization seemed to confirm their marginalization.

Gilsenan's analysis of the *ulama* in the Ottoman Empire and Morocco in the nineteenth century has captured two contrasting models of *ulama* subordination. In the first scenario, *ulama* were targeted as obstacles in the modernization of Muslim societies, and they themselves took on self-appointed roles as champions of tradition. The pressure to modernize the army and its state bureaucracy was felt acutely from the eighteenth century. As the Ottoman Empire lost wars against its rivals, mainly Austria and Russia, and was trapped in the diplomatic games of more powerful players, it sought to reform its military and state machineries. Sultan Selim III (r. 1789–1807) seemed to be the first Ottoman ruler to introduce modern forms of military organization and state bureaucracy. The *ulama* saw these changes as fundamentally conflicting with their own often privileged positions in the state, and vehemently opposed them. This opposition neither deterred the Sultan nor later Sultans from pursuing reforms. The fate of the *ulama* under pressure in the central Ottoman lands became symbolic and exemplary for most *ulama* elsewhere.

Gilsenan showed that the *ulama* in Morocco played no legitimizing role in pre-modern society, and thus played less of an oppositional one during modernization. Modern changes in Morocco were legitimized through a complex web of power relations of which the *ulama* constituted only one of its nodes (Gilsenan 1990, p. 38). In this case also, the *ulama* were progressively sidelined in the process of modern state-building. Since they did not enjoy the same role and prestige as Ottoman *ulama*, they could not be said to have retreated. And yet, modern states appear to have very little use for the *ulama*. Gilsenan's analysis of the *ulama* in retreat or in opposition was echoed in a number of other detailed studies. The widely read collection of essays edited by Nikki R. Keddie entitled *Scholars, Saints, and Sufis: Muslim Religious Institutions in the Middle East since 1500* presented such views across the length and breadth of Muslim societies.

This particular perception of the *ulama* changed after the success of the Iranian revolution of 1979. Then, in a way diametrically different from both the Ottoman and Moroccan examples, the *ulama* came into power in Iran. They took control of state and society and imposed their particular visions and aspirations on them. The case of Iran is a special case of what has happened in less spectacular ways in other countries.The power of the *ulama* has been witnessed in a number of other Muslim societies (Zubayda 1990). In academic circles, studies have since re-assessed the position of the *ulama* during the period of modernization. Apart from Iran, these studies have shed more light on Egyptian, Indian and Indonesian *ulama* (Lemke 1980; Eccel 1984; Mudzhar 1993; Zebiri 1993; Barton and Fealy 1996; Skovgaard-Petersen 1997; Zaman 2002). Unlike the earlier studies, these new studies have highlighted the transformed role of the *ulama* in modern Muslim societies. My own emphasis here is that the *ulama* have taken on new roles and identities within modern societies. They have not simply asserted their traditional authority against modernization and secularization. They have accepted the constraints and possibilities of the modern state and sometimes proved themselves capable of acquiring a dominant position within it. They have done this within the changing meaning of their authoritative pronouncements, within the plurality of voices speaking in the name of Islam, and within the changing contours of the modern Muslim state.

THE *FATWA* BETWEEN STATE AND SOCIETY

I propose to understand the changing role and authority of the *ulama* in modern societies by paying very close attention to the principal forms in which authoritative judgments are given and received in *fiqh* and *sharia* discourse. As religious leaders, *ulama* are usually approached for their views and judgments on a multitude of matters. They present such views as *fatwas* (juridical opinions), *hukm* (a ruling or a court order), or general advice (*nasihah, tawsiya*) depending on the position that they occupy in state and society. The *fatwa* is an opinion or judgement given by a scholar on a question posed by anyone, in either individual or statutory capacities. The manuals of *fiqh* consistently maintained the provisional and non-binding nature of the answer given. Discussions and definitions of *fatwas* are compared and contrasted with a judgment (*hukm*) given in a court. Thus, for example, the famous jurist Ibn Qayyim al-Jawziyyah, on *fatwa* and *hukm*:

> He (the mufti) issues a *fatwa* on the basis of what he is asked. If he (the questioner) wants to, he accepts his statement, and if he wants, he rejects it.

> But a judge, his statement (*hukm*) is binding. The judge and mufti participate in the giving of a ruling, and the judge is distinguished by the binding nature (of the ruling); and he is therefore more exposed to danger (Ibn Qayyim al-Jawziyyah, p. 1:36)

> The Mufti makes a universal, general rule that whoever does something will have such a consequence, and who does such and such is bound to do this; while the judge makes a specific decision on a specific person, and his judgment is specific and binding. The *fatwa* of a scholar is general and non-binding. Both have a great reward and great danger (Ibn Qayyim al-Jawziyyah, p. 1:38).

The balance between the *fatwa* and *hukm* has been recognized and debated in the literature. Sometimes, the term *ahkam* is also used to refer to general rulings on a particular subject, for example *ahkam al-awqaf* (pious foundations) or *hajj*. But when the *hukm* is contrasted with a *fatwa*, then the corresponding role of a political authority comes into play (Encyclopedia of Islam, s.v. ahkam). The *hukm* of a judge has by necessity to be supported by an executive authority of some sort. The balance and play between a *fatwa* and *hukm* can be particularly fertile for understanding the changing role of *ulama* in modern societies. Sherman Jackson (1996) has presented a fascinating account of the dynamic and constructive interplay between the *hukm* and the *fatwa* in pre-modern Mamluk Egypt of a prominent judge and mufti respectively. I wish to pay attention to a similar tension and play in contemporary societies.

In contemporary Islam, various protagonists have seized upon the *fatwa* as a means to instruct Muslims about the meaning of Islam, and as a means to elaborate opinions on new challenges and questions. Sometimes, a *fatwa* is simply a reminder about a simple Islamic teaching. At other times, though, it is a considered viewpoint on a new phenomenon. But there are two related considerations about the *fatwa* in modern Islam that impact directly on the nature of modern religious authority. Firstly, the plurality of voices brought about through new technologies has favoured the proliferation of those issuing *fatwas* (muftis). Secondly, modern political and legal changes have had a tremendous effect on the *fatwa* and thus on *ulama* authorities. Both of these conditions have actually favoured greater *ulama* authority.

The pluralist nature of the *fatwa* as a non-decisive opinion is ideally suited to the dispersive instruments of modernity. An opinion of a learned scholar or organization may be accepted or countered by another. A state-appointed mufti may be easily contradicted by an individual or competing group, by issuing a press statement, or an Internet posting. As much as the *fatwa* is constructed and made available, it is as easily contradicted. This proliferation of views on Islam has given the impression that the *ulama* have lost or are losing their authoritative positions in society. Studies that have focused on the diversity within the modern production of knowledge have stressed the challenges presented to older and established authorities. Reformists at the end of the nineteenth century, Islamists during the twentieth century and a more limited number of secularists, have robbed the *ulama* of their earlier monopoly of access to religious texts. The sheer proliferation of texts and new social groups speaking in the name of Islam have underlined the variety and conflicting positions on almost any issue (Eickelman and Piscatori 1996). The following statement from Eickelman on the possibilities of the civil public spaces captures the dominant sentiment of many analysts:

> Through fragmenting authority and discourse, the new technologies of communications combined with the multiplication of agency facilitated by rising educational levels, contribute significantly to re-imagining Middle Eastern politics and religion ... This fragmentation may contribute to political volatility in the short run but in the long run, it may become one of the major factors leading to a more civil society throughout the Middle East and elsewhere in the Muslim world (Eickelman 1999, p. 38).

My own assessment is that the access to texts and views has increased the authority of *ulama*, even though opinions have become highly contested. *Ulama* have themselves embraced these technologies after an initial period of hesitation. Such new technologies at first provoked an immediate and negative response from the *ulama* (Berkes 1998, pp. 40–41). As Robertson and others have pointed out, however, the *ulama* embraced these technologies once they recognized their potential in promoting the values of Islam, and the importance of representing Islam in the modern world. Printing presses at the end of the nineteenth century, Khomeini's audio cassettes during the Iranian revolution, the Internet and a myriad of multimedia technologies, have become the stock in trade of *ulama* (Rochlin 1933; Robinson 1993; Eickelman and Piscatori 1996; Eickelman and Anderson 1999). A comparison between the resistance to print in the nineteenth century and the embrace of the Internet at the end of the twentieth century underlines the transformed attitude of the *ulama* to new technologies. Moreover, the basic methodology promoted by the *ulama* has not been challenged. Their text-centred methodology has become the dominant discourse of Islamic knowledge production. Experience-based approaches like Sufism have come under general suspicion, the primary texts of the Qur'an and hadith have been promoted as the guarantors of morality, ethics, religious obligations and salvation. The *ulama* have proved themselves more adept than any of the more recent social groups to speak through and with the texts in public debates. In spite of the contestation, the *ulama* have maintained a dominant position in presenting judgements and views about the Qur'an, the Prophet and the *Shari'ah*.

Accessibility and religious methodology cannot by themselves guarantee a place for religious authority. The political and legal context for religions have had some decisive impact on the *ulama*. The *fatwa* and *hukm* have come under particular pressure in the development of the modern state. The relationship between the *mufti* and *hakim* has been redefined or completely shattered in the transformation of the state, the courts and the judicial system. Legal codes have redefined the role of *Sharia* experts and in many cases made them redundant. In other places, *Sharia* courts have been established, or special personal codes formulated, that have defined a very different practice of *fatwa* and *hukm*. Collective *fatwa* bodies have been formed to produce consensus among divergent opinions. Some states have gone out of their way to employ the *fatwa* as a legitimizing tool for a diverse set of political projects. (Masud et al. 1996, p. 19). The *ulama* have constructed their authorities within these changes, often turning them into opportunities. As those most easily recognized as the knowledge custodians of Islam, they have been able to claim their positions within the new institutions created for these new ventures. And in countries with more secular-oriented regimes, they have also formed independent organizations to represent their concerns and their interests.

Modern *ulama* authority has been transformed and refashioned by a relocation and reconstitution of *fatwa* and its official counterpart, the *hukm*. The increasing number of persons who claim to speak in the name of Islam has accentuated the method and role of the *ulama*. Even though their views are contested on every point, their position has been slowly enhanced over the course of the twentieth century. These challenges have been seized as opportunities to institutionalize *ulama* authority. In the examples presented here, I suggest some of the ways in which they have done so. The South African case helps to shed light on the importance of *ulama* organizations that try to mimic some of the state's role. As a country with a minority of Muslims, South Africa provides a striking example of the identity and power of the *ulama* in the context of modern non-Islamic social and state formation. But it also shows the need for some structure to take the responsibility for issuing the decisive *hukm*. The Egyptian example sheds light on the need for the state to obtain religious legitimacy from the *ulama* for social change and reformation. Whilst the *ulama* lost their authority in the court system, developments in Egypt show the state's need for legitimacy from the organizations that emerged and evolved. And finally, the Indonesian case presents a striking example of an elaboration of a particular religious space cultivated by *ulama* when the political space is neutralized. To varying degrees, the examples show how the authority and role of *ulama* have taken shape within organizations, providing legitimacy for political order, and maintaining the prerogative of determining the contours of an inherently religious space.

South Africa

In 2000, a dispute in a mosque in the Western Cape region of South Africa was presented at the local magistrate's court. This was not the first time that mosque disputes were raised in South African courts. Like previous ones over the past 150 years, this one too touched on the question of the limits and extent of religious authority and leadership within the Muslim community. South Africa has a minority of Muslims who mainly originated from Asia and to a lesser extent from Africa, since the first European occupation and settlement in the seventeenth century. They have built mosques and established various levels of madrasahs since the official declaration of freedom of religion in 1806. This small dispute may be analysed in the light of this local history, and illustrates the power and limit of religious leadership in a modern Muslim context.

The dispute involved an imam who had provoked two contradictory sentiments in a small community. On one side of the dispute were members of the congregation who wanted to fire him for negligence, and for behaving in an un-Islamic manner. Against them stood an equally committed group who supported the imam, and charged the first group with racial prejudice since the imam was a Zimbabwean of indigenous African descent. The first group approached the Muslim Judicial Council (MJC), a representative body of religious scholars in the Cape, to mediate in the dispute. The MJC established a tribunal to investigate the matter, and also empowered it to make a final and binding decision (a *hukm*). After some deliberation, the tribunal exonerated the imam of any wrong doing. The group that had accused the imam of misconduct did not accept the decision, however, and sought supportive opinions from other prominent *ulama*. One such scholar, Shaikh Faaik Gamieldien, presented a *fatwa* on the matter. He said that *if* the imam had actually been guilty of such behaviour, he should have been relieved of his post. He did not refer explicitly to the particular case at hand, but presented a general opinion. His was a classical *fatwa*, a pronouncement of a moral opinion on an issue. The dissenting group seized upon this *fatwa* to demand that the imam step down from his position. In response, the MJC, who had established the tribunal in the first place, surprisingly recommended that the imam vacate his position in the interest of the unity of the community. This recommendation further strengthened the resolve of the dissenters. Armed with the support of the *fatwa* and the new approach of the MJC, they threatened to physically remove the imam. The imam and his supporters sought the protection of the court, applying for an interdict to prevent the planned disruption. The court issued a final decision in their favour, and seemed to defer the dispute for a while.

The incident was a minor conflict in a small town, but its many dimensions bring into sharp relief the multifaceted changes and transformations of religious authority in this society. Imams in individual mosques in Cape Town have given their opinions on religious and non-religious matters since they were first established in the nineteenth century. The mosque in Cape Town was often established by a charismatic imam who exerted a powerful influence on its circle of congregants (called *murids*). The mosque as an institution inscribed a series of religious practices involving education and ritual services that bound the *murid* to the imam. This relationship was first founded in the political and social context of slavery and religious prejudice, and has survived the impact of successive new waves of Islamic thought including reformism, Deobandism, Islamism, and progressive Islam. New ideas, social and political changes, and disputes, posed particular challenges and opportunities for an imam. Who should be the Chief Priest of the Muslims in Cape Town? What is the value of pilgrimage for religious leadership? How can one accommodate different legal schools in the city? Is it permissible to eat crustaceans? Is it possible to have one Friday mosque in the city, and if so, where? Should Muslims support the anti-colonial movements or get as much as they could from the Afrikaner elite? These questions were all issues that plunged the mosques in a chain of disputes and conflicts (Davids 1980; Jeppie 1996; Tayob 1999).

In order to deal with competing opinions on these matters, a number of organizations were established over the second half of the twentieth century. One of the most prominent such organizations was the Muslim Judicial Council. It was founded in 1945 as a judiciary to deal with these issues in a decisive manner. The choice of "judicial" to describe the body does seem to have been deliberate at its founding. The MJC was a venture to settle disputes relating to marital discord within families, and to come to an agreement on differences of opinions on religious matters. When the need arose, it even convened a "court" in order to officially annul marriages on behalf of abused or abandoned spouses. In terms of the *Sharia* discourse of *fatwa* and *hukm*, the MJC imagined itself to be a judiciary (without an actual state), and pretended to issue final and binding judgments (*ahkam*).

This imagined fiction worked for the most part, but broke down when the disputes involved competing imams and the MJC itself. The local mosques and their supporters did not accept the MJC pronouncements as binding ahkam. From the point of view of the local mosque, the MJC viewpoints counted as non-binding *fatwas*. As a result, the authority of the *Sharia* coming from the MJC broke down when the individual mosque institutions themselves were brought into question. The fiction of the "judiciary" could not be sustained, and a higher authority was sought. In this dispute, the limits of the authority of a local imam, and indeed of the regional body representing religious leaders (the MJC), was exposed. In the case of mosques in South Africa, only the secular courts were decisive enough to produce a resolution. Only they could really issue the final "*hukm*".

It is not the failure of the MJC that I want to highlight, but their authority. The religious institution was constructed in order to deal with the absence of a higher political authority. Both the individual mosque and the MJC were institutional creations of the history of Islam in the Western Cape over a period of two hundred years. Unfettered directly by the state, religious institutions with distinctive powers and limitations came into being. In spite of their non-official nature, the mosque and the MJC had created competing levels of authority that this particular dispute in 2000 brought to the surface. The South African case clearly revealed the authority of the *ulama* within their respective locations. Both the alim/imam in his single mosque, and the association of *ulama* exerted authority and control in the Muslim communities. The problem arose only when disputes around imams presented themselves.

Egypt

The modern Egyptian state has regarded Islam, and Islamic authorities in particular, as a source of legitimacy. Unlike South Africa, where Islam has been at best a minor source of irritation for the modern state, the modern Egyptian state has generally regarded with apprehension any form of potential or actual religious authority. It may not be too inaccurate to say that the Egyptian state has assumed the final authority (*hukm*) in public matters. At the same time, however, the state has attempted to achieve legitimacy for this *hukm* by enlisting the support of *fatwas* within state-established institutions. Not surprisingly, this process in itself has multiplied the competing claims to *fatwas* from dissenting *ulama*, and from new social groups who have emerged over the course of its modern history. The various Islamic claims to authority in Egypt provide an interesting example of the vitality of *ulama* authority, and its present location.

The Napoleonic invasion of Egypt unseated the Ottomans and provided a short period of direct *ulama* power and prosperity. In this period of political instability, the *ulama* became influential as the guardians of pious foundations (*awqaf*) and the beneficiaries of land grants (Crecelius 1972). But they were not interested in taking over power from the retreating French forces, and asked Muhammad Ali Pasha to govern Egypt:

> Their self-image was that of the preservers of tradition, not of political innovators; tradition had decreed that though they become involved in the power process they neither direct nor lead it save indirectly. Perhaps there remained vestiges of the concept that power corrupts. They could not destroy that image of themselves, hence their limited involvement and the precipitation with which they abdicated power as soon as they acquired it (Marsot 1972, p. 165).

But they could not predict the power of the modern state over society and religion. Muhammad Ali began to build an Empire on the basis of the new modern possibilities, wherein an *independent ulama* class was regarded as a threat. He began the systematic dismantling of *ulama* authority by confiscating their land grants, and their control of pious foundations. Over the next two hundred years, his successors continued this trend, targeting the judiciary and the educational institutions for systematic change. They demanded that the *ulama* support and endorse their reign and particularly state-initiated reforms (Crecelius 1972; Marsot 1972; Gilsenan 1973; Crecelius 1980). These experiments have created the impression that the *ulama* were on the retreat in Egypt. A closer look at the transformation reveals that the *ulama* did not lose all their influence, and took on new roles and assumed new authoritative positions in society. These new roles were crafted in the very process of their modern institutionalization and apparent marginalization. The trajectories of the Dar al-Ifta (est. 1895) and the great educational institute, Azhar, illustrate the authority of the *ulama* in both state and society.

Skovgaard-Petersen has shown that the Egyptian modernizing state was marginalizing religious scholars with the one hand, but giving them due consideration with the other. The muftis were brought into the consultative chambers of Muhammad Ali and his successor Abbas (1849–54) (Skovgaard-Petersen 1997, p. 100). This advisory role was extended to a systematic introduction of the *fatwa* in the courts, both *Sharia* courts and then later the new national courts (*al-mahakim al-ahliyyah*). From the Ordinance of 1856 through to the Ordinance of 1897, *muftis* and their opinions were introduced as an important part of juridical practice. At the same time, an attempt was made to limit the extent to which individuals outside the courts could exercise the right to give a *fatwa*. Whilst stressing the important advisory role of *muftis*, the Ministry of Interior in 1865 stressed the need to control their different and conflicting pronouncements. The 1880 Code of Procedure for the *Sharia* Courts specified that only Hanafi law would apply. The pluralism of the *fatwa* could not be accommodated in the modern state. Two years later, therefore, a process was set in motion to reverse the role assigned to the *fatwa* in the courts. And finally, the Ordinance of 1897 imposed the obligation on the judges to rely entirely on the new legal codes. Prior to this, courts were obliged to consult with the officially appointed *muftis*. In the next century, completely closing the door to the *fatwa* the *Sharia* Court Ordinance of 1931 specifically prohibited the courts from consulting a *mufti* (Skovgaard-Petersen 1997, pp. 103–06). These courts were later abolished in 1956 (Eccel 1984, pp. 316–17). Skovgaard-Petersen summarized developments in the first hundred years as follows:

> ... while the 19th century witnessed an increasing attachment of the Hanafi mufti to legal institutions, during the first quarter of the twentieth century these links were once again loosened. The pendulum swung from *madrasa* [school] to *mahkama* [court] and then back again (Skovgaard-Petersen 1997, p. 106).

The mufti was first considered to be a vital part of the judicial process. However, with the systematization of the courts and the introduction of new codes, the free circulation of diverse *fatwas* had become a burden on the modernizing legal process. And thus began a process of limiting the role of the *fatwas* in the *courts*. The *hukm* in the court, obtained through new codes, could dispense with the *fatwa*.

But the *fatwa*, once brought into the state system, could be put to other uses. Skovgaard-Petersen suggests that the *Dar al-Ifta* did not entirely lose its relevance when *fatwas* were no longer necessary in the courts. What the Grand Mufti lost in the judicial process, he gained in the potential influence in the state. Whilst Egypt reduced the role of the mufti and non-codified *Sharia* in courts, it made a special provision for the mufti to advise and justify the state. Some of the most illustrious scholars in modern Egyptian history have held the post of Grand Mufti, including Muhammad Abduh at the beginning of the twentieth century and Muhammad Sayyid Tantawi towards the end. Both played an important role in the justification of the state's policies (Skovgaard-Petersen 1997, pp. 269–70; Zebiri 1993; Abduh 2000). With Abduh, the centralizing and modernizing state was justified, while under Tantawi, the power of the state against extremists was waged on both political and religious grounds. With some minor exceptions, Skovgaard-Petersen has pointed to the reformist character of the holders of the office, pointing to the supportive role that the office has played in the development of the modern state. In this case, the Dar al-Ifta points to the particular mobilization of *fatwa* by the state.

Another body in the history of modern Egypt has become equally authoritative in society and state. The old and venerable teaching institution of Azhar founded in the tenth century has become a parallel and competing source for religious justification and identity. Whilst the Dar al-Ifta was a creation of the modern state to provide support first for the courts and then the state, the Azhar has been enlisted for the various projects of modernization and social change. The modernizers of Egypt expected the Azhar to lead the nationalist transformation. As an indigenous organization, it was expected to carry this responsibility. Throughout the twentieth century, reforms were planned and sometimes implemented to direct the students and graduates to play a supportive and constructive role in modernizing Egyptian society. The institute neither resisted nor showed too great an enthusiasm for these projects (Crecelius 1972). Attempts to reorient the Azhar for the supply of judges and teachers in the new schools did not lead to positive results (Eccel 1984, pp. 165, 188). Political and social developments outstripped its capacity, its philosophy and willingness to work closely and independently with reigning governments. But in the context of an anti-colonial nationalism and an emerging Islamic voice, the hope for its potential never abated. Over the course of the twentieth century, the Azhar established itself as a state bureaucracy with a fundamental role in *religious* education (Eccel 1984, pp. 270–71). Both have ensured that Azhar provided employment to its graduates and to increase its influence in secular fields by reinventing the meaning and purpose of *religion* in society.

In effect, both the Dar al-Ifta and the University of Azhar have become sources for *fatwas* in modern Egyptian society. The process of modernization has given them an authoritative position within the state and the society. The state's policies to control the *ulama* and to direct them in useful projects of modernization have simply increased their presence in the public sphere. Through the institutionalization of a state *fatwa* body and a state-supported religious educational institute, the Egyptian *ulama* have secured a vital position within modern society. Even though their opinions are contested, their positions in both state and society are ensured (Abu-

Rabi 1996, p. 69). The state has literally and figuratively taken over the juridical *hukm*, but the *ulama* have been encouraged and allowed the prerogative of issuing *fatwas*. Further appraisal of their role should not ignore this institutionalization and authorization.

INDONESIA

Indonesia also presents an interesting example of particular religious space that *ulama* have occupied in modern society. Indonesia is the most populous Muslim country where Islam plays a large role in public life. However, unlike Egypt, Indonesia does not have a clearly defined role for Islam in the state. Its constitution ruled out that possibility with the adoption of the ideology of Pancasila. But this does not mean that religious issues are any less important in this country, or that the state has no interest in the religious opinions of its prestigious members. The political history of Indonesia cannot be written without taking into consideration the place of Islam as propounded by religious authorities and their political counterparts.

The first stirrings of national self-determination were accompanied by claims that Islam would and should have some important role to play in a future state. Nationalist questions early in the twentieth century debated the proper place of Islam. Post-independent constitutional questions about the place of Islam pushed the country to the brink of civil war. In this regard, all major religious parties from early in the twentieth century like Sarekat Islam (est. 1912), PERSIS (est. 1923), the Masjumi (est. 1942) umbrella organization during the Japanese occupation, and recent parties that have emerged after the fall of Soeharto, claimed a role for Islam. And the *ulama* have played some role within these organization. But these religio-political organizations have been dwarfed by two networks of *ulama* that have dominated Indonesian religious life since the beginning of the twentieth century. The Muhammadiyah and the Nahdlatul Ulama have become part of the deep fabric of the society (Mudzhar 1993; Barton and Fealy 1996; Hefner 2000).

The Muhammadiyah was founded in 1912, directly influenced by the reformists of Egypt, and has since championed Islamic rulings based directly on the Qur'an and the *sunnah*. In contrast, the Nahdlatul Ulama maintained its commitment to the Shafi'i tradition and other Indonesian practices. The Nahdlatul Ulama was formed in 1926. The *ulama* have elaborated their role and place in the state and society through *fatwas*, tausiyahs and amanat (Kaptein 2004). To these latter might be added a number of less carefully organized verbal representations in diverse media. This particular production of *ulama* counsel points to a process of identification and religious intervention in public life. Through the two organizations, the *ulama* have acquired a distinctive identity. Through the enunciations, they have created a religious space in public life.

The authority of *ulama* was created through state initiatives to guide and control the direction and development of their involvement. The Japanese during the Second World War promoted the formation of a federation of Muslim bodies, including the Muhammadiyah and the Nahdlatul Ulama, in the name of the Masjumi. Masjumi included both the nationalist aspiration for independence, and the voice of Islam against Dutch colonialism. After Independence, this trend continued and intensified. Both Sukarno and Soeharto tried to curtail the presence of Islam within the state, but also claimed its legitimacy in the accumulation of power. Sukarno relied directly on the Islamic parties, and the NU network in particular, to crush his communist rivals. Soeharto also followed a policy of keeping his Islamic rivals at a comfortable distance. The *ulama* were not to obtain too much power, but they were also directed to form non-political religious authorities to advise the government and the people.

Simply looking at the state initiatives cannot exhaust the modern formation of *ulama* in Indonesia. More careful attention to the *ulama* production of counsels points to an important aspect of their authority. Already in 1926, the NU established a *fatwa* body, thereby attempting to replace individual opinions given by its members:

> Since that time, each congress of the Nahdlatul Ulama, in addition to making organizational and political declarations, has produced *fatwas* on issues related to Islamic law, compiled and published under the title *Ahkam al-fuqaha* (Mudzhar 1993, p. 3).

The Muhammadiyah also felt the need soon thereafter to form its own *fatwa*-issuing body in 1927 (Mudzhar 1993, pp. 3–4, 19). In contrast to the Nahdlatul Ulama, the rival Muhammadiyah established a committee called *Majlis Tarjih* to issue *fatwas* compiled in a collection called *Himpunan Putusan Majlis Tarjih*. With these early and modest beginnings, the *ulama* bodies have recorded a history of *fatwas* on diverse matters.

It seems that the Indonesia *ulama* organizations have been aspiring to transform their opinions (*fatwas*) into *ahkam*. The *ahkam* of the Nahdlatul *Ulama* and the *tarjih* (preference) clearly illustrate the ideological conceptions of *fiqh* authority of the two bodies. The Nahdlatul Ulama issued clear rulings (*ahkam*) that it considered binding on both its registered members and the Sunni Muslims in Indonesia in general. The *ahkam* of the Nahdlatul Ulama underlines their commitment to the exclusive fidelity to the Shafi'i school. But the context of these compilations leads one to question if this usage of *ahkam* was simply an alternative meaning of *fatwas*. Perhaps the NU fuqaha expected their followers to regard the *fatwas* as binding *ahkam*. This becomes clear when considering the Muhammadiyah's position. The Muhammadiyah advocated the acceptance of rulings from all Sunni legal schools, as long as they were based on the Qur'an and sunnah. The use of *tarjih* seems an appropriate term for their philosophy. But the Muhammadiyah also issued *keputusan* (decisions) which were binding upon their members (Kaptein 2004, pp. 8–9). The *fatwas* and other opinions of the Indonesian *ulama* aspired to be binding decisions (*ahkam*) issued from these organizations.

The Indonesian history of issuing *fatwas* received a tremendous boost in the 1970s with the formation of regional and provincial councils of *ulama*, and a national council, Majelis Ulama Indonesia (MUI) (est. 1975). This organization and centralization was supported and favoured by Soeharto to turn the *ulama* away from politics. Both the Muhammadiyah and Nahdlatul Ulama occupied key positions on the MUI. Since the MUI included representatives from all the various groups, their directives and counsels provide a good indication of *ulama* authority at the end of the twentieth century. Mudzhar and Nur Ichwan have shown how carefully the MUI has charted its relationship with the ruling politicians (Mudzhar 1993; Ichwan 2005). It generally maintained a careful approach towards the Soeharto regime, but it was not averse to taking an independent stand on a religious matter such as Muslims attending Christmas celebrations. In spite of the state ideology of Pancasila that decreed inter-religious dialogue, the MUI seemed to inscribe a religious prerogative beyond the control of the state. After the fall of Soeharto, the MUI supported B.J. Habibie and the general elections but did not explicitly ask Indonesians to vote for one particular party. With the accession to power of Abdurrahman Wahid, a scholar in his own right, the MUI took an independent stand on the impermissibility of a food additive, monosodium glutamate (MSG), made from pork (Hosen 2004; Ichwan 2005).

In order to make some observations about the authority and legitimacy of the MUI and the *ulama* of Indonesia, it is important to return to the question of the *fatwa* as a fiqh category. The *fatwas* of the MUI, the nationally constituted body, cannot ignore challenges from other *ulama* and the two leading Islamic organizations. The example of the impermissibility of MSG from pork issued during the presidency of Abdurrahman Wahid presented the clearest example of both the effectiveness and limitation of MUI *fatwas*. The President, as an '*alim* himself, issued a directive to the MUI to review its decision on the basis of *Sharia*. In spite of its membership within the MUI, the Muhammadiyah produced an opposing view in support of the President. Hosen has discussed differing views emanating from different regional councils that have sometimes given conflicting opinions (Hosen 2004, p. 167). *Ulama* from differing backgrounds, and from opposing organizations, are ready to challenge the *fatwas* of the MUI (or any other organizations). It seems, then, that the national *fatwas* of the MUI will always be open to challenge from other individual *ulama* and organizations. In this sense, they cannot be the *ahkam* of the state.

A careful examination of the *fatwas* by the MUI may be found to be inscribing a religious public space. It seems that on some issues like the halal character of MSG, the MUI ruling won popular support in spite of differences among the *ulama*. Earlier in 1981, the MUI's ban on Muslims attending Christian celebrations also struck a chord with the masses. Hosen believes that the support for the MUI on the halal issue was a reflection of the rejection of President Abdurrahman Wahid. This is probable, but the *fatwas* may also be seen as a discourse that was creating the limits of a field of religious activity that reflected Indonesian concerns. Avoiding haram food may be a reflection of an emerging space of religiosity in public life that many Indonesians feel strongly about. A more thorough review of the *fatwas* for their religious significance may suggest the constitutive nature of the *fatwas*. Once the *fatwas* are delinked from any engagement in the legal structures, they may be seen more clearly as important indicators of public religious life.

GENERAL REMARKS AND CONCLUSION

This essay has presented a case for a modern *ulama* authority that is plural in terms of the intellectual backgrounds and particular social and political interests. The range of tendencies from modernist, revivalist to traditional, is represented among *ulama*. But this diversity is managed by the formation of *ulama* bodies that try to represent the voice of the *ulama* to the state and to society. In many cases, as in Egypt and Indonesia discussed here, the *ulama* bodies are formed or encouraged by states who desire to manage the plurality of religious voices. In other cases, *ulama* have themselves formed associations in order to represent themselves in complex and diverse societies, and in response to their needs. Whether independently formed or state-engineered, the organizations have emerged as the representatives of a moral/religious authority in modern states. These institutions have projected the identity of *ulama* in different contexts. Thus, the MJC in South Africa, the Azhar and Dar al-Ifta in Egypt, Nahdlatul Ulama and Muhammadiyah in Indonesia, and other less well-known organizations, articulate the identity of *ulama* in broader society.

Within the parameters of *Sharia* discourse, they attempt to present some of their views as authoritative and binding on their followers. Muslim majority states like Indonesia and Egypt also hope to benefit from their authoritative views to serve the interests of the state. But the instrument that the *ulama* and the states use, the *fatwa*, is inherently prone to challenge and debate. This challenge is ever-present when the rival *fatwa* emanates from other muftis (individual or organisation). And so the nature of *ulama* legitimacy is constrained by the competition inherent in the instruments being used. Among the *ulama* themselves, they attempt to create the fiction that they can issue rulings (*ahkam*). This was evident in the most unlikely context of South Africa, but it is also clear in the *fatwas* issued in Indonesia by non-governmental organizations as well.

The rulings cannot ignore the all-powerful states that keep the *ulama* at some distance, and employ their potential to create legitimacy. The modern state has progressively taken over the capacity to issue rulings (*ahkam*) without too much *ulama* participation and interference. The deliberation over conflicting and competing *fatwas* obscures the supervising or absent role of the state. In minority contexts such as South Africa, the state can afford to be aloof in most cases. In majority Muslim cases, the *fatwas* have to be put under surveillance for fear that they may turn into bids for complete control. They may turn into a bid for assuming rule (*hukm*). Given this potential to legitimize, *ulama* institutes and organizations engage their *fatwa*-authority in the domain of public morality. The *ulama* are very successful at determining the nature of a moral and religious space in modern society. It seems even likely that the states are prepared to support and tolerate this domain in their hands. In Egypt and Indonesia, the many *fatwas* merit further study in terms of the particular articulation of a religious/moral space which is free from political interference, or can easily be defended from political interference. It is in this domain that the *ulama* are likely to obtain significant popular support. And it is here that they can blur the lines between a *fatwa* and *hukm* in order to appear decisive and authoritative. Occupying the space of public morality, *ulama* can consolidate their authority.

Returning to the review of Gilsenan on the role of the *ulama* in modern state and society, I would venture to say that the *ulama* are neither unreserved defenders of the modern state nor in full opposition. At the end of the twentieth and the beginning of the twenty-first centuries, they have adjusted themselves to the state and society and made a bid for their moral direction.

This role does not rely on a clear differentiation of spheres, but it tells us a great deal about the meaning of religious obligations and devotion in Muslim public spheres.

References

Abduh, Muhammad. "The Necessity of Religious Reform". In *Contemporary Debates in Islam: An Anthology of Modernist and Fundamentalist Thought*, edited by Mansoor Moaddel and Kamran Talattof. New York: Palgrave Macmillan, 2000.

Abu-Rabi, Ibrahim. *The Intellectual Origins of Islamic Resurgence in the Modern Arab World*. Albany: State University of New York Press, 1996.

Barton, Greg, and Greg Fealy, eds. *Nahdlatul Ulama, Traditional Islam and Modernity in Indonesia*. Clayton, Australia: Monash Asia Institute, Monash University, 1996.

Berkes, Niazi. *The Development of Secularism in Turkey*. London: Hurst & Company, 1998.

Crecelius, Daniel. "Non-Ideological Responses of the Egyptian Ulama to Modernization". In *Scholars, Saints, and Sufis: Muslim Religious Institutions in the Middle East Since 1500*, edited by Nikki R. Keddie. Berkeley: University of California Press, 1972.

Crecelius, Daniel. "The Course of Secularization in Modern Egypt". In *Islam and Development: Religion and Sociopolitical Change*, edited by John L. Esposito. Syracuse: Syracuse University Press, 1980.

Davids, Achmat. *The Mosques of Bo-Kaap: A Social History of Islam at the Cape*. Cape Town: The S. A. Institute of Arabic and Islamic Research, 1980.

Eccel, A. Chris. *Egypt, Islam and Social Change: Al-Azhar in Conflict and Accommodation*. Berlin: Klaus Schwarz Verlag, 1984.

Eickelman, Dale F., and Jon W. Anderson, eds. *New Media in the Muslim World: The Emerging Public Sphere*. Bloomington, Indiana: Indiana University Press, 1999.

Eickelman, Dale F., and James Piscatori. *Muslim Politics*. Princeton, New Jersey: Princeton University Press, 1996.

Eickelman, Dale F. "Communication and Control in the Middle East: Publication and Its Discontents". In N*ew Media in the Muslim World: The Emerging Public Sphere*, edited by Dale E. Eickelman, and Jon W. Anderson. Bloomington, Indiana: Indiana University Press, 1999.

Gilsenan, M. *Saint and Sufi in Modern Egypt: An Essay in the Sociology of Religion*. Oxford: Clarendon, 1973.

Gilsenan, Michael. *Recognizing Islam: Religion and Society in the Modern Middle East*. New York; London: I. B. Taurus, 1990.

Hefner, Robert W. *Civil Islam: Muslims and Democratization in Indonesia*. Princeton, NJ: Princeton University Press, 2000.

Hosen, Nadirsyah. "Behind the Scenes: Fatwas of Majelis Ulama Indonesia (1975–1998)". *Journal of Islamic Studies (Oxford Centre for Islamic Studies)* 15, no. 2 (2004): 147–998.

Ibn Qayyim al-Jawziyyah, Shams al-Din Abu Abd Allah Muhammad b Abi Bakr. *Ilam Al-Muwaqqi'in an Rabb Al-Alamin*. Beirut: Dar al-Jil, 1350.

Ichwan, Moch. Nur. " 'Ulama, State and Politics: Majelis Ulama Indonesia after Suharto". *Islam Law and Society* 12, no. 1 (2005): 45–72.

Jackson, Sherman A. *Islamic Law and the State: The Constitutional Jurisprudence of Shihab Al-Din Al-Qarafi*. Leiden: E.J. Brill, 1996.

Jeppie, Shamil. "Leadership and Loyalties: The Imam of the Nineteenth-Century Colonial Cape Town, South Africa". *Journal of Religion in Africa* 26, no. 2 (1996): 139–62.

Kaptein, Nico G. "The Voice of the 'Ulamâ': Fatwas and Religious Authority in Indonesia". ISEAS Working Paper on Visiting Researchers Series No. 2. Leiden: Institute of Southeast Asian Studies, 2004.

Keddie, Nikki R. *Scholars, Saints, and Sufis: Muslim Religious Institutions in the Middle East since 1500*. Berkeley: University of California Press, 1972.

Layish, Aharon. "The 'Fatwa' as an Instrument of the Islamization of a Tribal Society in Process of Sedentarization". *Bulletin for the School of Oriental and African Studies* 54, no. 3 (1991): 449–59.

Lemke, Wolf-Dieter. "Mahmud Shaltut (1893–1963) und die Reform Der Ashar: untersuchungen Zu Erneurengsbestrebungen Im Agyptisch-Islamischen Erziehungsystem". *Islam Und Abendland*, edited by Dr A. Falaturi, Vol. 1. Frankfurt: Peter D. Lang, 1980.

Marsot, Afaf Lutfi al-Sayyid. "The Ulama of Cairo in the Eighteenth and Nineteenth Centuries". In *Scholars, Saints, and Sufis: Muslim Religious Institutions in the Middle East since 1500*, edited by Nikki R. Keddie. Berkeley: University of California Press, 1972.

Masud, M. Khalid. "Adab Al-Mufti: The Muslim Understanding of Values, Characteristics, and Role of the Mufti". In *Moral Conduct and Authority: The Place of Adab in South Asian Islam*, edited by Barbara Daly Metcalf. Berkeley: University of California Press, 1984.

Masud, Muhammad Khalid, Brinkley Messick, and David S. Powers, eds. "Introduction". In *Islamic Legal Interpretation: Muftis and Their Fatwas*. Cambridge, Massachusetts: Harvard University Press, 1996.

Mudzhar, Mohammed Atho. Fatwas of the Council of Indonesian Ulema: A Study of Islamic Legal Thought in Indonesia 1975–1988. Jakarta: Inis.

Robinson, Francis. "Technology and Religious Change: Islam and the Impact of Print". *Modern Asian Studies* 27, no. 1 (1993): 229–51.

Rochlin, Samuel A. "Early Arabic Printing at the Cape of Good Hope". *Bulletin for the School of Oriental and African Studies* 7, no. 1 (1933): 49–54.

Skovgaard-Petersen, Jakob. *Defining Islam for the Egyptian State: Muftis and Fatwas of the Dar Al-Ifta*. Leiden: Brill, 1997.

Tayob, Abdulkader I. *Islam in South Africa: Mosques, Imams and Sermons*. Gainesville: University of South Florida Press, 1999.

Zaman, Muhammad Qasim. *The Ulama in Contemporary Islam: Custodians of Change*. Princeton: Princeton University Press, 2002.

Zebiri, Kate. *Mahmud Shaltut and Islamic Modernism*. Oxford: Clarendon Press, 1993.

Zubayda, S. "De Ulama en het Moderne Politieke Denken". In *Schriftgeleerden in de Moderne Islam*, edited by J.G.J. Ter Haar, and P.S. van Koningsveld. Muiderberg: Dick Coutinho, 1990.

5

AUTHORITY CONTESTED
Mathla'ul Anwar in the Last Years of the New Order

Didin Nurul Rosidin

INTRODUCTION

Mathla'ul Anwar (*Matla'u al-Anwar*) along with its madrasah was founded in 1916 by a group of Bantenese religious teachers (*kiyai*)[1] as an immediate response towards both the massive introduction of secular schools by the Dutch colonial government following the issuance of the Ethical Policy and the declining effectiveness of the *pesantren*- (traditional Islamic boarding school) based education in providing an attractive place to study religion for Muslim youth in Banten. Mathla'ul Anwar's madrasah was to be the first modern Islamic school in the Banten region before the foundation of the Al-Khairiyah (*al-Khairiyya*) in Serang in 1923. From its foundation to the present, there have been seven different leaders who have acted as the general chairman of the central board of Mathla'ul Anwar, including Kiyai Haji Muhammad Yasin (1916–37), Kiyai Haji Abdul Mu'thi (1937–39), Kiyai Haji Uwes Abu Bakar (1939–72), Kiyai Haji Muslim Abdurrahman (1972–74), Haji Nafsirin Hadi (1974–85), Kiyai Haji Burhani (1985–91) and Haji Irsyad Djuwaeli (1991–up to now). Except Nafsirin Hadi and Irsyad Djuwaeli, all leaders have a similar education background, pesantren. Meanwhile, both Nafsirin Hadi and Irsyad Djuwaeli represented the alumni of the madrasah. For instance, Irsyad Djuwaeli spent his early studies at the madrasah of the Anwarul Hidayah (*Anwar al-Hidaya*) before continuing his study at the Religious Teacher Training (*Pendidikan Guru Agama*, PGA) of Mathla'ul Anwar in Jakarta. Educational background is important to see the style and orientation, as well as their acceptability among traditional members of Mathla'ul Anwar. Members of this organization would not qualify Nafsirin Hadi as a true leader of Mathla'ul Anwar due to his lack of religious expertise,[2] while they highly admired Kiyai Uwes Abu Bakar as an example of the perfect leader due to his exceptional expertise in religious matters.[3] Yet, authoritative knowledge in religious matters as the only referred parameter for judging the leadership in Mathla'ul Anwar does not do justice to reality as is shown in the case of Irsyad Djuwaeli's leadership. His ability to combine a variety of sources of authority paved the way for him to exercise unparalleled influence within Mathla'ul Anwar. So, this chapter will elaborate the leadership of Irsyad Djuwaeli who has taken dominant roles since the 1985 congress and was elected as the general chairman in the 1991 congress.

MATHLA'UL ANWAR AT A GLANCE

As mentioned above, the foundation of Mathla'ul Anwar was followed by the opening of the madrasah located at Simanying in the sub-district of Menes in Pandeglang on the land attained from people's endowment (*waqf*). Up to 1929, it offered nine years of study from class A, B, I, II until VII exclusively for male students. Each class had a fixed curriculum and was supervised by one teacher. From 1929, Mathla'ul Anwar opened classes for female students. Unlike the males, female students only took six years of study up to class IV. In all of their educational activities, both male and female pupils were totally separated.[4]

In addition to their main concern on Islamic education, the leaders of Mathla'ul Anwar were active in the Islamic missionary (dakwah) activities either through organizing public sermons in prayer houses or sending their envoys to areas surrounding Menes sub-district and even as far away as Bogor and Serang. Through these activities, they established their influence in those places and, because of this, local Muslim leaders in most cases sent a request to the central board of Mathla'ul Anwar to also operate its madrasah in their neighbourhood. After that, Mathla'ul Anwar supported the setting up of the madrasah through providing the curriculum and qualified teachers who were actually alumni of the madrasah of Menes. In the mid-1930s, it was reported that there had been forty new madrasahs founded in a variety of regions, including some villages in Pandeglang, Serang, Lebak and even Bogor. During its first congress in 1936, Mathla'ul Anwar issued regulation classifying its *madrasahs* into two general groups. The first was the Central Madrasah (*Madrasah Pusat*) that was located in Simanying in Menes where the first madrasah was founded and the second was the Branch Madrasahs (*Madrasah Cabang*) that included all of the *madrasahs* outside the Central Madrasah. For those branch madrasahs, Mathla'ul Anwar provided a restricted authority to operate their teaching activities with only six years of study in which class IV was to be the highest level. Graduates who wished to upgrade their level of knowledge were obliged to study at the Central Madrasah in Menes.[5] Prior to Independence, most, or even perhaps all, of its local *madrasahs* were located in villages and other remote areas. The political separation from the hegemonic power of the colonial government in the urban areas that was the main feature of religious teachers' movements in Banten in the second half of the nineteenth and early of twentieth centuries[6] had a great influence over Mathla'ul Anwar's early orientation. So, Mathla'ul Anwar prominently represented itself as a rural-based socio-religious movement.

Mathla'ul Anwar operated this system of education until 1950 when the independent Indonesian government implemented a new regulation dealing with the national system of education. In this new framework, there were four levels of school in the country: six years for elementary school, three years for junior high school, three years for senior high school and the university level. Mathla'ul Anwar fully adopted the system as it decided to divide its nine years of study into two levels of schools: elementary (*Madrasah Ibtidaiyah* or MI) and junior high (*Madrasah Wustho* or MW), while its branch *madrasahs* with their six years of study changed into MI.

Furthermore, Mathla'ul Anwar also included some secular subjects such as Indonesian and English in its curriculum. The decision to introduce English brought about bitter internal fractures as senior teachers led by Kiyai Abdul Latif, who was at that time the director of education affairs of the organisation succeeding Kiyai Mas Abdurrahman who died in 1943, could not agree with this notion. These teachers believed that secular subjects, particularly English, were non-Islamic. On the basis of this belief, they suspected the introduction of such subjects as the main instrument for the colonial powers to re-establish their influence in the country.

In spite of this resistance, the central board firmly maintained its policy and even went further to support the government in a number of projects aimed at reforming or modernizing Islamic education. In 1958, it took part in the compulsory education project for the *madrasahs* known as the *Madrasah Wajib Belajar* (MWB), aimed at intensifying the introduction of secular subjects in the madrasah. During its congress in 1975, Mathla'ul Anwar again showed its strong support for the government-designed reform of curriculum for the madrasah when it decided to fully accept the controversial introduction of the newly composed curriculum in which secular subjects were more dominant than religious subjects in all levels of the madrasah education. Yet, again, resistance towards the reform resurfaced as not all of its local madrasahs took the same side. They attempted to maintain the existing curriculum in which religious subjects were dominant. The intensified enforcement of the uniformity of the education system by the government in the early 1980s resulted in all madrasahs of Mathla'ul Anwar applying the unified national curriculum by 1984. As a result, Mathla'ul Anwar since then was "fully nationalised", like other secular and religious schools in the country.

All of the founders of Mathla'ul Anwar were religious teachers who had a high status in Banten society and, therefore, were influential with the masses. Their strong power brought about close contact with a variety of social movements either at the local level of Banten or the national one. One year before the foundation of Mathla'ul Anwar, both Kiyai Haji Muhammad Yasin and Kiyai Haji Mas Abdurrahman had established a close link with the first ever established political party, *Sarekat Islam* (Islamic League or SI) and both were chairmen of the executive board and the religious advisory board of the Menes branch of SI respectively. Their active roles remained until 1928 when SI changed its name into the Islamic League Party (*Partai Sarekat Islam* or PSI) and was apparently under the domination of the Muslim modernist leaders. However, both leaders continued to maintain their political activities through associating themselves with the *Nahdlatul Ulama* or *Nahdatal al-'Ulama'* (Resurgence of Muslim Scholars or NU), an association founded by traditionalist leaders in 1926, soon after announcing their withdrawal from SI. Ten years later, Mathla'ul Anwar played a great role in the history of NU when its Central Madrasah in Menes became the venue of the thirteenth National Congress of NU. Still under the banner of NU, it supported the foundation of Masyumi in 1945. However, their intimate relationship for more than two decades ended when they took different standpoints over the internal fractures within Masyumi. In 1952, NU founded its own political party, while, in the same year, Mathla'ul Anwar proclaimed its non-political affiliation, which for years to come would remain one of its basic principles. Although formally independent, the majority of its leaders were known as supporters and even leading figures of Masyumi in their regions.[7] Largely assumed as a part of the party, in the last years of Sukarno's rule, Mathla'ul Anwar was among the targets of Sukarno's loyalists, particularly those from NU and *Partai Komunis Indonesia* (Indonesian Communist Party, PKI). In 1964,

Mathla'ul Anwar worked together with other anti-communist groups in the creation of *Sekretariat Bersama Golongan Karya* (The Joint Secretariat of Functional Groups or *Sekber Golkar*).

After the collapse of Sukarno, Mathla'ul Anwar along with other former supporters of Masyumi, set up a federative association, named *Badan Koordinasi Amal Muslimin Indonesia* (the Coordination Council of Indonesian Muslim Works or BKAMI) with one of its prime goals to rehabilitate Masyumi. Unable to implement their goal due to the strong resistance of the military forces, they agreed to set up a new party, *Partai Muslimin Indonesia* (Indonesian Muslim Party or Parmusi). The formal involvement of the central board of Mathla'ul Anwar in the foundation of the party brought widespread protests from young leaders who felt the central board had betrayed the long-preserved commitment to keep the organization away from any forms of political association. The failure of Kiyai Uwes Abu Bakar, who had been the general chairman of the central board of Mathla'ul Anwar since 1939, to gain a parliamentary seat in the 1971 general election drove Kiyai Uwes to announce his resignation from Parmusi and other political roles. Furthermore, he instructed all elements in Mathla'ul Anwar to no longer formally associate their organization with the party. Both decisions again brought Mathla'ul Anwar back to its stance as a non-political affiliated association.

In 1972, one year after his political retirement, Kiyai Uwes Abu Bakar died at the age of 70. Kiyai Muslim Abdurrahman, who was at that time the first chairman of the central board, was appointed as the new general chairman. The new leader strongly advocated the full application of Islamic law and opposed Pancasila as the ideology of the state and brought a new political approach to Mathla'ul Anwar vis-à-vis the New Order government. Mathla'ul Anwar not only maintained its non-political affiliation policy but also acted as an opposition force. Kiyai Muslim's leadership was short-lived, he died in 1974. However, his radical approach in politics survived as another radical leader, Haji Nafsirin Hadi, was elected as the new general chairman during the 1975 congress. Under the leadership of Nafsirin Hadi, Mathla'ul Anwar was frequently in conflict with the New Order regime and some leaders, including Kiyai Haji Nafsirin Hadi, were put in jail. Mathla'ul Anwar's political resistance put it under the bitter political pressures of the ruling administration. Consequently, its activities declined, if not totally ceased. Under such hostile circumstances, it failed to organize its already scheduled national congress in 1980 in Lampung following the refusal of the local government to give permission. Up to 1985, Mathla'ul Anwar was under political pressure from the government and this finally gave the opportunity for the accommodationist leaders led by Irsyad Djuwaeli who attained strong backing from some ruling figures, prominently Alamsyah Ratu Prawiranegara, one of the closest assistants of Soeharto,[8] to take over the leadership of Mathla'ul Anwar. This changing leadership marked a new chapter for Mathla'ul Anwar against the New Order regime.

Just like in politics, Mathla'ul Anwar encountered dramatic changes in religious thought. Prior to Independence, Mathla'ul Anwar was a strict follower of the Shafi'ite school and developed the traditionalist's religious thought.[9] Its withdrawal from PSI and joining NU was mainly because of religious thought. This type of religious thought was one of the major factors for the Islamic foundation of Anwariyah of Bandung to fuse with Mathla'ul Anwar in the early months of 1952. Following its political separation from NU, Mathla'ul Anwar began to entertain itself with a new religious thought that was to be close to that of reformist or modernist groups. The arrival of a number of the reformist leaders such as Abu Bakar Aceh, Saleh Syu'adi and others, intensified the propagation of new religious ideas among members of Mathla'ul Anwar. Kiyai Uwes as the general chairman played a pivotal role in this effort as he also composed a book titled *Ishlahul Ummah dalam menerangkan arti Ahlusunnah wal Jama'ah* (*al-Ahl al-Sunna wa al-Jama'a*) in which he boldly underlined his objection to some ideas of the traditionalist groups and furthermore championed those of the reformist ones.[10] However, the massive introduction of reformist ideas did not mean that those who supported the traditionalist ideas totally vanished. Instead, they continued to exist, although weakened. Furthermore, the moderate approach applied by Kiyai Uwes guaranteed their survival. Yet, his tolerant approach in introducing new religious ideas declined as both Kiyai Muslim and Haji Nafsirin Hadi tended to exercise radical approaches. To purify all supposedly non-Islamic elements, Kiyai Muslim set up a special team consisting of students of the Central Madrasah whose main duties were to rid society of all practices not explicitly defined by the Qur'an and the Sunnah. Due to this radical approach, Mathla'ul Anwar was then associated with the Wahhabi, the leading group of fundamentalist movements in the history of Islam. The radical approaches exercised by both leaders nonetheless failed to totally eradicate all traditionalist elements within Mathla'ul Anwar since some of those who supported the purification notion opposed the radical approach. Thus, the collapse of Haji Nafsirin Hadi's leadership in the mid-1980s left at least three important streams of religious thought within Mathla'ul Anwar: the radical, moderate or reformist, and traditionalist. All of them would compete to be the dominant religious thought and this would be seen clearly in the creation of the *khittah* (Basic Guideline) in the mid-1990s.

THE RISE OF IRSYAD DJUWAELI

Irsyad Djuwaeli, who was born in Lebak in 1949, first rose to the elite level of Mathla'ul Anwar as he led Mathla'ul Anwar's students in Jakarta to take active roles in the anti-communist student movements in 1966. Responding to the widespread appeal of the anti-communist student movements, he (at that time registered as a student of the Religious Teacher Training (*Pendidikan Guru Agama*, or PGA) of Mathla'ul Anwar in Jakarta) took the initiative to set up an organization through which Mathla'ul Anwar's students could express their anti-communist aspiration. He named this organization the *Ikatan Pelajar Mathla'ul Anwar* (the Mathla'ul Anwar's Student Association or IPMA). Representing the IPMA, Irsyad Djuwaeli then took a role in the anti-communist movements at the national level through his participation in the *Kesatuan Aksi Pemuda Pelajar Indonesia* (the United Action of Indonesian Youth and Student or KAPPI), in which he was elected treasurer.

His active roles in both the IPMA and KAPPI soon brought him fame among the elites of Mathla'ul Anwar. In the 1966 congress, Kiyai Uwes, who was elected as the general chairman for his seventh term, named Irsyad Djuwaeli as chairman of the newly composed autonomous organization for students. His political career progressed rapidly. For instance, in 1970 Kiyai Uwes appointed him to represent Mathla'ul Anwar in the *Gerakan Usaha Pembaharuan Pendidikan Islam* (Islamic Education Reform Endeavour Movement, or GUPPI) that later became a vehicle of the New Order to politically mobilize Muslims in order to support Golkar.[11] Indeed, in the GUPPI, Irsyad Djuwaeli began to establish his political link with the elite circle of the ruling regime, including Ibnu Hartomo, Soeharto's brother-in-law, and Alamsyah Ratu Prawiranegara. Particularly, with the latter, Irsyad Djuwaeli acted as a private secretary in the 1970s. In Mathla'ul Anwar, his political rise also rapidly moved forward following his election at the 1975 congress as the general secretary under the leadership of Haji Nafsirin Hadi. However, their conflicting attitudes towards the ruling regime brought about their separation. In 1977, the general chairman decided to dismiss Irsyad Djuwaeli as general secretary and replaced him with another figure, Haji Damanhuri, who was an activist of *Partai Persatuan Pembangunan* (United Development Party or PPP), one of the three existing parties as the result of the fusion in the 1970s. Being ejected from the central board of Mathla'ul Anwar, Irsyad Djuwaeli then focused on establishing his political network within the ruling elites. In the mid-1980s, as the government attempted to overwhelm all Muslim forces through the adoption of *Pancasila* (Five Principles) as the sole state ideology, Irsyad Djuwaeli acted as the "bridge" between the government and Mathla'ul Anwar.

In order to attain significant support from members of Mathla'ul Anwar, Irsyad Djuwaeli exploited the prevalent internal conflicts within Mathla'ul Anwar. These conflicts were the result of the leadership failures of Haji Nafsirin Hadi along with the controversies he aroused, in particular over his ideas on the new approaches in religious thought and over a number of his decisions on reshuffling the central board. Some instances can be mentioned here. First, he failed to organize the already scheduled congress in 1980 that brought about the crises of legitimacy of his leadership. The second example was his decision to relieve a number of important figures from their posts in the central board. Nahid Abdurrahman was ousted from his position at the central board after allegedly being involved in a scandal concerning the recruitment of government employees. In cooperation with some officers in the Department of Religious Affairs, he asked for money from candidates in order to be accepted as the government employee. The matter became public when one of the candidates reported the case to the Jakarta-based *Pelita* daily newspaper.[12] Mohammad Amin, a son-in-law of Kiyai Uwes Abu Bakar, was dismissed as chairman of the board of the Central Madrasah due to his alleged misuse of donations from Saudi Arabia.[13]

Backed by a number of government officials who were alumni of Mathla'ul Anwar's madrasahs, prominently Sayaman, the head of the Department of Religious Affairs office of Pandeglang, Chowasi Mandala, an official at the provincial government of Jakarta, and Uwes Corny, an official of the provincial government of West Java, Irsyad Djuwaeli entered the arena through stressing the importance of changing the central leadership. To effectuate his plan, he then recruited Kiyai Burhani, a government employee at the Department of Religious Affairs of Pandeglang, who was the second chairman of the central board, to act as the leading figure. Under the direction of Irsyad Djuwaeli, Kiyai Burhani led the campaign that finally succeeded in forcing Nafsirin Hadi to set up a team to make some necessary preparations for the congress in which a new central board would be elected. Chairman of this team was Kiyai Burhani. Instead of preparing for a congress, the team created a new central board in which Kiyai Burhani acted as the temporary general chairman and Irsyad Djuwaeli as the general secretary. It was this new central board that finally organized the Congress, while Nafsirin Hadi, who saw this endeavour as a coup, was left without any role.

In the 1985 congress, both Kiyai Burhani and Irsyad Djuwaeli gained a formal legitimacy following their election as general chairman and general secretary respectively. The adoption of Pancasila as the sole ideological base of Mathla'ul Anwar was clearly ratified at the congress and the declaration of political alliance with Golkar in 1986 brought fruits to Kiyai Burhani who was elected as a member of the district parliament of Pandeglang in the 1987 general election. Meanwhile, Irsyad Djuwaeli perpetuated his dominating influence within the organization that finally resulted in his election as general chairman at the 1991 congress, replacing Kiyai Burhani who was elected as general chairman of the *Majelis Fatwa* (Religious Advisory Board). More than Kiyai Burhani, Irsyad Djuwaeli's successful effort in bringing Mathla'ul Anwar to Golkar was rewarded by his election as a member of parliament both in the 1992 and 1997 general elections.

MATHLA'UL ANWAR UNDER THE LEADERSHIP OF IRSYAD DJUWAELI

Irysad Djuwaeli's rising influence brought several changes in Mathla'ul Anwar. Among the most important were the adoption of Pancasila as the sole ideology of the organization, the declaration of political loyalty to Golkar and, finally, the massive establishment of Mathla'ul Anwar's branches in vast areas of the country. These three changes marked the development of Mathla'ul Anwar in the last years of the New Order.

Anxious over the impact of sectarian ideologies, including religious ones, on stability and order, the New Order enforced all organizations, whatever their form and character to adopt a government-designed uniform worldview, Pancasila. To implement the concept, the government issued a special law giving it the ultimate authority to promote the idea, while, at the same time, it made all civil associations powerless to resist. Mathla'ul Anwar, known as one of the main sources of political resistance in the 1970s, but facing acute internal ruptures in the early 1980s, became one of the main targets of this drive for uniformity. It was through Irsyad Djuwaeli's group that this campaign manifested itself. The notion started when Irsyad Djuwaeli's group was in urgent need of both political and financial support to organize the planned 1985 congress. Irsyad Djuwaeli had established close contacts with a number of prominent political figures, the most important one being Alamsyah Ratu Prawiranegara, and proposed to all members of his group to express their support to those ruling elite members. To minimize suspicion over the involvement of Alamsyah Ratu Prawiranegara, Irsyad Djuwaeli attempted to convince leaders of Mathla'ul Anwar about the latter's religious educational background. He said that Alamsyah was a former student of one of the madrasahs of Mathla'ul Anwar in Lampung and therefore had a moral obligation to save the organization from a further decline. Although Irsyad Djuwaeli never showed any convincing evidence about this claim, questions about its validity were rarely raised. This was perhaps due to a number of reasons, one being that in later years, Alamsyah played a dominant role within Mathla'ul Anwar. So, the questioning over the validity of the claim was irrelevant and even unproductive.

Members of the group soon agreed and visited Alamsyah who had showed his willingness since the very beginning. Yet, Alamsyah also presented three conditions. Firstly, Mathla'ul Anwar should fully adopt Pancasila as its sole ideology. Secondly, it should support the re-election of Soeharto for a third term. Thirdly, it should support the awarding of Soeharto as the Father of Development (*Bapak pembangunan*). The first condition meant that Mathla'ul Anwar had to lose its Islamic identity. Actually, since 1975 it had adopted Pancasila as its ideology but still maintained its Islamic identity. When the condition to fully endorse Pancasila was presented, the law on the sole ideology regulating this was still in the process of deliberation in Parliament. Because of this, Irsyad Djuwaeli's group encountered strong opposition from the majority of the members who felt it was too early to adopt this secular ideology while the situation was still unclear. The second and third requests had their consequences. In order to back Soeharto's re-election, Mathla'ul Anwar also had to support Golkar which clearly campaigned for Soeharto. It was also forced to show a blind loyalty to all policies applied by the government to assure that Soeharto was the true Father of Development. Resistance to the development programmes of the government would endanger the title. Under the strong influence of Irsyad Djuwaeli, Mathla'ul Anwar accepted those three conditions without significant objection.

The 1985 congress was crucial as during this event Mathla'ul Anwar introduced a number of decisions that would change its political character. Under the tight control of the military officers who played an important role in preventing a radical group led by both Nafsirin Hadi and Wahid Sahari from taking part in the congress as well as in muting all kinds of opposing notions within the congress arena, Mathla'ul Anwar decided to adopt Pancasila as the sole ideology. Pancasila was also declared as the product of the *ijma ummat*, the general consensus of all Muslim communities in the country, which thus bound all Muslims to fully adhere to it. The congress also declared its support to the development programme of the government that was considered to have protected the genuine interest of Muslims as the majority of the population. On the basis of these considerations, Mathla'ul Anwar went on to proclaim that it was religiously justified to show full loyalty to the government. To justify this notion, it referred to the principles of the *Ahl al-Sunna wa al-Jama'a*. According to Kiyai Uyeh Balukiya, one of the most neglected principles of the *Ahl al-Sunna wa al-Jama'a* was the loyalty to the legitimately ruling government. He argued that the New Order government was religiously legitimate because it was elected by a People's Assembly (*Majelis Permusyawaratan Rakyat* or MPR) as a concrete manifestation of the concept of the *Ahl al-Hilli wa al-'Aqd* (those who bind and solve) where all groups of society were represented. So, in the final conclusion, Mathla'ul Anwar declared its readiness to cooperate with the government in developing society and uplifting all the problems faced by people, particularly Muslims, in the country.

During the congress, however, the representatives still declared the political independence of Mathla'ul Anwar as had always been enunciated in every congress since 1952. The dominant resistance to radically shift its political orientation was the prime cause of its relatively consistent standpoint of self-assured political independence. In spite of this, the politically pragmatic leaders succeeded in enforcing the more accommodative political stance. In the final statement of the congress, Mathla'ul Anwar underlined the need to establish a close and mutual cooperation between the organization and the state. It was even argued that Mathla'ul Anwar had a moral as well as religious obligation to take an active part in supporting the development programmes set up by the government in order to achieve the ultimate goal of a prosperous Muslim society. In the following year, this declaration became the ground of multiple interpretations. Those who tended towards keeping Mathla'ul Anwar politically independent saw this statement as the way for Mathla'ul Anwar to preserve its politically independent status, while accepting other matters related to social welfare. Meanwhile, those who expected Mathla'ul Anwar to be a part of the ruling power, viewed this pronouncement as the main argument to give a more flexible attitude for Mathla'ul Anwar to take political roles. The second notion finally won the battle. A year later in July 1986, the central board of Mathla'ul Anwar held a mass rally in Menes, in which thousands of its members participated to declare its political association with Golkar. Alamsyah Ratu Prawiranegara, a member of the Supervisory Board of Golkar, accepted this joint statement on behalf of Golkar. Since then, Mathla'ul Anwar, like GUPPI, was politically a part of Golkar.

To further justify Mathla'ul Anwar's political alignment with Golkar, the central board made the first move to set up a political guideline for members of the organization. The central board then requested the *Majelis Fatwa* to undertake a number of steps to compose the guideline. In response, the *Majelis Fatwa*, under the leadership of Kiyai Haji Uyeh Balukiya, organized a meeting where it was decided that all members of the organization, as the true followers of the *Ahl al-Sunna wa al-Jama'a*, were obliged to support the ruling government. Although not stated explicitly, it meant that supporting the ruling government should be manifested through giving full support to

Golkar as the ruling party. This decision prompted harsh criticism from a number of leaders, including those who were actually pragmatic in politics. They considered it to have violated the sacred doctrine of Islam in order to justify worldly affairs that were profane in nature. Therefore, they demanded that the central board form a special team to evaluate the decisions made by the *Majelis Fatwa* and then to draft a more acceptable text of the guideline. Another important factor fanning opposition was the inclusion of a number of important New Order figures with no kind of background link with Mathla'ul Anwar, in its boards since Mathla'ul Anwar had declared its political association with Golkar. To preserve the identity of the organization, the creation of the fundamental guideline was deemed essential.

Under these enduring pressures, the central board held a meeting inviting a number of religious leaders of Mathla'ul Anwar from a variety of branches. This meeting took place in Cikaliung in July 1995. A number of respected religious teachers such as Kiyai Abdul Hadi Muktar of Tangerang, Kiyai Uyeh Balukiya of Bandung, Kiyai Wahid Sahari of Pandeglang, and Kiyai Bai Ma'mun of Pandeglang presented their points of view. Conflicting ideas over religious issues as well as political standpoints brought all participants to conclude the meeting with the creation of a special team consisting of five members to elaborate the contents of the guideline in details. Kiyai Wahid Sahari became chairman of the team. After organizing a number of meetings, the team finally succeeded in drafting the guidelines and submitted them to the central board in November 1995. The draft was then brought to the 1996 congress in order to be ratified as the formal guidelines of the organization. In this congress, the term *khittah*,[14] an Arabic derivative word that means a primarily guideline, was taken as the formal name.

In this newly formalized *khittah*, there were some changes made. First, the principle of loyalty to the legitimate government gained a stronghold but there were some additional requirements. The *khittah* defined the legitimate government to be based on its formation procedure; that is, through the election, but also its policies should not be contradictory with the principles of Islamic doctrines. However, the *khittah* did not elaborate in detail whether this legitimate government should also apply the *Sharia* (Islamic law) for instance. Wahid Sahari said that this statement did not imply that Mathla'ul Anwar supported the enunciation of the *Piagam Jakarta* (Jakarta Charter) in which the implementation of the *Sharia* is explicitly mentioned. Instead, the Mathla'ul Anwar's view was that the condition in which Muslims could perform the five principles of Islam, including giving aims, fasting, five daily prayers and going on pilgrimage, was enough to decide whether or not a ruling government was legitimate. Another important point was that members of Mathla'ul Anwar should be "sophisticated in politics" (*berpiawai dalam politik*). According to Wahid Sahari, this point was among the most hotly debated issues during the meetings of the team since there were two important streams within the team that also reflected the major political notions of members of the organization. Some members attempted to maintain the political independence of Mathla'ul Anwar, while others tended to be more moderate and pragmatic. As the political circumstance of the New Order would not tolerate a politically independent notion, the team finally opted for a compromise which at the same time was an ambiguous political stance; being sophisticated in politics. This phrase was, on the one hand, according to the members of the team, expected to accommodate both conflicting notions. On the other hand, it also provided a strong legitimacy for the central board under the leadership of Irsyad Djuwaeli to further promote the notion of supporting Golkar.

The pro-Golkar groups grew stronger as they succeeded in rapidly developing the organization. Prior to the 1985 congress, Mathla'ul Anwar, under the political pressures of the New Order due to its opposing stance, only had branches at the district levels in three provinces, Lampung, Jakarta and West Java. During its 1991 congress, it was reported that Mathla'ul Anwar had established branches in fourteen out of twenty-seven existing provinces. At the time of the 1996 congress, it was only in provinces like Irian Jaya, East Timor and Bali where Muslims constituted a minority status, that Mathla'ul Anwar did not have branches. In its expansion strategy, Mathla'ul Anwar employed its close affiliation with the ruling elites, particularly under the direction of Alamsyah Ratu Prawiranegara[15] who was at that time Minister of Social Welfare but still enjoyed a tremendous influence in the Ministry of Religious Affairs. Through the networks of both Golkar and the Department of Religious Affairs, Mathla'ul Anwar recruited local political and religious leaders in its attempts to set up its local chapters.

Mathla'ul Anwar's political affiliation with Golkar was the major factor for a number of local Islamic schools that sought a political channel at the centre of the power to declare their fusion with the Mathla'ul Anwar. Unlike previous expansions in the 1930s and 1950s when Islamic educational empowerment was the core of the mission, the new expansion was clearly political. The idea was not to expand its educational institution but rather to establish a political representation in almost every region in the country. As the result of such a method of expansion, Mathla'ul Anwar in the 1990s was more urban-oriented. Most of its new chapters were now located at district capitals. It was very different from the 1930s when Mathla'ul Anwar leaders were more concerned with providing Islamic education for rural people.

With such a method of expansion, many viewed Mathla'ul Anwar as a mass-based Muslim association, without real mass support. Yet, the leaders of the organization believed this expansion to be a spectacular achievement and proudly used the phrase *Ayam Kampung Masuk Kota* (literally means a free-range chicken from the village comes into the city). In other words, Mathla'ul Anwar had transformed itself from a rural-based and identified organization due to its previously concentrated activities in rural areas into an urban and modern-oriented organization.

OPPOSITION TO IRSYAD DJUWAELI'S LEADERSHIP

The new developments in fact had implications for both the organization and its members. Among them was the loss of traditional support as a consequence of the massive arrival of "alien" figures without a clear standard, and the loss of its critical stance against the ruling power. A number of opposing movements used both issues as the main weapon to attack the leadership of Irsyad Djuwaeli.

One of the most visible consequences of the political closeness to Golkar was the massive change in the board structure of Mathla'ul Anwar, along with the inclusion of a significant number of Golkar's men. In its 1985 congress Mathla'ul Anwar created a new body above the central board named the Supervisory Board (*Dewan Pembina*), mirroring a similar institution in Golkar. This body replaced the Advisory Board (*Dewan Penasehat*) that had been created since the 1966 congress and was designed to accommodate government officials. Unlike the latter which did not have a significant influence on the decision-making processes, the *Dewan Pembina* had an accumulation of powers including that to appoint the members of the central board. Its first general chairman was General (ret.) Alamsyah Ratu Prawiranegara. Because of this position, he had unlimited powers within Mathla'ul Anwar. All other members were ministers or military officers who were mostly also members of the Supervisory Board of Golkar such as Munawir Sjadzali, who succeeded Alamsyah as the Minister of Religious Affairs in 1983. Golkar's men were placed not only at the Supervisory Board, but also at other existing boards including the *Majelis Fatwa* and the Central Board (*Pengurus Besar* or PB). This kind of board structure was reflected at all levels of the organization. For instance, at the provincial level, governors, military officers and Golkar's leaders acted as the members of the Supervisory Board. Furthermore, in all newly created branches, both local government officers and Golkar's leaders dominated the board structure of the organization.

The radical method of recruitment of the leaders without any standardized procedures had grave consequences for those who were traditional members of Mathla'ul Anwar, particularly in those areas known as the traditional bases of the organization such as Banten, Lampung and parts of West Java. Leaders of those areas grew alienated, as the newly recruited figures, mostly without even having enough knowledge about Mathla'ul Anwar, took dominant roles in the boards of Mathla'ul Anwar. One of the most controversial events was the appointment of Yusuf Alamsyah, a son of Alamsyah Ratu Prawiranegara, as the general chairman of the Central *Perguruan* (a complex of a number of madrasahs along with their various levels of schooling) of Mathla'ul Anwar in Menes. His selection was to be the first "incident" when the Central Perguruan was not in the hands of former graduates of Mathla'ul Anwar madrasahs. Many who believed that the Central Perguruan was the core symbol of the identity of Mathla'ul Anwar accused Irsyad Djuwaeli of having damaged the already long-preserved convention of selecting the leadership of the Central Perguruan. They saw the appointment of Yusuf Alamsyah as political in nature rather than an attempt at educational empowerment since its main goal was to weaken the opposition against the ruling government, which were clearly dominant in the first two decades of the New Order.

The issue of political expenditure of Irsyad Djuwaeli in inviting "alien" figures became the main criticism of a number of opposition movements, mostly led by young leaders. In 1991, just a few months before the national congress, hundreds of teachers from a number of madrasahs in Banten organized a demonstration in front of Irsyad Djuwaeli's house in Rangkasbitung protesting the lack of concern of the central board in dealing with the improvement of education and teachers' salary. In 1995, led by Humaidi Hasan and Huriyudin, a number of opposition leaders gathered in the Central Perguruan of Mathla'ul Anwar in Menes complaining against the "politization" of Mathla'ul Anwar for the sake of Irsyad Djuwaeli's political interest and, thus, demanding the replacement of Irsyad Djuwaeli as the general chairman in the 1996 congress. Their demand failed as Irsyad Djuwaeli was re-elected for a second term. Another attempt to prevent Mathla'ul Anwar from being further politicized was the creation of the *khittah* in which it was laid down that the members controlled the central board. This last attempt succeeded as in the 1996 congress, the *khittah* was ratified as the formal guideline of the organization along with the statutes (*Anggaran Dasar*) of the organization. However, some compromises, particularly in relation to political issues, made the *khittah* ineffective preventing from the central board from further bringing the organization into the fields of practical politics. The vague conception of the *khittah* on political matters in fact provided more legitimate grounds for some leading politicians of Mathla'ul Anwar to strengthen their efforts to keep the organization under the political hegemony of Golkar.

Another impact of the politically accommodative stance was the loss of the politically critical stand of Mathla'ul Anwar that was one of the main credits in the first two decades of the New Order. Furthermore, this change of political feature created internal ruptures. The radical approach of the central board in dealing with political opponents poured oil on the fire. Following the Firm Declaration (*Kebulatan Tekad*) of Mathla'ul Anwar to vote for Golkar in 1986, many members of the organization who had been PPP activists strongly protested that decision. Some of them, such as Haji Abdul Malik and Haji Dhoifun of Kepuh, even publicly declared their political support to PPP and were ready to be placed on the list of the candidates for the PPP in the 1987 general election. In reaction, Irsyad Djuwaeli, in his capacity as general secretary, vehemently condemned such steps and issued a letter dismissing both leaders from their positions as members of the board of Mathla'ul Anwar's branch of Serang District.

Another source of resistance was a group led by alumni of the Middle Eastern Universities. Those who were critical of New Order Islam policy frequently criticized the central board blindly justifying all policies of the government. Irsyad Djuwaeli accused this group of not having enough loyalty to the state. He even proposed to the government to hold a personal screening through forcing such critics to take part in the *Pedoman Penghayatan dan Pengamalan Pancasila* (the Guideline of the Internalization and Implementation of Pancasila, or P4) training before their return to society in order to minimize the impacts of their radical points of view. Wars of words between both opposing groups dominated the political discourse within members of Mathla'ul Anwar in the last years of the 1980s and the early 1990s.

The powerless stance of the first group drove some of them to finally withdraw from Mathla'ul Anwar and establish their own Islamic educational institutions independent from Mathla'ul Anwar. For instance, Kiyai Wahid Sahari, before his return to Mathla'ul Anwar in 1995, and Kiyai Zainal Abidin Syuzai in cooperation with the *Dewan Dakwah Islamiyah Indonesia* (Indonesian Islamic Missionary Council, DDII) established an Islamic foundation named *Al-Ishlah* that literally means Reconciliation[16] in 1989. Meanwhile, sponsored by the *Rabita al-Alam al-Islami* (the Islamic World League), Syadeli Karim founded another Islamic foundation named *Al-Izzah* in 1991 in Serang. These institutions then in the early 1990s became the centre of opposition leaders within Mathla'ul Anwar before their return either in the last years of Soeharto's rule or after the demise of Soeharto.

Political changes as the result of Soeharto's new approaches on Islamic affairs in the mid-1990s and the newly democratic circumstances after the collapse of Soeharto's rule were to be the major factors inducing those opposition leaders to return to Mathla'ul Anwar. Yet, their attempts to overthrow Irsyad Djuwaeli in the 2001 congress failed following his re-election for a third term. There were at least two major factors contributing to this failure. First, since most of the participants of the congress represented new branches that were created by Irsyad Djuwaeli, the political machine of the incumbent general chairman could easily convince them to maintain the status quo. Second, the lack of financial resources to run such a huge organization like Mathla'ul Anwar was to be the main obstacle for other candidates, particularly proposed by opposing groups, to compete in the election.

CONCLUSION

From the above description, some conclusions can be drawn. First, Mathla'ul Anwar like NU and Muhammadiyah since the early twentieth century represents an organized form of religious authority to which its members refer their religious questions. In spite of the fact that since the demise of Soeharto or even before that moment, individual religious men from a variety of political and social backgrounds come to the surface in the religious discourse, those mass-based organizations still hold a prominent role as the source of religious reference. Second, since associations such as Mathla'ul Anwar and NU were a source of both cultural and political identification, the state paid a high interest in attempting to control them. At the same time, Muslim leaders like those of Mathla'ul Anwar who were aware of the pivotal position of their associations made use of them to express their political aspirations against the state. Third, in the development of Mathla'ul Anwar in the last years of the New Order, the contest of authorities, either religious or non-religious, within Mathla'ul Anwar manifested itself especially in the change of political orientation and in the drafting of the *khittah*. From this competition for authority came to the fore issues such as the dominant versus the marginalized and the "genuine" versus the "alien". These issues are perhaps useful to study other social movements under the hegemony of politics.

NOTES

This article is a revision of the paper presented at the Final Conference of the Dissemination of Religious Authority in Twentieth Century Indonesia Programme, 7–9 July 2005, Hotel Salak Bogor. The original version has also been published in the

Jurnal Wahana Akademika. My thanks go to Prof Van Dijk and Dr Kaptein; both have given me a number of very valuable critical suggestions.

1. They were Kiyai Haji Entol Muhammad Yasin, Kiyai Haji Tubagus Muhammad Soleh, Kiyai Haji Mas Abdurrahman, Kiai Arsyad Tegal, Kiyai Abdul Mu'thi, Kiyai Soleman of Cibinglu, Kiyai Daud, Kiyai Rusydi, Kiyai *Entol* Danawi, Kiyai Mustaghfiri, Kiyai Saiman, Kiyai Muhammad Rais, and Kiyai Entol Ismail. Pengurus Besar (PB) Mathla'ul Anwar. *Sejarah dan Khittah Mathla'ul Anwar*, Jakarta: PB Mathla'ul Anwar, 1996, p. 10. Tim Penyusun, "Mathla'ul Anwar dalam Perspektif Sejarah Gerakan Islam di Indonesia", a paper presented at the Seminar on the History of Mathla'ul Anwar, May 1991, p. 16. See also Malnu's website, <www.malnupusat.tripod.com/aboutmalnu.htm> (accessed March 2005).
2. This could be seen in the case of his introduction of a more "rational" interpretation of the Qur'anic verses. For instance, Nafsirin Hadi interpreted the word "*as*" a belonged to Musa not as a stick in the true sense, but as a kind of power or authority given by God to his Prophet. Many religious teachers of Mathla'ul Anwar strongly rejected his idea and blamed his lack of expertise in religious matters as the major factor for his false understanding of the Qur'anic verses. Interviews with Kiyai Haji Rafiuddin, 20 July 2002, Haji O. Boman Rukmantara, 17 July 2002, Kiyai Haji Mahnun, 18 July 2002, and Kiyai Haji A. Wahid Sahari, 7 August 2003.
3. One of the most referred to evidence of his outstanding expertise in religious subjects was his book titled *Ishlahul Ummah dalam menerangkan arti Ahlussunnah wal-Jama'ah* (Reconstructing Islamic Community through Explaining the True Description of the Adherents of Prophet Tradition and Community) published in 1969. Along with those books composed by Kiyai Haji Abdurrahman, the ultimate teacher in Mathla'ul Anwar, like *Al-Jawa'iz fi Ahkam al-Jana'iz* (The Religiously Acceptable Acts in Dealing with Muslim Corpses), the *Ishlahul Ummah* has constituted itself as the primary reference for religious matters for members of Mathla'ul Anwar.
4. PB Mathla'ul Anwar, *Sejarah dan Khittah*, pp. 11–12.
5. Ibid.
6. For more details about this development, see Martin van Bruinessen, "Shari'a Court, Tarekat and Pesantren: Religious Institutions in the Banten Sultanate", *Archipel* 50 (1995).
7. Kiyai Uwes Abu Bakar was a Member of Parliament on behalf of Masyumi and Kiyai Mas Abdurrahman was also a Masyumi representative at the district parliament of Pandeglang in the 1955 general election before he resigned in 1957.
8. In the early years of Soeharto's rise to power, Alamsyah, who had established a close friendship with the second President of the Republic of Indonesia since the 1950s, was a member of the so-called "inner core group" of the New Order. He was the coordinator of the private staff (*staf pribadi* or SPRI) that was first set up

in August 1966 but dissolved in June 1968 after being fiercely attacked by students and the press. In this "non-structural" institution, Alamsyah, along with other members, Ali Murtopo, the mastermind of OPSUS, Sujono Humardani, Yoga Sugama, Suryo Wirjohadiputro, and others "enjoyed greater powers than the cabinet, particularly in the policy formation". Due to this powerful influence, many regarded this group as an "invisible government". After the abolishment of this institution, Alamsyah did not immediately lose his influence, as several months before he was already appointed as the state secretary, through which he fully controlled all matters related to the policy decision-making in the New Order government. In 1971, however, he lost Soeharto's favour following continuous political intrigues within Soeharto's inner groups and was sent to The Netherlands as an ambassador. After three years of service in The Netherlands, he was called back and was appointed deputy chairman of the Supreme Adviser Council (*Dewan Pertimbangan Agung*, DPA) in which he once again showed his critical view towards the government's policies, particularly in the deepening wealth gap within society. Instead of losing an important position, he was recruited by Soeharto in the 1978 cabinet portfolio as Minister of Religious Affairs in which he neutralized Muslims' oppositions towards the recognition of the *Kebatinan* that was under his direction brought under the Ministry of Education and Culture instead of the Ministry of Religious Affairs. David Jenkins, *Suharto and His Generals: Indonesian Military Politics 1975–1983* (1984), pp. 22–23 and 77–78. See also Masykuri Abdillah, "Alamsyah Ratu Prawiranegara: Stabilitas Nasional dan Kerukunan", in *Menteri-menteri Agama RI: Biografi Sosial-Politik*, edited by Azyumardi Azra and Saiful Umam (1998), pp. 334 and 357–60. For a full coverage of the biography of Alamsyah, see Suparwan G. Parikesit and Krisna R. Sempurnadjaja, *H. Alamsyah Ratu Prawiranegara: Perjalanan Hidup Seorang Anak Yatim Piatu* (1995).

9. See Kiyai Mas Abdurrahman's work, particularly, *Al-Jawa'iz fi Ahkam al-Jana'iz*, n.p., n.d.
10. See Kiyai Uwes Abu Bakar, *Ishlahul Ummah* (1969).
11. Established in Sukabumi, West Java by a group of traditionally oriented religious teachers led by Kiyai Badri Sanusi and Kiyai Mansur, GUPPI was very much concerned with the declining significance of Islamic education institutions, particularly pesantrens, vis-à-vis both public schools and modern-based madrasahs. Its founders strongly rejected the government-made rules that put religious instruction in public schools as an optional choice based on the decision of the parents. In its early stages, GUPPI was very much restricted to a number of pesantrens in Sukabumi as its members. Furthermore, matters became much worse as GUPPI encountered other problems, including lack of human resources as well as of finance. Another important factor for the stagnancy of GUPPI was that its members became the targets of PKI-inspired attacks. It was only after 1968, in order to accommodate the interest of Islamic education institutions, that some GUPPI leaders took an initiative to revive their organization. The first

event was the holding of the GUPPI congress that took place in December 1968 in Malang, East Java, in which a modernist-oriented kiyai and former Masyumi activist, Anwar Sanusi, was elected as new chairman. At the time of this congress, GUPPI had also succeeded in expanding its influence in Java as a number of religious teachers coming from different places in Java took part in the congress. The absence of financial resources had driven GUPPI to finally affiliate with Golkar to seek an effective channel to entail support from Muslims. Its decision to affiliate with Golkar also meant the end of its non-political affiliation status underlined in its early foundation. Under the tightly orchestrated actions led by Ali Murtopo and Sujono Humardani, the building up of GUPPI was successful as many Islamic education groups were among its supporters, including Mathla'ul Anwar that sent Uwes Abu Bakar and Irsyad Djuwaeli to attend the inauguration of GUPPI. The last name was furthermore recommended as a Mathla'ul Anwar's representative on the board of GUPPI. Interview with Irsyad Djuwaeli, 16 June 2002. About GUPPI and its roles in politics, see Arif Subhan, "GUPPI: Pembaruan Pendidikan Melalui Politik?", *Jurnal Komunikasi Dunia Perguruan Madrasah* I, no. 4 (1998): 15–23; Ken Ward, *The 1971 Election in Indonesia: An East Java Case Study* (1974), p. 130; and Heru Cahyono, *Peranan Ulama dalam Golkar 1971–1980: Dari Pemilu sampai Malari* (1992).

12. See "Pembaca Menulis", *Pelita*, 25 October 1978 and 30 November 1978.
13. In 1977, Mathla'ul Anwar received financial support from Saudi Arabia to build new classrooms at the *Perguruan Pusat*, a new term applied since 1961 for the Central Madrasah. To deal with this project, the central board appointed the board of the *Perguruan Pusat* to manage this project. Haji Muhammad Amin, who was at that time the chairman of the board of the *Perguruan Pusat*, became the head of the project. Other members of the board, such as Boman Rukmantara and Lili Suhaeli, assisted him in this project. Within a year, this team succeeded in constructing a new building which was later used as classrooms for students of Madrasah Tsanawiyah (MTs). However, after the smooth construction project had ended, the scandalous issue of corruption committed by the members of the team, particularly Muhammad Amin and Boman Rukmantara, arose. Failing to assure Nafsirin Hadi about the falsity of this allegation and their innocence, both project managers were suspended from their posts as the chairman and vice-chairman of the board of the *Perguruan Pusat*. The furious general chairman soon appointed his man, Wahid Sahari, as the chairman replacing Muhammad Amin, while the post of vice-chairman was left unfilled. Interview with Haji O. Boman Rukmantara, 17 July 2002, and with Lili Suhaeli, 13 September 2002.
14. The issue of the *Khittah* also came up in NU when it finally declared the Return to the *khittah* of 1926 (*Kembali ke Khittah 1926*) in its 1984 congress following its decision to withdraw from "practical" politics. Like NU, the nature of the notion of the *khittah* in Mathla'ul Anwar was political, although the term itself according to some writers of Mathla'ul Anwar had been popular since the late 1950s. The difference was that this idea in Mathla'ul Anwar did not come from

those who demanded that the organization keep its political independence, but from those who sought a legitimacy for the new political orientation of Mathla'ul Anwar following the adoption of Pancasila as its sole ideology and its political approaching with the New Order government. So, if NU through its *kembali ke Khittah 1926* campaign broke away from politics, Mathla'ul Anwar through it threw itself into politics. For the case of NU, see Martin van Bruinessen, *NU: Tradisi, Relasi-relasi Kuasa, Pencarian Wacana Baru* (1994). Andrée Feillard, *NU vis-à-vis Negara: Pencarian Isi, Bentuk dan Makna* (1999, chapter X), and Douglas E. Ramage, *Politics in Indonesia: Democracy, Islam and the Ideology of Tolerance* (1995, particularly chapter 2 on Abdurrahman Wahid and Nahdlatul Ulama).

15. The dominant role of Alamsyah in Mathla'ul Anwar's expansive endeavours have even brought an observer to suggest that it was Alamsyah who actually founded Mathla'ul Anwar. Andrée Feillard, *NU vis-à-vis Negara*, p. 291.
16. According to Wahid Sahari, the name of *Al-Ishlah* was based on his own reflection about the necessity of creating reconciliation between members of Mathla'ul Anwar after being parted because of their different political inclinations. So, the name was to be the manifestation of his criticism of the development of Mathla'ul Anwar at that time. However, prior to the last congress of Mathla'ul Anwar held in July 2005, Wahid Sahari was among the candidates for the general chairman of the organization. Many considered that his notion to found a new educational institution separate from Mathla'ul Anwar whatever the reasons showed his lack of loyalty to the organization. In response, Wahid Sahari argued that people should closely observe the historical context of his temporary departure in which he was forced to stay away from the organization because of his political stance against the New Order government. Interview with Wahid Sahari, 8 April 2005.

References

Abdurrahman, Haji Mas. *Al-Jawa'iz fi Ahkam al-Jana'iz* [The Religiously Acceptable Acts in Dealing with Muslim Corpses]. N.p., n.d.

Abdillah, Masykuri. "Alamsyah Ratu Prawiranegara: Stabilitas Nasional dan Kerukunan". In *Menteri-menteri Agama RI: Biografi Sosial-Politik*, edited by Azyumardi Azra and Saiful Umam. Jakarta: INIS, PPIM and Badan Litbang Agama Departemen Agama RI, 1998.

Abu Bakar, Uwes. *Ishlahul Ummah dalam menerangkan arti Ahlussunnah wal-Jama'ah* [Reconstructing Islamic Community through Explaining the True Description of the Adherents of Prophet Tradition and Community]. Jakarta: PB Mathla'ul Anwar, 1969.

Cahyono, Heru. *Peranan Ulama dalam Golkar 1971–1980: Dari Pemilu sampai Malari*. Jakarta: Sinar Harapan, 1992.

Feillard, Andrée. *NU vis-à-vis Negara: Pencarian Isi, Bentuk dan Makna*. Yogyakarta: LKIS, 1999.

Jenkins, David. *Suharto and His Generals: Indonesian Military Politics 1975–1983*. Monograph Series 64. Ithaca New York: Modern Indonesia Project, Cornell University, 1984.

Parikesit, Suparwan G. and Krisna R. Sempurnadjaja. *H. Alamsyah Ratu Prawiranegara: Perjalanan Hidup Seorang Anak Yatim Piatu*. Jakarta: Pustaka Sinar Harapan, 1995.

Pengurus Besar (PB) Mathla'ul Anwar. *Sejarah dan Khittah Mathla'ul Anwar*. Jakarta: PB Mathla'ul Anwar, 1996.

Ramage, Douglas E. *Politics in Indonesia: Democracy, Islam and the Ideology of Tolerance*. London: Routledge, 1995.

Subhan, Arif. "GUPPI: Pembaruan Pendidikan Melalui Politik?". *Jurnal Komunikasi Dunia Perguruan Madrasah* I, no. 4 (1998).

Tim Penyusun. "Mathla'ul Anwar dalam Perspektif Sejarah Gerakan Islam di Indonesia". Paper presented at the Seminar on the History of Mathla'ul Anwar, May 1991.

van Bruinessen, Martin. "Shari'a Court, Tarekat and Pesantren: Religious Institutions in the Banten Sultanate". *Archipel* 50 (1995).

———. *NU: Tradisi, Relasi-relasi Kuasa, Pencarian Wacana Baru*. Yogyakarta: LKIS, 1994.

Ward, Ken. "The 1971 Election in Indonesia: An East Java Case Study". Monash Papers on Southeast Asia No. 2. Clayton, Victoria: Monash University, 1974.

Website and Newspaper

<www.malnupusat.tripod.com/aboutmalnu.htm>

Pelita

6

STRUGGLE FOR AUTHORITY
Between Formal Religious Institution and Informal-local Leaders

Machasin

INTRODUCTION

In the history of Indonesian Islam, especially in Java, *ulama* (*kiai, ajengan, tuan guru, tengku, buya*) played a hugely significant role in the life of the people because of their position in the "Islamic" community. For centuries they had a dominant position in the Islamic communities because they were the only source of Islamic expertise. It was only after the ideas of democracy spread, modern institutions of learning were introduced, modern organizations were established and the state formation got underway that their authority began to be challenged or — better — that they found competitors.

Theoretically speaking, when every individual is equal, knowledge (including religious knowledge) is accessible to everyone, and public affairs are handled by institutions, there will be no place for individuals to dominate authority. The reality, however, can always break the theory. Until the present time, local *ulama* still manage to maintain their religious authority in their "territory", i.e., among groups of people who are loyal to them. A decision on a religious matter made by the highest decision bodies of, for example, Muhammadiyah and Nahdlatul Ulama, sometimes turns out to be inapplicable in a place where one or two *ulama* express a different opinion on the same issue.

AUTHORITY OF *ULAMA* IN RURAL SOCIETY

When Islam came to the Indonesian archipelago and became the religion of the majority of its inhabitants, some old traditions survived although they got new garbs. One example is in rural Islamic societies where *ulama* replace the position of exalted religious leaders functioning as a "medium" between the divine world and the profane; the divine world is believed to be inaccessible to common people but has much influence on what happens in the profane. For the lay believers, the *ulama* possess sacred knowledge and magical power due to their proximity to God. This position was partly a result of the *ulama*'s pivotal role in spreading Islamic teachings. For many communities — especially in villages — *ulama* are the only source — of what the believer should know concerning religious obligations and rules. They have taught the people, guided them how to behave properly and led them in prayer and rituals. The *ulama* are always with the people any time they need help.[1]

These activities resulted among other things in the psychological dependence of the common people on the *ulama*. Not only for matters of religious rituals and obligations do these people turn to the *ulama*, but also on many other matters about which they think they are in need of advice or guidance. For example, they will ask them to find a suitable name for a new born child, to heal sicknesses, to find stolen property, to determine a suitable date for a wedding etc.[2]

In return, the people will give money, agricultural products and other gifts to the *ulama*. Some will work for them as a sign of gratitude and are ready to do any job the *ulama* ask them to do. This *symbiosis mutualis* is a logical consequence of the absence of the idea of church in the Islamic world. The propagation of Islamic teachings (dakwah) is basically a voluntary activity performed by any pious believer who believes it is his/her obligation to share God's guidance with other human beings. Since there is no church in Islam, such pious believers who put the duty of dakwah on their shoulders have to find themselves the money needed for such activities and even their own expenditure.

For people in rural areas, the *ulama* with their esoteric and privileged knowledge are often seen as personal guarantees providing a sense of safety. They know the will and the law of God, and they function as intermediary persons through whom people's wishes and prayers will be known and eventually fulfilled by God. Thus, the *ulama* function as *the* institution of religion, meaning that every religious activity should only be performed under their guidance and leadership and with their permission.

MODERNITY AND ITS IMPACT ON RELIGIOUS INSTITUTION

Modernity means a change in human attitude towards nature and man. To some extent, the dependence of human beings upon one another is replaced in modernity by independency and rationalized relations. Some "sacred knowledge" that was before the privilege of an elite is now open to everyone. Religious obligations and restrictions are accessible to those who are willing to read books and learn in learning institutions. In short, a personal guarantee is no longer needed since everybody can have access to knowledge.

With that change and its consequences, modernity brings competitors to *ulama* in the field of religion. In the case of Indonesia, two processes need thorough attention, i.e., the formation of the nation-state and the establishment of socio-religious organizations. No one argues that the formation of the Indonesian state is a blessing for Muslims in this country, including their leaders, the *ulama*. They look at it as a vehicle — among other things — to realize the genuine ideal of *Sharia* implementation. However, the course of time forces them to face a number of difficulties caused by the ever-growing power of the state that compromises their own religious authority and psychological grip on the people.

A good example is the case of education. The pesantren or Islamic religious boarding school used to be the only institution of education for Muslims. With the introduction of modern education after the beginning of the last century — first by the Dutch colonial government and then by the Indonesian Republic — and the type of life that came with the modern world, it seemed that the pesantren could no longer meet the educational needs of Indonesian Muslims. They needed skills, knowledge and expertise that most pesantrens could not offer. The formation of the state and its administration require knowledge and skills other than Islamic knowledge studied in pesantrens. So do positions and occupations that came up as result of the state formation. Pesantrens were thus forced to change themselves or otherwise face marginalization in the process of the country's development.[3]

The recent development that shows parents' growing interest in sending their children to pesantrens is not yet proof that they have won the battle of gaining public trust — on which the authority of local *ulama* rests — but indicates that people think that these pesantrens provide some complementary benefits lacking in public schools. Among other things, these pesantrens give parents in big cities a feeling of security when they are worried by the dangers of modern life such as drug abuse and irresponsible youth relations. This could only happen, however, after pesantrens changed their education system in compliance with national requirements of education. This change — either in a form of a madrasah or of an Islamic general school[4] — will assure theoretically that those who study there will have access to modern life without being cut off from their Islamic tradition.

In short, after the formation of the Indonesia state, parents sent their children to pesantrens because they were not expensive and because of the religious education they provided. Pesantrens in or near big cities have an additional advantage. They became places for cheap lodging and additional religious education for students of other institutions of higher education. In Yogyakarta, for example, we can find students of universities like Gadjah Mada University, State Islamic University Sunan Kalijaga, Indonesian Islamic University and Yogyakarta State University, who stay in pesantrens in Krapyak (al-Munawir, Ali Maksum, etc.) and Kota Gedhe (Nurul Ummah and Nurul Ummahat) and the Aji Mahasiswa and Wahid Hasyim pesantrens. In short, after the formation of the Indonesian state and the arrival of a modern lifestyle, pesantrens changed their system of education and were now one among many choices of secondary and high educations — and not the most popular.

Modernity brought about the establishment of nation-wide Islamic organizations, like Muhammadiyah and Nahdlatul Ulama. Although, in theory, local *ulama* have access to the decision-making process in these organizations and their administration, in reality, some of them feel abandoned and, as a result, they are in a state of tension or even competition with them. It is not uncommon for some local kiais to maintain their own opinions concerning religious and political issues when they feel that the decision of the organization is not appropriate. In Nahdlatul Ulama, the tension between the organization and local kiais happens more often since the autonomy of the latter is so great that they sometimes see the former more as a nuisance and hindrance than as a unifying means to build up power or as an appropriate channel of communication with the government and other groups. An organization aims to unify many scattered individuals who otherwise would have little power and could never accomplish great deeds. Nevertheless, in the course of Indonesian history — especially in the instance of contacts with the centres of political power and the state bureaucracy — many kiais enjoyed more fruitful directed relations with these institutions than they thought they might get through an organization. Thus, such an organization was seen as a restriction and an obstacle to the possibilities to profit from such contacts.

An interesting example is the RMI (*Rabita al-Ma'ahid al-Islamiyya*, Association of Islamic Boarding Schools), a body in the Nahdlatul Ulama concerning pesantrens. The vision and programme of this organization get little attention from students of universities like Gadjah Mada University, State Islamic University Sunan Kalijaga, Indonesian Islamic University and Yogyakarta State University. Two facts are indicative of this lack of interest. First, not all pesantrens are willing to be members of RMI or are involved in the management or leadership of it. Second, often pesantren leaders send only their assistants to take part in meetings of the RMI and then do not feel bound by its decisions.

Ulama have great sensitivity where it concerns issues on which they will issue a religious decision (*fatwa*) and have a good understanding of opinions in their community about the matter. They will think twice before issuing a decision that will harm their reputation among the people who look up to them, and will be much more inclined to come with a *fatwa* when their ruling enhances their reputation in the community.[5] The same goes for their attitude towards any movement and organization. The reliance of *ulama* on their communities is very important since it is thereon that their existence rests. An *ulama* without any community is beyond the bounds of the possible. His function is not in the first place that of a scholar in the academic sense of the word, but that of a figure on whom the surrounding community leans, especially in religious matters. The coming of modernity with its freedoms and ways of acquiring knowledge of everything for almost everyone affects to some extent their position in society and their religious authority. Organizations and institutions established by the process of modernity are thus seen as competitors for *ulama* in the field of religious authority.

One more thing can be added: those religious organizations and institutions need skilled people — which pesantrens usually cannot provide and a capacity for which *ulama* usually do not qualify — for their administration and management. That is why the *ulama* stay outside the bureaucracy and management of religious institutions in Indonesia, especially those which belong to the government. Together with the autonomy they have in their local Islamic community, this remaining outside the management of organizations will perpetuate the tension or at least the difference of opinions between the local *ulama* on the one hand and the religious organizations and institutions on the other. The state which is responsible for the prosperity of its citizens, the Islamic organizations which see it as their duty to channel the aspirations of their members and the local *ulama* who function as leaders of local communities, are bound to collide at times; since every one can be a citizen of the state, a member of an organization and a member of a religious community at the same time.

campaigning for another candidate. Also, some local *ulama* challenged a *fatwa* issued by MUI (Majelis Ulama Indonesia, the Council of Indonesian *Ulama*) in March 1981 ruling that Muslims are not allowed to be present at Christmas celebrations.[10] The MUI said that the prohibition aimed to protect Muslims' faith, but some *ulama* countered that attending such celebrations functioned more as maintaining good relations with Christian neighbours and had little or nothing to do with proselytization. The same argument was put forward in discussing a *fatwa* prohibiting praying together with people of different religions and even the saying of amen after a prayer said by a non-Muslim.[11] A young kiai from Yogyakarta challenged the prohibition not only by issuing a *fatwa* allowing such practices, but also by taking part in a public praying with adherents of different faiths and denominations.

The collecting of zakat, especially zakat al-fitr, is another good example of conflicting interests between organizations and individual *ulama*. Traditionally, *ulama* receive *zakat al-fitr* from the people at the end of Ramadan and distribute it among those who have the right to a share. There are eight categories of people[12] who have such a right, one is those who work for it. Some *ulama*, considering themselves administrators of zakat, keep a portion of zakat for themselves and when in the 1970s the government decided to establish public foundations to administer zakat, they resisted.[13]

In all such examples, the important thing is not that there are differences of opinion between the local *ulama* and Islamic organizations, but that both sides try their best to convince Muslim communities that they are right. This is done either by giving arguments or by acting in the way thought to be in accordance with the right teaching of Islam. Nevertheless, in religious matters, religion is not always the only consideration and sometimes one can detect economic and political interests when *ulama* endorse an opinion and oppose another.

Other areas that are worthwhile mentioning are the management of dakwah and religious education. Here, economic interests are very easy to detect. As said before, some individuals voluntary engage in dakwah and — in return — get their income from donations by the community. When organizations come to take over dakwah activities, the most obvious consequence for such individuals is that they will lose support and income. Modern management of dakwah means that any reward that formerly went to the *ulama* will go to organizations and that *ulama* have to find another source of income.

The hajj also provides a clear example of the economic interests at stake in the business of religion. By the growing number of pilgrims to Mecca, many individuals — motivated — firstly by religious — reasons and then by economic ones — offer private guidance for which pilgrims have to pay. Organizations do the same thing. The problem or tension arises from the fact that there are always people who claim that such and such congregation should go to such and such individual guide or organization. Usually it is the proximity of a person who wants to go on a pilgrimage to any of the local *ulama* or representatives of the organizations offering guidance which in the final analysis determines the choice.

In determining subject matters of Islamic education, sometimes there are conflicting views. The government usually displays an inclusive attitude and tries to minimize any teachings which call for the unfair treatment of some of its citizens, while some *ulama* — basing their opinions on religious texts — sometimes are not sensitive enough to propagate inclusive opinions. Formally speaking, the government is winning the struggle so far, but there is still room for private institutions of learning — including those that are run by *ulama* — to add subject matters other than those decided by the government, thus leaving space for exclusive teachings.

Relations with the government is yet another field where competition is frequent. It is true that as a rule, the government should always recognize the representative of the mainstream. Otherwise it will lose its popularity. It is also usually the case that Islamic organizations and, especially MUI and its regional branches, are more likely to represent the Islamic community. However, it is not always easy to decide who actually holds authority. In some cases, local political leaders listen more to a single *ulama* — having great charisma — than to MUI. The representativeness of MUI is at times challenged by some Muslims.

WHY SUCH A STRUGGLE

Differences in understanding religion at a practical level may be one cause for the rivalries outlined above, but very often such differences themselves are a pretext for conflict. There is always more than one opinion on almost every religious problem and everybody has the right to chose one of them in accordance with his/her situation and thoughts. However, the very existence of options does not automatically mean that someone has to be in conflict with others who have made a different choice. There must be "something" that causes the rivalry. Among the factors may be economic interest, political relations, jealousy, and the feeling of being excluded.

In many cases, it is usual that Islamic organizations in Indonesia use a wider consideration in making religious decisions, while local *ulama* use more genuine teaching of Islam — meaning the teaching they get from the traditional understanding of the Qur'an. An example is the case of Muna/Mina *jadida* (the place where pilgrims have to spend the night when they stone the *jamarat* during the hajj). In view of the fact that the Muna proper had become too small to accommodate all pilgrims, the Saudi government enlarged the area to include land across the hills that used to be its border, calling it Muna *jadida* or new Muna. Muhammadiyah and NU accepted this enlargement, saying that it is religiously valid for pilgrims to spend the night there. However, many local *ulama* say the opposite.

Sometimes local *ulama* resist decisions by the state or Islamic organizations based on practical reasons by holding to more suggested (*afdal*) practice, as in the case of the first day stoning (*jumrat al-'aqaba*) during the hajj. The majority of past *ulama* suggested that it be carried out between *duha* (some time after sunrise) and noon. The Indonesian Ministry of Religious Affairs, seeing that a great mass of people usually jostle at that time resulting in injuries and even death, suggested that Indonesian pilgrims should perform the ceremony at night; an allowed, but not suggested practice. Some *ulama*, however, prefer to bring their folk to do the stoning at the suggested, but risky moment.

Another example is the use of prohibited food and drinks (*al-muharramat*) for curative purposes. Some *ulama* say that it is not allowed, except in a state of necessity (*darura*), basing on the alleged saying of the prophet: *inna Allah lam yaj'al shifa'akum fi-ma haruma 'alaykum* (Indeed, God does not make your cure in what He prohibits you).[14] For some local *ulama*, such considerations go beyond the guidelines of religion and accordingly they think it is their responsibility to remind the people of — and to protect them from practising — the unwarranted teaching.

CONCLUSION

The struggle for religious authority that takes place between Islamic organizations or institutions and local *ulama* basically comes from the problem of representation of Islamic communities: an organization is not enough, since there is no binding relation from it to the community, while cultural and psychological dependence on or trust in local *ulama* of some segments of the community is still operative. The reliance of the believers on personal guarantees is sometime greater than that on religious institutions, especially in matters where a behavioural example is needed rather than a rigorous argument. Sometimes people see contestable opinions of some leaders of an organization as "proof" that the organization is not sincere enough in representing their religion.

In the Islamic community, political and economic interest will always play a significant role in the struggle for authority between the personal, trust-based leadership of local *ulama* and the rational leadership of Islamic organizations and institutions. The struggle will always be there, although the forms in which it manifests itself and the matters it concerns can change from time to time. This does not mean that modernization fails in rationalizing the way in which people think and act, but there are always segments in society that are more inclined to irrational behaviour and those who take advantage — involuntarily perhaps — of this inclination.

Notes

1. Cf. the study of Hiroko Horikoshi of *ulama* in West Java in the 1970s: *Traditional Leader in a Time of Change: The Kijaji and Ulama in West Java*, translated by Umar Basalim and Andy Muarly Sunrawa as "Kiai dan Perubahan Sosial" (Jakarta: P3M, 1987), pp. 148–49.
2. Similar practices can be found in every Islamic community throughout the world. See, for example, Henri Chambert-Loir and Claude Guillot, eds., *Les Cultes des saints dans le monde musulman* (Paris: École Française d'Extrême-Orient, 1995), especially in two articles of Samuel Landell-Mills, pp. 217–34.
3. Cf. Karel Steenbrink, *Pesantren, Madrasah, Sekolah: Pendidikan Islam dalam Kurun Modern*, translated by the author and Abdurrahman from *Pesantren, Madrasah, Sekolah: Recente ontwikkelingen in Indonesisch islamonderricht* (Jakarta: LP3ES, 1986).
4. In *madrasah*, the curriculum contains more religious subject matters, while in general schools in pesantren it contains more general subject matters.
5. Cf. Horikoshi, *Traditional Leader in a Time of Change*, pp. 169–71.
6. Cf. my "Muhammadiyah and Nahdlatul Ulama in the Reformation Era" Cleveringa Lecture, 4 December 2004 at Universitas Indonesia Depok (Jakarta: KITLV, 2005).
7. See Imam Ghazali Said and A. Ma'ruf Asrori, eds., *Ahkamul Fuqaha, Solusi Problem Aktual Hukum Islam: Keputusan Muktamar, Munas dan Konbes Nahdlatul Ulama (1926–1999 M.)* (Surabaya: LTN NU Jawa Timur and Diantama, 2nd/revised edition, 2005), pp. 624–27.
8. The Qur'an, chapter 4/the Women: 34.
9. This saying of the Prophet Muhammad, reported by al-Bukhari, al-Turmuzi, al-Nasa'i and Ahmad, in relation to the Persians who decided to have a daughter of the late Chosroes the Emperor replace her father on the throne.
10. Cf. M. Atho Mudzhar, *Fatwa-Fatwa Majelis Ulama Indonesia: Sebuah Studi tentang Pemikiran Hukum Islam di Indonesia, 1975–1988* (edisi dwibahasa) (Jakarta: INIS, 1993), pp. 71, 117–23 (Indonesian version) and pp. 61, 101–8 (English version).

11. Find the *fatwa* in Said and Asrori, eds., *Ahkamul Fuqaha, Solusi Problem Aktual Hukum Islam*, pp. 561–64.
12. As described in the Qur'an sura 9/the Redemption: 60, "Alms are for the poor and the needy, and those employed to administer the (funds); for those whose hearts have been (recently) reconciled (to the truth); for those in bondage and in debt; in the cause of Allah; and for the wayfarer: (thus is it) ordained by Allah, and Allah is full of knowledge and wisdom."
13. Such resistance does not fade. Nevertheless, today zakat foundations are everywhere in the country bearing the names of Bazis (Badan Amil Zakat, Infaq dan Sadaqah or Administering Body of Alms) and Lazis (Lembaga Amil Zakat, Infaq dan Sadaqah or Institution for Administering Alms). A bill on how alms are administered was passed by the Indonesian Parliament a couple of years ago.
14. Reported by al-Bukhari as the interpretation of Ibn Mas'ud, a companion of the Prophet Muhammad, on the verse "It is allowed to you to consume good things" (chapter 5/the Table: 4). Cf. the use of this saying as argument against the use of *al-muharramat* (the prohibited kinds of food and drink) for curative purpose, in *Fiqhus Shihhah*, Pondok Pesantren "Al Munawwir", Krapyak Yogyakarta, 2.

7

THE INDONESIAN MADRASAH
Islamic Reform and Modernization of Indonesian Islam in the Twentieth Century

Arief Subhan

The madrasah is one of the important Islamic educational institutions in Indonesia. Emerging in the late nineteenth century, in the early period of its development the madrasah tended to compete with the Dutch education offered by the colonial government and became a symbol of Islamic reform. The madrasah is an Islamic institution of education which teaches both Islamic and secular subjects, uses a grading system, and offers a certificate to its graduates. In the Indonesian context, the madrasah is located between the pesantren and *sekolah* (public school). According to the Ministry of Religious Affairs (*Education Management and Information System* (EMIS, 2003), the number of madrasahs in Indonesia is 37,363. They have 5,698,143 students. This chapter discusses the madrasah and the influence of the educational policy of the Indonesian state on its development. It deals with the negotiating process between people representing madrasah education and the state about the time allocated to secular subjects in the curriculum and draws attention to the emergence of salafi madrasahs and the *Sekolah Islam* (Islamic School) in recent years.

INDONESIAN ISLAMIC REFORM AND MADRASAH

In the late nineteenth century, Indonesian Islam began to create a new centre of learning later called madrasah. The emergence of the Indonesian madrasah cannot be separated from two important events. The first one is the Dutch Government policy to build modern schools, *volkscholen*, which were designed to provide basic education for indigenous Indonesians, in line with the changing colonial policy that began to be concerned with the welfare of the people of the Netherlands Indies, the Ethical Policy. The second concerns the Islamic reform movement that emerged in Indonesia as a result of intensive contacts between Muslims in Indonesia and the Middle East (Van der Mehden 1993; Azra 2004).[1] The growing number of Indonesians who performed the pilgrimage and studied in Mecca and Cairo is one good example to indicate the close relation and interaction between the two regions.[2] Such a connection encourages cultural exchanges between Indonesia and the Middle East. Indonesian students staying in Mecca and Cairo played a vital role in this (see Abaza 1994).

The media have also strongly influenced the introduction of the ideas of Islamic reform in Indonesia. Among the periodicals which contributed to this was *al-Manar*, published in Cairo from 1898–1936. *Al-Manar* served as one of the main references of the Islamic reform movement in the Malay world. It inspired three reformist periodicals in the Malay world: *al-Imam, al-Munir*, and *Azzachierah al-Islamijah* (Expression of Islam).[3]

Through *al-Imam,* Sheikh Tahir Jalaluddin (1869–1956), who had studied in Mecca and Cairo, advocated reforms to the traditional system of education. He encouraged Muslims to teach secular subjects at Islamic schools. In this regard, *al-Imam* was instrumental in establishing a modern madrasah in Singapore, al-Madrasah al-Iqbal Islamiyah (Islamic School al-Iqbal), in 1908. Haji Abdullah Ahmad, the major reformer in Minangkabau, took it as a model to found such a modern Islamic school in Padang, West Sumatra, the Adabiyah School (School of civilization) (Noer 1973, p. 34). Indeed, it could be said that the expansion of modern Islamic education in Indonesia was part and parcel of the Islamic reform movement at the beginning of the twentieth century.

The Minangkabau was the first region in Indonesia where such new centres of learning were established. The Adabiyah School mentioned above is one example. Founded in 1909 by Haji Abdullah Ahmad (1878–1933), it offered secular and religious subjects to its pupils. It was the first school in

Minangkabau that combined religious and secular subjects in its curriculum. Others included the Diniyah School (School of Religion) founded by Zainuddin Labai El-Yunusi (1890–1924) in 1915, and the Diniyah Putri (School of Religion for Women) built by Rahmah El-Yunusi for Islamic female students in 1923. Especially active in the field of education was the Sumatra Thawalib, an organization set up by Haji Abdul Karim Amrullah (1879–1945) and other prominent Muslim leaders to establish modern madrasah. Deliar Noer (1973, p. 41) notes that these schools offered languages, mathematic, history, geography and other secular subjects beside religious ones. They even had music clubs. Lee Kam Hing (1995, p. 10) states that in 1922 there were fifteen religious schools using the word *diniyah* in their name although none had any connection with Zainuddin Labai's institutions.[4] There also emerged many institutions of learning under the banner of the Persatuan Tarbiyah Islamiyah (Perti) (Union of Islamic Education), Jam'iyatul Wasliyah (Mediator Organization) in Medan, Persatuan Ulama Seluruh Aceh (PUSA) (Union of Ulama in Aceh), and other Islamic organizations.[5]

The same development took place in Java. Muslim reformists created modern organizations and used education as a means to reach their goals. One of the leading reformist groups was the Muhammadiyah, founded in November 1912 by Haji Ahmad Dahlan. Muhammadiyah established many madrasahs or Islamic schools in various parts of Indonesia, introduced modern styles of teaching and learning under the concept of *HIS met de Qur'an* (lit. HIS with the Qur'an, Islamic denominational HIS). Seventeen years later, in 1929, the Muhammadiyah, as stated by Deliar Noer (1973, p. 83), had 8 HIS (*Hollands Inlandsche School*, Dutch Native [Elementary] School); 1 teachers' training school; 32 "second class" five-year course elementary schools; 1 *schakelschool* (Dutch language elementary school); and 14 madrasahs.

Many educational Islamic institutions were also founded in Java by socio-religious organizations such as the *Persatuan Islam* (Persis) (Islamic Union), founded in September 1923 in Bandung; *Al-Jam'iyah al-Khairiyah* — known as — *Jamiatul Khair* (Association for the Good) — established in July 1905 by Arab merchants in Jakarta; *Jam'iyah al-Islam al-Irsyad al-Arabia* (Association of Islam and Arabian Guidance), also on the initiative of Arab merchants, and others (Noer 1973, p. 83; Federspiel 2001).

THE EXPANSION OF THE MADRASAH SYSTEM

At the end of the nineteenth century, the strong wave of transformation in Islamic education eventually touched on the pesantrens, the traditional institutions of Islamic learning, which has been the target of criticism by reformist Muslims. While they continued to maintain traditional aspects of the educational system, a number of pesantrens in Java began to modernize management and curricula, and finally adopted the madrasah system. Based on the increasing number of madrasahs and the emerging perception among Muslims that the madrasah was a symbol for modernizing Islamic education, many pesantrens began to adopt the madrasah system to enrich their learning system, although it does not necessarily mean that the *ulama* of the pesantrens agreed with the ideas of Islamic reformists, which were behind the emergence of madrasah education. Consequently, at the end of the nineteenth century, many pesantrens took on certain features of the madrasah system, such as the use of graded classes and planned curricula (Dhofier 1994, p. 38).[6]

In discussing pesantren reform, the Pondok Modern in Gontor, East Java, has to be mentioned. Established in 1926, the Pondok Modern became a new type of Islamic school in Indonesia known as modern and independent pesantren. Modern meant that such pesantrens not only adopted a madrasah system, but also offered their pupils classes in English and Arabic. They also used new texts of Islamic studies such as Muhammad Abduh book's on theology. Independent meant that the pesantrens had no relation with the differences in ideological orientation as reflected in the disputes between Nahdlatul Ulama (NU) and Muhammadiyah. The Pondok Modern became the prototype of this new pesantren model in Indonesia. Many Pondok Gontor graduates founded similar pesantrens in their own region such as the Pondok Modern Pabelan in Magelang, Central Java, Pondok Modern Gintung in Tangerang, West Java, and Pondok Modern Darunnajah in Jakarta. The "pondok alumni" then became an effective network for the development and spread of the Pondok Gontor system.

The objective of Pondok Modern, as stated by Lance Castle (1966, pp. 30–45), was above all to provide cadres for the Muslim community by combining the virtues of the old pesantren system with those of modern education. To reach this objective, the Pondok Modern introduced secular subjects, encouraged students to study foreign languages, and organized sport and music events and other extra-curricula activities. The Pondok Gontor differed from common pesantren in the sense that its education was more systematic and disciplined, and that it devoted considerable time to secular subjects. Students were forbidden to use Indonesian in daily conversation in the pesantren. They had to speak English or Arabic.

SECULARIZING THE MADRASAHS?

After 1945, the madrasahs came under the direction of the Ministry of Religious Affairs. Almost immediately problems arose when the Ministry decided to modernize the madrasahs in line with public schools. One of the measures the Ministry took concerned the proportion of secular subjects in the madrasah curriculum. Officials of the Ministry, especially those of the Japenda (Jawatan Pendidikan Agama, the Directorate of Religious Education) such as Drs Sigit and Arifin Temyang — two key figures in formulating the madrasah "blue print" in 1950 — insisted on having more secular subjects taught.

In 1950, in order to accelerate the modernization of madrasahs, Japenda transformed a number of private madrasahs into Madrasah Negeri (Public Madrasah). These became the model for other madrasahs, especially for the standardization of the proportion and quality of secular subjects. The Japenda also opened Pendidikan Guru Agama (Schools for Religious Teachers) in many places to train teachers of secular subjects in madrasahs.[7]

To enforce this policy, the Ministry linked the subsidy granted to the madrasahs with the proportion of secular subjects taught. The Ministry also encouraged pesantrens to adopt the madrasah system. The reason for this was to provide pesantren graduates with the opportunity to enter universities. This policy was supported by many Islamic organizations. In a meeting held by the Ministry in Jakarta on 12 and 13 February 1958, representatives from the Muhammadiyah, NU and other Muslim organizations expressed their support for the Ministry's decision to strengthen'the teaching of secular subjects at *madrasahs*. In addition, the authority to formulate the subjects and allocate time for religious subjects was in the hands of the madrasah leaders or leaders of Islamic organizations (Almanak 1959, p. 185).

The next question that came up was to decide how much time should be devoted to secular subjects in the madrasah curriculum. The Ministry suggested 70 per cent. Some Muslim organizations proposed 50 per cent. Still others wanted 30 per cent to be reserved for secular subjects and 70 per cent for religious subjects. In 1962, based upon the many opinions that emerged during the debate the Ministry stipulated that 68 per cent of the madrasah curriculum should be filled with secular subjects and 32 per cent with religious ones.[8] This was not the end to the issue. Private madrasahs in particular did not comply. New negotiations about the proportion of secular subjects in the curriculum had to be conducted.

In the New Order, a drastic change took place following the issuing in 1975 of the Joint Decision of Three Ministers; that is those of Religious Affairs, Education and Culture, and the Interior.[9] The decision stipulated that graduates from madrasahs would have the same status as those from public schools of the same level. It meant that madrasah graduates would encounter no obstacles in entering public schools. The same applied to the graduates of public schools if they wanted to study at a madrasah. The Joint Decision also stipulated that madrasah had to reserve 70 per cent of their curriculum for secular subjects and 30 per cent for religious ones. Many Muslims could not agree. They feared that the conditions set would transform the madrasah into a secular institution, moving far away from its main mission as an Islamic educational institution (Munhanif 1998, p. 315). Although the Joint Decision was controversial, in the end, almost all madrasahs complied with its stipulation. The Ministers' directive even came to be seen as an important step towards the modernization of the madrasah.

In 1989, the Indonesian government released Law No. 2 of 1989 on the National Education System. It transformed the madrasah into a public school with an Islamic identity. When the law was revised and refined by Law No. 20 of 2003 on the National Education System, the madrasahs became almost identical to public schools as they offered the same proportion of secular subjects. Some Indonesian Muslims indeed concluded that the madrasah system of education no longer differed from the secular system.

To preserve the traditional function of the madrasah as an institution to produce religious leaders (*ulama*), the Ministry of Religious Affairs then established a pilot project called Madrasah Aliyah Program Khusus (MAPK) (Senior High School for Special Programmes) in which religious subjects took up 70 per cent of the curriculum and secular subjects 30 per cent. The MAPK graduates were mainly prepared for entering the State Institute of Islamic Studies (Institut Agama Islam Negeri, IAIN) where they could study Islam at university level. They were expected to became *ulama-intellectual*, a new term for Islamic leaders introduced by Munawir Sjadzali, the then Minister of Religious Affairs. In 1988 the MAPK project started. Schools were established in several cities in Indonesia such as Padang Panjang, Ciamis, Yogyakarta, Ujung Pandang, Jember, Banda Aceh, Lampung, Solo, Banjarmasin, and Mataram (Effendy inter alia 1998). The MAPK then became Madrasah Aliyah Keagamaan (MAK). There is no substantial differentiation between MAPK and MAK.

Although, "state madrasahs" had become almost similar to public schools, there are two kinds of madrasah which continued to play the traditional role as centres for turning out Islamic leaders. One has already been mentioned, the MAK. The other is the "private madrasah". The private madrasahs, especially those which are located in pesantren, still devote more time to the teaching of Islamic subjects. They usually supplement the national curriculum as stipulated by the government with Islamic subjects and use textbooks from the classical era, the famous *kitab kuning* (yellow books).

In 2001–02 there were 37,363 madrasahs with 5,698,143 students in Indonesia. Less than 20 per cent of these madrasahs fell under the direct supervision of the Ministry of Religious Affairs. More than 80 per cent are private madrasah run by Muslim individuals and organizations. Most are financially weak and located in rural areas.[10] The conditions of these madrasahs are generally bad with respect to the quality of education and facilities. Relying on the students' parents is not an option. About 36 per cent of these parents do not have a stable income and only 11 per cent of them earn more than Rp 500,000 (about US$60) per month.[11]

MAPPING THE INDONESIAN MADRASAH

The madrasahs provide a modern way of education in which Indonesian Muslims are taught both traditional Islamic and secular subjects. Nevertheless, they do not present a uniform picture. Indonesian madrasahs vary. They range from madrasahs belonging to modernist groups to the madrasahs managed by members of the traditionalist groups; and from "secular madrasahs" which offer more secular than religious subjects in their curriculum to the "salafi madrasahs" where the opposite is the case. Than there is also the *Sekolah Islam*, a type of school whose history can be traced back to the *HIS met de Qur'an* of the Muhammadiyah.

This means that madrasahs differ greatly in objectives, textbooks used, and teaching-learning systems. The objectives of the madrasah managed by people from modernist groups mirror the aims of the reform movement. Through madrasahs, its members want to imbue the younger Muslim generation with the spirit of Islamic reform. They urge them to purify Islamic practices from all accretions (*bida'*) and return to pristine Islam based on the Qur'an and Sunnah; liberate Islam of the blind acceptance of the dogmas of former scholars (*taqlid*); and reopen the doors of independent reasoning (*ijtihad*) to enable Islam to respond to the demands of modern life. The madrasahs which belong to traditionalist groups stress traditional values. They function as guardians of the legal doctrines which were formulated by four Muslim scholars, the founding fathers of the schools of Islamic law (*imam madzhab*). The textbooks they use are from the classical era, the *kitab kuning*.

It is important to note that the efforts made to develop and modernize pesantrens and madrasahs both by Islamic individuals and organizations and by the government have significantly changed the image of Islamic educational institutions. This gained momentum when a new religious consciousness took hold in the 1990s among the new and younger generation in Jakarta,

Bandung, Yogyakarta, Surabaya and other large cities, a phenomenon often referred to as *santrinisasi* (santrinization or becoming more pious) or *Islamisasi* (Islamization). Many of those attracted by this upsurge of religiosity came from middle class families. They had graduated from prominent Indonesian and foreign universities, were at ease with the advancement of science and technology, but felt that they lacked profound religious education. Some state that this new urban identity and consciousness is the result of the improvement in education, steady economic growth and a worldwide increase in Islamic awareness. The latter is said to be stimulated by the activities of international organizations, personal contacts, and information obtained via television, radio broadcasting and the Internet and, especially, by easy access to a huge amount of religious information in books, journals and magazines. This, in turn, has led to greater *ghirah* (courage) to develop and advance the Muslim community vis-à-vis the other communities in Indonesia.

In view of the educational background, it is understandable that these people pay great attention to the quality of the Islamic school they select for their children. They insist on advanced education for their children, if possible in the field of science and technology, and also expect them to become familiar with religious traditions and practices.

It is these middle class people who are the main actors or at least staunch supporters of the development of a new trend in Islamic educational institutions. They initiated and financed the development of the *Sekolah Islam*, a new genre of Islamic education that differs from the pesantren and madrasah. Indeed, this new institution is a "secular" or general school in terms of its system and curriculum. It follows the system and curriculum of public schools administred by the Ministry of Education. Some of these schools are explicitly called "Sekolah Islam" while others are called "*sekolah model*" (model schools).

What makes a *Sekolah Islam* substantially different from a pesantren or madrasah is the practical emphasis on religious education. Pesantrens and madrasahs are well known for the specific knowledge taught there such as Islamic history (*tarikh*), Islamic jurisprudence and law (*fiqh*), theology and any other subjects on Islamic texts, in conjunction with general knowledge like mathemathics, economy and the natural and social sciences. Rather than emphasizing Islamic knowledge in subjects taught regularly in classes, the *Sekolah Islam* provide a more practical emphasis on Islamic values in daily life. It does not consider religion to be a core subject of the curriculum as a pesantren or *madrasah* does, nor does it see them just as supplementary subjects as is the case at a public school. The *Sekolah Islam* aim to build the Islamic character of the student based on religious ethics and values. In other words, religion is not considered a part of the cognitive aspect of detailed subjects in the curriculum, but rather has to manifest itself in the daily life of the students. Accordingly Islam should be transformed into values and ethics to which the students become accustomed. Consequently, detailed subjects of Islamic sciences commonly taught in pesantrens and madrasahs are hardly taught in a *Sekolah Islam*.

A *Sekolah Islam* is relatively expensive in terms of entrance fee and monthly cost. They are well equipped with facilities such as air-conditioned classrooms, libraries, laboratories and sport arenas as well as other teaching and education facilities such as computers and Internet connections. They also have well organized extra curriculum activities. And as a modern institution, a *Sekolah Islam* is run by professionals in terms of management and curriculum development. Teachers, managers and administrative staff are recruited by highly competitive selection and most of them have advanced degrees. The requirements for a student to be admitted are also high. Only those who gain a high score in an entrance examination and pass an interview are accepted. As the *Sekolah Islam* is geared to the interests of the middle class, in many cases, this type of private school, is of higher quality that the public schools and madrasahs which are administered by the Ministry of Education and the Ministry of Religious Affairs.

An outstanding example of a *Sekolah Islam* is the SMU (Sekolah Menengah Umum, Senior High School) Insan Cendekia (Man of Learning) located in Serpong in Banten. This school was founded on the initiative of a number of prominent scientists, most of whom were employed at the BPPT (*Badan Pengkajian dan Penerapan Teknologi*, The Agency for the Assessment and Application of Technology) of the *Kementerian Riset dan Teknologi* (Ministry of Research and Technology).[12] The SMU Insan Cendekia aim to produce Muslim students, and after they have graduated, scientists who are also proficient in Islamic knowledge. It puts a strong emphasis on science and technology. To further the career of its students the SMU Insan Cendekia maintains links with the ITB (Bandung Institute of Technology) and IPB (Bogor Agriculture Institute). It also awards scholarship to graduates to study science and technology abroad, especially in Germany. The SMU Insan Cendekia adopts a boarding school system in which the achievements of each student are closely monitored. Their daily interaction is supervised twenty-four hours a day. The admission requirements of SMU Insan Cendekia are high. It only accepts candidates who have graduated from Madrasah Tsanawiyah (junior high school) with A-grades in all subjects. Graduates from the SMP (junior high school) under the supervision of the Ministry of Education cannot enter the school. This means that the school is especially intended to attract the madrasah graduate in subjects of science and technology. In addition, the candidates should also pass an entrance examination, an interview and other tests.[13]

Another important institution that has emerged especially after the fall of Soeharto in May 1998 is the Salafi madrasah. The Salafi madrasahs are Islamic teaching centres which cater specifically for those who explicitly identify themselves as salafis, literally meaning the followers of the pious forefathers, *Salaf al-Salih*. These people believe that to follow the *Salafi al-Salih* means to submit to the absolute truth as underlined in the Qur'an and Sunnah, and this submission will define whether one can be called Muslim or not. These "salafi" worldviews have been partly responsible for the raise of fundamentalism in Indonesia (Hasan 2004).[14]

One of the basic characteristics of fundamentalism is the belief in the finality of Islam. Islam is understood as a static religion that should be followed literally. There is no variety in Islam. Islam is one and the same forever. This is an example of fundamentalist attitude. Ulil Abshar Abdallah, a young Indonesian intellectual Muslim, chose the term "fossilized Islam" to describe this way of thinking (as a result he was issued with the death sentence from a number of religious leaders). The "*Islam warna warni*" (colourful Islam) advertisement from JIL (Jaringan Islam Liberal, Liberal Islamic Network), to which Ulil Abshar Abdallah belongs, was stopped on one TV station because of protests by a number of Muslims. The TV station did not want to take any risk.

According to salafi-fundamentalists, education is mainly oriented towards maintaining the established order, values and traditions. The idea that education is a vehicle for change is not appreciated. The belief in the finality of Islam implies that they view Islam as self-sufficient and consider learning from other cultures, traditions, religions and civilizations irrelevant. There is no urgency to incorporate social and natural sciences, which are considered to be "outside of Islam". Developing school networks, through which different ideas and communities are connected and mutual enrichment can take place is not a priority. The idea that participation is based on hierarchy (especially in terms of religious knowledge) and the uncritical acceptance of religious authorities are a barrier to the salafi participation in other types of education.

Salafi-pesantrens emerged in many cities in Indonesia. Among them are the Pesantren Ihya al-Sunnah (the Revival of the Sunnah), and the Pesantren al-Turast al-Islami (Islamic Heritage) founded in Yogyakarta in 1994 and 1995 respectively. Between 1995 and 2000 many more salafi-pesantrens were founded such as the Pesantren al-Madinah (Prophet City) and the Pesantren Imam Bukhari in Solo, the Pesantren al-Ittiba' al-Sunnah (Follower of the

Sunnah) in Sukoharjo, the Pesantren Lu'lu wal Marjan (precious stone mentioned in the Qur'an) in Semarang, and the Pesantren al-Sunnah in Cirebon and Makassar (Hasan 2004). Almost all are small pesantren with around 100 pupils.

This overview shows that Indonesian madrasahs are diverse in nature. The variety of madrasahs indicates that every institution of education has a special raison d'être and ideology. Some madrasahs emphasize secular subjects along the lines of public schools, others maintain their traditional role of producing *ulama*. This is an indication of the fact that Indonesian madrasahs remain a medium in the reproduction of religious authority in Indonesia. This function is confirmed by a survey conducted by the Center for the Study of Islam and Society (PPIM) State Islamic University Syarif Hidayatullah Jakarta on Islam and good governance (2006). The survey found that 60 per cent of Muslims in Indonesia expected that religious leaders should come from madrasah and pesantren in term of the background of their education.

Notes

1. Fred R. von der Mehden, *Two Worlds of Islam, Interaction between Southeast Asia and the Middle East* (Gainesville: University Press of Florida, 1993). Azyumardi Azra's book, *The Origins of Islamic Reformism in Southeast Asia, Networks of Malay-Indonesian and Middle Eastern 'ulama in Seventeenth and Eighteenth Centuries* (Leiden: KITLV Press, 2004), extensively described the connection and network between *ulama* in both countries focusing on the emergence of the Islamic reform in the Malay-Indonesian world.
2. From about 1890, the number of Indonesians who were going to Mecca for the pilgrimage (*haji*) was about 10,000 each year, in the years 1910 to 1930 this had grown to more than 20,000 each year. Bernhard Dahm, *History of Indonesia in Twentieth Century* (London: Pall Mall Press, 1971), pp. 10–11 and 40.
3. *Azzachierah al-Islamiyah* was published in Arabic and Malay in Jakarta in 1923 under the editorship of Ahmad Soorkattie, a Sudanese who come to Jakarta in 1911 inspector of the *al-Jami'ah al-Khairiyah* school. Then he was known as one of al-Irsyaâd founders, one of the important organizations to promote Islamic reform. *Al-Munir* was founded by Haji Abdullah Ahmad and published in Padang from 1911 to 1916. This periodical translated and published several articles in Malay from *al-Manar*. *Al-Imam* was published from 1906 till 1908 by a group of reformist Muslims in Singapore. This periodical tended to spread the ideas of Islamic reform to the Malay Archipelago. Jutta Blum-Warn, 'Al-Manar and Soorkati, "Links in the Chain of Transmission of Muhammad 'Abduh Ideas to the Malay-Speaking World" in Peter Riddel and Tony Street eds., *Islam: Essays on the Scripture, Thought, and Society, a Festschrift in Honour of Anthony H. Johns* (Leiden: Brill, 1997), h. 297.

4. For example, Mahmud Yunus (1888–1982) built the Diniyah School in Batusangkar to replace a madrasah built by Muhammad Thaib Umar which closed in 1913.
5. Karel Steenbrink, *Pesantren, Madrasah, Sekolah, Pendidikan Islam dalam Kurun Modern* (Jakarta: LP3ES, 1996), pp. 62–83. For PUSA see Lee Kam Hing, *Education and Politics in Indonesia 1945–1965*, pp. 98–104.
6. Dhofier also notes that in 1910 some pesantren in Jombang began to enrol female students.
7. Actually Pendidikan Guru Agama (PGA) had two objectives. The first objective was to produce teachers for religious subjects in public schools, the second was to train teachers of secular subjects in Islamic schools (madrasahs).
8. SK Menteri Agama No. 104/1962.
9. Known as SKB (Surat Keputusan Bersama) Tiga Menteri No. 6, 1975 and No. 037/U/1975.
10. Indonesia has many small Islamic foundations beside the big organizations such as Nahdlatul Ulama and Muhammadiyah. There is no adequate information about the number of under-qualified madrasahs and to which organizations these madrasahs are atttached.
11. The source of the data is *Education and Management System* (EMIS) of the Ministry of Religious Affairs, 2003.
12. This state-sponsored council is strongly connected with Professor B.J. Habibie, a former President of Indonesia, who graduated from a German university and the former prolific chairman of ICMI (*Ikatan Cendekiawan Muslim se-Indonesia*/ Indonesia Muslim Scholars Association).
13. Profile Insan Cendekia, VCD, 2005.
14. For detailed information see Noorhaidi Hasan, *Laskar Jihad: Islam, Militancy and The Quest for Identity in Post-New Order Indonesia* (Ithaca NY: Cornell Modern Indonesia Project, 2006).

References

Abaza, Mona. *Indonesian Students in Cairo: Islamic Education Perceptions and Exchanges*. Paris: Cahier d'Archipel 23, 1994.

Azra, Azyumardi dan Saiful Umam, eds. *Menteri-Menteri Agama RI: Biografi Sosial-Politik*. Jakarta: PPIM, Litbang Depag, INIS, 1998.

Azra, Azyumardi. *The Origins of Islamic Reformism in Southeast Asia: Networks of Malay-Indonesian and Middle Eastern 'Ulama in the Seventeenth and Eighteenth Centuries*. Leiden: KITLV Press, 2004.

Blum-Warn, Jutta. "Al-Manar and Soorkati, Links in the Chain of Transmission of Muhammad 'Abduh Ideas to the Malay-Speaking World". In *Islam: Essays on the Scripture, Thought, and Society, a Festschrift in Honour of Anthony H. Johns*, edited by Peter Riddel and Tony Street. Leiden: Brill, 1997.

Castle, Lance. "Notes on the Islamic School at Gontor," *Indonesia*, no. 1 (1966): 30-45.

Dahm, Bernhard. *History of Indonesia in the Twentieth Century*. London: Pall Mall Press, 1971.

Departemen Agama RI. *Almanak Djawatan Pendidikan Agama*. Djakarta: Departemen Agama RI, 1959.

Dhofier, Zamakhsyari. *Tradisi Pesantren, Studi tentang Pandangan Hidup Kyai*. Jakarta: LP3ES, 1994.

Effendy, Bahtiar, Hendro Prasetyo, and Arief Subhan. "Munawir Sjadzali, MA: Pencairan Ketegangan Ideologis". In *Menteri-Menteri Agama RI: Biografi Sosial-Politik*, edited by Azyumardi Azra dan Saiful Umam. Jakarta: PPIM, Litbang Depag, INIS, 1998, pp. 369–412.

Federspiel, Howard. *Islam and Ideology in the Emerging Indonesian State: The Persatuan Islam (PERSIS) 1923 to 1957*. Leiden: Brill, 2001.

Hasan, Noorhaidi. "The Salafi Madrasa in Indonesia: History, Profile, and Network". Paper presented at the International Workshop, "The Asian Madrasa: Transnational Lingkages and Real or Alleged Political Roles", organized by ISIM (Leiden) in co-operation with ZMO (Berlin), Leiden, 22–24 May 2004.

Hasan, Noorhaidi. *Laskar Jihad: Islam, Militancy and the Quest for Identity in Post-New Order Indonesia*. Ithaca, New York: Southeast Asia Program, Cornell University, 2006.

Lee Kam Hing. *Education and Politics in Indonesia 1945–1965*. Kuala Lumpur: University of Malaya Press, 1995.

Mehden, Fred R. von der. *Two Worlds of Islam, Interaction between Southeast Asia and the Middle East*. Gainesville: University Press of Florida, 1993.

Ministry of Religious Affairs. *Education Management and Information System (EMIS)*. Jakarta: Ministry of Religious Affairs, 2003.

Munhanif, Ali. "Prof. Dr. A. Mukti Ali: Modernisasi Politik-Keagamaan Orde Baru". In *Menteri-Menteri Agama RI: Biografi Sosial-Politik*, edited by Azyumardi Azra dan Saiful Umam. Jakarta: PPIM, Litbang Depag, INIS, 1998, pp. 271–319.

Noer, Deliar. *The Modernist Muslim Movement in Indonesia 1900–1942*. Singapore: Oxford University Press, 1973.

Steenbrink, Karel. *Pesantren, Madrasah, Sekolah, Pendidikan Islam dalam Kurun Modern*. Jakarta: LP3ES, 1996.

PPIM, UIN Syarif Hidayatullah. Survey on "Islam and Good Governance". Jakarta: PPIM (Center for the Study of Islam and Society) UIN Syarif Hidayatullah, 2006.

Yunus, Mahmud. *Sejarah Pendidikan Islam di Indonesia*. Jakarta: Mutiara Sumber Widya, 1995.

8

FROM APOLITICAL QUIETISM TO JIHADIST ACTIVISM

"Salafis", Political Mobilization, and Drama of Jihad in Indonesia

Noorhaidi Hasan

Jihad is often perceived as an expression of religious fanaticism and is mostly associated with the outrageous acts of irrational, insane individuals inspired by their firm belief in radical religious doctrines. Although there is some plausibility in this perception, it fails to uncover the deeper meaning of jihad. Jihad is also a language of protest that can be used by marginalized individuals to construct their identity and thereby their position in the public sphere. For them, jihad is a message conveyed to display attempts to transform and empower their marginalization and break out of their own sense of frustration.

The rise of Laskar Jihad, which from April 2000 until its disbanding in October 2002 mobilized more than 7,000 members to fight jihad against Christians in the Moluccas and other Indonesian trouble spots, perfectly represents an attempt made by a group of people to negotiate their identity through the call for jihad and the particular kind of violence it enacted. This organization was a paramilitary division of the Forum Komunikasi Ahl al-Sunnah wal-Jama'ah (Communication Forum of the Followers of the Sunna and the Community of the Prophet) established by those who identify themselves as "Salafis", followers of the pious ancestors (*Salaf al-Salih*), active under the banner of the salafi dakwah movement.

THE SALAFI DAKWAH MOVEMENT

The salafi dakwah movement began to exert its influence throughout Indonesia in the mid-1980s, by developing a stance of apolitical quietism. Unlike other Islamic organizations, both home-grown and transnational, which had proliferated earlier, this movement was squarely within the puritanical classic Salafi-Wahhabi tradition. Its main concern covered matters of creed and morality, such as strict monotheism, anti-sufism, divine attributes, purifying Islam from accretions, and developing the moral integrity of the individual.[1] True to their advocacy of the espousal of the return to the doctrine of the *Salaf al-Salih*, members avoided discussing politics, or, more precisely, engaging questions of political power. They considered the *dakwah hizbiyya*, meaning Islamic movements that are perceived to value political engagement over the purification of the individual Muslim's religious beliefs and practices, a form of bida (heretical innovation), thus an anathema to Islam. From their point of view, the main error committed by the groups promoting the *dakwah hizbiyya* stems from their loyalty to the followers of bida. This mistake is believed to have caused division among Muslims because it teaches fanaticism to each separate group, prompting members to renounce any truths that might belong to the others.[2]

The salafi movement can be called a form of reconstituted Wahhabism, an official school of Saudi Arabia. This is indicated by the determination of its proponents to codify and follow more systematically the thoughts formulated by both the classic Wahhabi inspirators, including Ahmad bin Hanbal (780–855), Ahmad ibn Taymiyya (1263–1328), and Muhammad ibn Qayyim al-Jawziyya (1292–1350), and contemporary Wahhabi authorities, such as 'Abd al-'Aziz 'Abd Allah bin Baz (1912–99) and Muhammad Nasir al-Din al-Albani (d.1999). In fact, it was part of the transnational salafi society, representing the most puritanical Saudi style of Islam. It is apparent that the term Salafi has preferably been used as the banner of the movement because of the pejorative connotation of the term Wahhabi among many Muslims in the world, thus crucial for political convenience.

The efflorescence of the salafi movement cannot be isolated from Saudi Arabia's immensely ambitious global campaign for the Wahhabization of the Muslim *ummah* (community). This campaign aimed to reinforce the Kingdom's position as the centre of the Muslim world, bolstered by its permanent status as the *Khadim al-Haramayn*, the Guardians of the Two Holy Sanctuaries.

Thanks to skyrocketing world oil prices, which provided considerable economic benefits during the 1970s, the Kingdom sponsored a variety of dakwah activities throughout the Muslim world, working with local agents. In Indonesia, for instance, it collaborated with the *Dewan Dakwah Islamiyah Indonesia* (Indonesian Council for Islamic Propagation, DDII), a dakwah organization set up by Muhammad Natsir (1908–93) and other former Masyumi leaders in 1967. From its inception, DDII became the Indonesian representative of the Rabitat al-'Alam al-Islami, acting as the main organization to spearhead the Kingdom's campaign.[3] In this way Wahhabism was exported and disseminated. This campaign was later intensified, particularly in the aftermath of the Iranian Revolution and the takeover of al-Haram al-Sharif in Mecca by a Juhayman al-Utaybi-led group in 1979.[4]

Signs of the expansion of the salafi movement were first and foremost strikingly seen in the appearance of young men wearing long, flowing robes (*jalabiyya*), turban (*imama*), trousers right to their ankles (*isbal*) and long beards (*lihya*), and women wearing a form of enveloping black veil (*niqab*) in public places. Initially its presence was most significantly felt in the area around university campuses where it formed an exclusivist current of Islamic activism. Under the changing political circumstances during the first half of the 1990s, the movement spread beyond campuses. Members openly organized meetings, called *halqas* and *dauras*,[5] in mosques located on city outskirts and rural villages. As a result, enclaves of members sprung up, followed by the construction of mosques and Islamic schools under the banner of the movement.

Through religious activities organized systematically and openly, a sense of solidarity and group identity was born that fostered a growing network. The publication of pamphlets, bulletins, journals, and books provided communication channels through which salafi messages were disseminated to a broader audience. The multiplication of salafi activism led seamlessly to the emergence of foundations with names like al-Sunna, Ihya al-Sunna, al-Turath al-Islami, al-Sofwa, Lajnat al-Khairiyya, and Wahda Islamiyya. These foundations received considerable financial support from Saudi Arabia, Kuwait and other Gulf countries through, among other foundations, the Mu'assasat al-Haramayn al-Khayriyya (Haramayn Charitable Foundation), known as al-Haramayn, and the Jam'iyyat Ihya' al-Turath al-Islami (Reviving of Islamic Heritage Society).[6]

The attraction of the salafi movement is rooted in its ability to provide a domain in which a resistance identity is created through discourses, symbols, and everyday practices. Within this context, members are required to organize themselves into small tight-knit communities that stand distinctly apart from the "anything goes" open society around them. To some extent it can be identified as a sect, demanding complete loyalty, unwavering belief, and rigid adherence to a distinctive lifestyle.[7] Such an organization acts as a kind of refuge for believers who have undergone an internal *hijra* (migration) to shelter themselves from the stains and temptations of the outside world.

The fast currents of modernization and globalization, which provided the opportunities for young people from rural villages to migrate to big cities in order to pursue higher education or seek jobs, contributed to the growth of the movement. Ironically, the social mobility of these youths has been mired in the failure of the New Order regime to fulfill its development promises, particularly to make good on its promise to distribute public goods and resources for all. This deficiency has been aggravated by rampant corruption and a lack of public accountability. The upshot is that many of the young rural migrants have become discontented and frustrated, and more importantly, experienced a sort of relativization of identity.

In the modern, global society, the relativization of identity can undermine the more conventional anchors of social life that provide a measure of stability, and this makes the quest for individual identity a central pursuit of modern life. As a source of meaning for social actors, identity organizes meaning by determining how the purpose of certain actions is symbolically identified. Alberto Melucci refers to the "homelessness of personal identity" when describing the sort of alienation people experience when identities are relativized, and he proposes that this condition requires individuals to reestablish their identity and thus their "home" continually.[8] In a similar analysis, Manuel Castells suggests that the need to reconstruct an identity shaken by the swift current of social change encourages global, modern people to return to a primary identity established by working on "traditional materials in the formation of a new godly, communal world, where deprived masses and disaffected intellectuals may reconstruct meaning in a global alternative to the exclusionary global order."[9]

Small tight-knit exclusive communities developed by the salafi movement serve as a kind of enclave facilitating an attempt of the deprived youths to return to the primary identity. It is a closed system, which distinguishes itself by an exclusive pattern of dress, interactions, and relationships, whereby members usually construct a "wall of virtue" based on moral values. This wall separates the saved, free, and morally superior enclave from the hitherto tempting central community.[10] The emphasis on a distinctive lifestyle in the enclave culture is clearly associated with the problem of identity. By joining a particular, exclusive movement, members' pride in being different is emphasized and a sense of certainty reached. Simultaneously, they achieve control over the social space by shrinking the world to the size of their community.[11]

Ironically, however, the rapid expansion of the salafi movement was coupled with an eruption of tension among its protagonists, particularly following the outbreak of the Gulf War in 1990. This tension developed as competition intensified among those who had just returned from salafi teaching centres in the Middle East for prized positions as the movement's legitimate representatives. As a result, fragmentation and conflict became inevitable. The movement split into two currents: the so-called Sururis and non-Sururis. This split was triggered by the spread of the *Sururiyya* issue associating some salafi leaders, including Abu Nida, Ahmad Faiz Asifuddin, Yusuf Usman Baisa, Muhammad Yusuf Harun, Ahmad Zawawi and Abdul Hakim Abdat, with Muhammad Surur bin Nayef Zayn al-'Abidin.[12] A critic of Saudi Arabia's decision to invite American troops following the Gulf crisis in 1990, Muhammad Surur was condemned by prominent salafi authorities linked to Bin Baz as a proponent of the *takfir* doctrine developed by Sayyid Qutb (1906–66), the main ideologue of the Muslim Brotherhood, and was consequently expelled from the Kingdom. This doctrine considers that a regime is necessarily apostate if it does not follow the *sharia* and that violence can be used to topple such a regime and replace it with a true Islamic state.

The central figure who defined the dynamics of the salafi movement in Indonesia was Ja'far Umar Thalib, the founder of Laskar Jihad. He joined the movement when it had already solidified its existence on university campuses. Alongside the opportunities he had gained to deliver religious lectures and sermons among university students, his central role soon became apparent. He has been known among the salafis as a preacher who dared to stridently criticize all other Islamic movements and demonstrate mistakes committed by them. This reputation made him the movement's centre of attention and leading authority.

Born into a Hadrami (Arab) family in Malang, East Java, and raised in the puritanical atmosphere of al-Irsyad, an Indonesian reformist, modernist Muslim organization predominant among the Hadramis,[13] Ja'far Umar Thalib emerged as a typical cadre of Islamism, an ambitious youth with a rebellious streak. He was a student at the Pesantren of Persis, another reformist, modernist Muslim organization, in Bangil, East Java,[14] where he sharpened his insights into Islamic reformism. Next, he moved to Jakarta to study at the Lembaga Ilmu Pengetahuan Islam dan Bahasa Arab (the Institute for the Study of Islam and Arabic, LIPIA), a Jakarta-based institute of high-learning established and directly sponsored by Saudi Arabia.[15] In this institute, Ja'far Umar Thalib studied Arabic and explored the militant views of Qutb. His uncompromising attitude showed in his outspoken repudiation of the *Asas Tunggal* (Sole-Foundation) policy enforced by the New Order regime requiring all mass and political organizations to base their existence on the Pancasila, the ideology of the state, for which he suffered stern investigations by military intelligence agents. After a falling out with a member of the teaching staff, he dropped out of LIPIA. In spite of this, the then LIPIA director, 'Abd al-'Aziz 'Abd Allah al-'Amr, paved the way for him to study abroad at the Mawdudi Islamic Institute in Lahore, Pakistan, in 1987.

The militancy of Ja'far Umar Thalib grew to maturity in Pakistan, which was directly engaged in mobilizing Muslim youths around the world to fight shoulder to shoulder with Afghan mujahideen to defeat the Red Army of the then Soviet Union. Pakistan was among several countries, including Saudi Arabia, that formed an axis created by the United States to halt communist influence in Central Asia. In Pakistan, Ja'far Umar Thalib began his jihad adventure by first joining the al-Khairiyah Base Camp in Peshawar. He was said to have supported the factions of both Abu Sayyaf and Gulbuddin Hikmatyar in the Afghan mujahideen. However, the puritanical insights cultivated previously at al-Irsyad, Persis and LIPIA eventually led him to join the Jama'at al-Qur'an wa Ahl al-Hadith, a Saudi-supported faction led by Jamil al-Rahman, a fanatical supporter of Wahhabism.[16] Within this faction, Ja'far Umar Thalib shared experiences with thousands of jihad volunteers from all over the Muslim world and established contacts with the transnational salafi dakwah movement.

The involvement of Ja'far Umar Thalib in salafi activism ousted the leadership of Abu Nida, the first proponent of the salafi movement in Indonesia. He became the most important figure in the informal social network interlocking a dozen salafi teaching centres scattered throughout various regions in the country. This achievement was partly determined by his success in establishing a special linkage with Muqbil ibn Hadi al-Wadi'i, a salafi ideologue par excellence in Yemen,[17] and other prominent salafi authorities in the Middle East. Its non-hierarchical and open character notwithstanding, this network played an important role in the spread of the salafi movement and in the fame of Ja'far Umar Thalib himself. Lessons, study circles, informal meetings and a myriad of other dakwah activities were firmly established in the network, serving as a vehicle for the production, articulation and dissemination of salafi messages. Its centre was the Pesantren Ihya al-Sunna led by Ja'far Umar Thalib, which published the periodical *Salafy* as its mouthpiece. Despite its remarkable influence, the network barely registered among Middle Eastern funding sources, thus it remained marginal and poor. "Established salafi foundations" led by the rivals of Ja'far Umar

Thalib, however, received generous financial support. He attempted to remedy this situation by exploiting the *Sururiyya* issue, as mentioned earlier, in the hope of seizing the advantage. But this attempt appears to have backfired. It simply kept him away from the financial support of the foundations, which consistently demanded the unity and solidarity of the salafis in working together to achieve the salafi dakwah goals as a funding criterion.

Nevertheless, the austere conditions in the pesantrens associated with the Ihya al-Sunna seemingly strengthened the ties that had been built among their ustadhs (religious teachers) in the form of an informal social network. This relationship is not simply a nexus that links network clusters together but also an engine for network expansion. All the ustadhs were active in organizing their own activities independently. There was no formal organization available to effect movement mobilization, which defined the hierarchy between the centre and the "branches", between the leaders and common followers. Only on certain occasions, did they mobilize their students and surrounding people to gather in one city to conduct *tabligh akbar*, a mass religious gathering, in which Ja'far Umar Thalib had the opportunity to stir the emotions of his followers. There is no doubt, however, that in a certain context this passive network can be activated for collective action through the art of mobilization.

TOWARDS POLITICAL MOBILIZATION

The salafis began to make their appearance in the arena of the *Realpolitik* of Indonesia shortly after the collapse of the New Order regime in May 1998. In response to the escalation of the bloody communal conflict in the Moluccas that erupted in January 1999,[18] they issued a jihad resolution and simultaneously mobilized thousands of volunteers to join Laskar Jihad. No doubt the key to the success of the Laskar Jihad formation, as a form of social movement, lies in the ability of its main actors to organize discontent, reduce the costs of action, utilize and create solidarity networks and achieve internal consensus.[19] Centres of salafi activism served as the recruitment pools through which voluntary fighters were recruited. The cohesiveness of the network reduced the free-riding problem, a situation commonly arising in public good contexts in which players may benefit from the actions of others without contributing.[20] All salafis associated with the network felt themselves necessarily part of the mobilization. It was therefore natural that they competed to clamber on board the ships that would take them to the Moluccas. The magnificence of jihad, which had frequently been discussed in religious lectures and glorified in their religious publications, had apparently borne fruit.

Despite the importance of the network, the establishment of Laskar Jihad benefited enormously from the political conditions following the collapse of the New Order regime and its ensuing transitional processes. As indicated by Sidney Tarrow, the changes in the pattern of political opportunities and constraints encourage people to engage in contentious politics.[21] In fact, this dramatic event stimulated the growth of a free political space, which enabled all members of Indonesian society to discuss and develop opinions on issues affecting their lives. Consequently, a variety of groups, identities, and interests emerged, competing for the newly liberated public sphere. Paradoxically, this openness offered the remaining powers of the status-quo (the old elite) room to manoeuvre and orchestrate a game that could hold the seeds of the destruction of the emerging civil society and help them, in turn, to recover their lost power.[22] The key to reach this end was to manipulate the public sphere, the main arena in which ideas, interests, values, and ideologies are formed and relations of civil society are voiced and made politically efficacious.

Keeping pace with the opening of political opportunity structure, actors in a social movement produce, arrange, and disseminate discourse that may resonate among those they intend to mobilize. This so-called "framing" process determines the success of attempts at mobilization.[23] During this process, the salafis sought to frame their actions by placing the Moluccan issue coherently within the context of global conflicts in the Muslim world. In what can be described as a manifesto, they stated that having succeeded in winning the Cold War against the Soviet Union, the United States lost no time in proclaiming itself the sole superpower. It continued to say that this superpower had thereby given itself the right to subjugate Islam which it saw as the greatest and most dangerous enemy of the globalized world. The salafis interpreted the success of the United States as a victory of Zionists and (Christian) Crusaders, who had long been nurturing a hatred of Islam. Conflicts and violence that had erupted in different parts of the Muslim world, including Bosnia, the Philippines, North Africa, and Chechnya, they declared, were all evidence of the fierceness which the enemies of Islam displayed in their efforts to eliminate all Muslims from the face of the earth. Confronted with the complexity of the Moluccan conflict, the salafis saw no solution except jihad. They were convinced that with jihad the manoeuvres of the enemies of Islam seeking to undermine the growth of Islam in Indonesia could be halted and, at the same time, the fate of Moluccan Muslims could be turned.[24] To legitimize this position, they requested *fatwas* (legal opinions) from Middle Eastern salafi authorities, including 'Abd al-Razzaq ibn 'Abd al-Muhsin al-'Abbad, Muqbil ibn Hadi al-Wadi'i, Rabi' ibn Hadi al-Madkhali, Salih al-Suhaymi, Ahmad Yahya ibn Muhammad al-Najm, and Wahid al-Jabiri.[25]

The establishment of Laskar Jihad confirms that under certain conducive political circumstances a resort to violence is an elective choice among Islamic militant groups, even among the non-political wings that reject the use of revolutionary means in the struggle to reach the final goal. As we have seen before, a dakwah community concerned with the purity of the faith and the subsequent moral integrity of individuals, the salafis had previously considered political activism, not to mention violence, an anathema to Islam. The resort to violence by Laskar Jihad proves that the repudiation of political activism by the salafis was not a rigidly adhered-to point; it was more a strategy to deal with the distressing and discouraging political situation under an uncompromising secular ruling regime, rather than a desirable form of activism. The basic premises in their doctrines were in fact political in nature. The themes of reform centred on the issue of the purity of faith, though they had been isolated from the idea of revolutionary jihad, not only demanded that salafis be concerned with the comprehensive implementation of *sharia*, but also required them to repudiate democracy and consequently the system of the nation-state. Democracy is considered to be in opposition to the principle of God's Sovereignty, which derives from the absolute Oneness of God. More importantly perhaps, these themes provided the foundation for the call for jihad in the Moluccas, where it was regarded as a mechanism to defend Muslims from the attacks of war-mongering infidels.

Furthermore, the fact that the salafi community resort to violence went hand-in-hand with the radicalization of its discourse casts light on the position held by ideology in a militant Islamist movement: This is not static, but rather dynamic, and develops in line with the contextual changes. The ideology of a social movement is best understood in relation to the struggle of the movement's actors over the production of ideas, meaning that it does not merely stand as a carrier of extant ideas that flow from the movement's underlying strains.[26] Yet, the role of ideology remains crucial to the establishment of a social movement, serving primarily as an ethical, moral and normative principle that guides individual members towards an understanding of the frame constructed by movement actors. In other words, ideology functions as a resource of culture at the service of framing.[27]

DRAMA OF JIHAD IN THE MOLUCCAS

Under the banner of Laskar Jihad, the salafis started their mission in the Moluccas by staging a spectacular collective action in the Senayan Main Stadium in Jakarta on 6 April 2000. At that time, some 10,000 salafis joined and presented themselves majestically: a sea of swarming, writhing people, clad in white, absorbed in chants of "Allah Akbar", whose echoes reverberated throughout the stadium. Sunlight flashed from their swords like strobe lights. In the background, banners and posters fluttered magnificently, emblazoned with the slogans "Wage jihad fi sabil Allah" and "Defend Muslims in the Moluccas". At the height of his public exposure, commander-in-chief Ja'far Umar Thalib mounted the podium and delivered a speech in which he decried the "disaster" afflicting Moluccan Muslims, confronted as they were by a genocidal threat.

The salafis' mission to fight jihad in the Moluccas is better conceptualized as a drama, because this apparently frenzied action was motivated not so much by the hope for a resounding victory as by the intention to fabricate a heroic image. It was the moment in which the salafis proclaimed their rightful place in the political arena of Indonesia. Through the staging of theatrical scenes, they emerged on the political scene as a bunch of militant youths willing to martyr themselves for the cause of God. Wearing the distinctive uniform (white *jalabiyya* and turban) complete with arms on proud display, they portrayed themselves as the most heroic jihad combatants, aching to go to the frontlines.

The salafi fighters, cast as heroes or villains, destined for some great ideal according to differing scenarios, acted in a plot that could end either in a happy or tragic ending. The plot might have been written beforehand or it might have been improvised, or it might have crystallized only after the drama was underway. Any of these possibilities is of little account as long as there is no public to side with the play's main character and applaud their warring spectacle against the hegemonic global order.[28]

The Moluccan province constituted the primary stage on which Laskar Jihad recruits acted out their drama. This stage is figuratively located in the huge theatre building called the Republic of Indonesia, where the New Order had successfully managed political power by expertly using symbols and state rituals for more than thirty-two years. As described by Clifford Geertz, in the case of nineteenth-century Bali, in a theatre state, political symbology — ranging from myth, insignia, and etiquette to palaces, titles, and ceremonies — is the instrument of purposes concealed behind it. Its relations to the real business of politics are therefore all extrinsic. But the isomorphic aspects of "practical" instrumental politics and expressive actions cannot be isolated from the exercise of power itself.[29]

The main actor in this drama was no doubt Ja'far Umar Thalib, himself a sign among signs. But it was the drama of jihad that created him, raised him from the ranks of a modest salafi ustadh to an icon of jihad, for without this drama the image of the hero could never have taken form. Nevertheless, in order to leave a lasting impression, he needed to mobilize, and more importantly be seen mobilizing, the forces that would carry him onto the political stage. Mobilizing men for jihad was, thus, his primary task. The flow of fighters from various provinces in Indonesia, who came to proclaim their support for this call to action, contributed to both strengthening his position as the icon of jihad and to facilitate the process by which he could claim central leadership among Indonesian Muslims.

As players in a drama, the salafi fighters acted intentionally to capture public attention. They enjoyed the coverage in the media, including television, radio, newspapers, bulletins, and magazines, although their underpinning doctrine should have prevented them from doing so. They warmly welcomed reporters from the media who used the event (and at times sensationalized it) to sell their publications. Yet, ironically, because most of the salafi fighters were actually unskilled combatants, their only success lay on the symbolic level, that is, in creating propaganda that influenced public opinion through the media. They published *Maluku Hari Ini* (Moluccas Today), a pamphlet printed on a single double-sided sheet of paper, *Buletin Laskar Jihad,* a sixteen-page, large lay-out, weekly bulletin featuring colour photos and advertisements, and the *Laskar Jihad Online.*

Shifts in the political landscape determine the sustainability of a drama staged in a transitional situation. Four or five months after the arrival of Laskar Jihad in the Moluccas, the room to manoeuvre available to this group began to narrow. This was particularly felt after pressures exerted by various elements in Indonesian society and the international community succeeded in forcing the Indonesian government to take necessary political measures. In the aftermath of the 11 September tragedy, the situation deteriorated for Laskar Jihad. It had to confront not only the Indonesian government but also the United States administration.

The United States saw Southeast Asia, notably Indonesia, as one of the most important targets in the global campaign against terrorism, owing to the emergence of radical Islamist groups suspected to have linkage with al-Qaeda terrorist cells.[30] Allegations linking Laskar Jihad — as well as two other paramilitary organizations, Laskar Pembela Islam (the Defenders of Islam Force) and Laskar Mujahidin Indonesia (Indonesian Holy Warriors Force) — to al-Qaeda became more widely spread. In tandem with the increasing pressure that Laskar Jihad felt after 11 September, opposition to its jihad arose among Indonesian Muslims advocating liberal Islam.

The Malino Agreement in February 2002, when seventy members of the Christian and Muslim delegations agreed an eleven-point joint declaration that promised to end all conflict and violence, eventually closed the space that had enabled Laskar Jihad's drama. Under this agreement, Laskar Jihad was to be expelled from the Moluccas. Just five days after the bombing of Paddy's CafÈ and the Sari Club at Legian, Bali, on 12 October 2002, Laskar Jihad surprisingly disbanded. In retrospect, some veterans of Laskar Jihad concluded that Laskar Jihad's mission in the Moluccas was a political manouevre by group leaders at the expense of a sincere religious commitment. Some even claimed that their participation was a "black stain" on their lives. This admission can be regarded as proof that the drama of jihad initiated by Ja'far Umar Thalib, and his attempt to become the grand hero of Indonesian Muslims, ended in failure.

CONCLUSION

Despite this failure, the engagement of some 7,000 people in the jihad operation in the Moluccas indicated the strength of jihad as the concept whose symbols and discourses can be used by marginalized individuals to express themselves and their interests. Its use reflects the impotence of the deprived citizens in the face of uncertainty arising from modernization and globalization. Jihad is considered an appropriate choice as they believe that the globalized world flaunts its victories and shows no awareness of their frustration. By glorifying the symbols of jihad, they are in fact trying to resist their own impotence and frustration, and thereby establish their identity and claim dignity. The zeal of purity and martyrdom fuels and completes their struggle. For these people, the desire to resist the globalized world will continue to burn bright as long as their frustration is not addressed or ameliorated. This resistance will oscillate between two poles: enclave and jihad. The former is implicit, and the latter is explicit. Under certain favourable political situations, implicit resistance in the form of an enclave can resort to explicit resistance in the form of jihad. In contrast to the enclave, jihad can transform marginality into centrality and defeat into patriotism. But it should be noted that these strategies all remain predominantly rhetorical. Global hegemonic war machines are certainly strong enough to withstand the swords drawn in jihad, although these swords have been embellished with the slogan of "*La ilaha illa Allah*".

NOTES

1. In older academic parlance, the term Salafi is usually distinguished from the term Wahhabi. The former denotes the nineteenth-century Islamic reform movement centred in Egypt under the leadership of Muhammad 'Abduh (1865–1935), while the latter is identical to the eighteenth-century purification

movement in the Arabian Peninsula pioneered by Muhammad ibn 'Abd al-Wahhab (1703–87). For further discussion, see Emad Eldin Shahin, "Salafiyah", *The Oxford Encyclopedia of the Modern Islamic World*, ed. John L. Esposito (New York, Oxford: Oxford University Press, 1995), pp. 463–64; John Obert Voll, *Islam: Continuity and Change in the Modern World*, 2nd ed. (Syracuse: Syracuse University Press, 1994); and Albert Hourani, *Arabic Thought in the Liberal Age, 1798–1939* (Cambridge: Cambridge University Press, 1983).

2. Abdul Mu'thi, "Memerangi Dakwah Hizbiyyah", Salafy 9 (1996): 16–19; Ibnu Syarif al-Bengkului as-Salafy al-Atsary, "Semangat Hizbiyyah, Semangat Jahiliyyah", *Salafy* 9 (1996): 51–54; Ja'far Umar Thalib, "Akhlaqul Muwahhidin dan Akhlaqul Musyrikin", *Salafy* 16 (1997): 12; Tim Redaksi, "Fatwa-Fatwa Ulama tentang Larangan Membentuk Jama'ah-Jama'ah Hizbiyyah", *Salafy* 9 (1996): 24–28.
3. On this organization, see Saad S. Khan, *Reasserting International Islam: A Focus on the Organization of the Islamic Conference and Other Islamic Institutions* (Oxford: Oxford University Press, 2001); see also Reinhard Schulze, *Islamischer Internationalismus in 20. Jahrhundert* (Leiden: Brill, 1990), pp. 215–16.
4. For a further account, see Cary Fraser, "In Defense of Allah's Realm: Religion and Statecraft in Saudi Foreign Policy Strategy", in *Transnational Religion and Fading States*, edited by Susanne Hoeber Rudolph and James Piscatori (Oxford: Westview Press, 1997), pp. 226–34; Stephen Schwartz, *The Two Faces of Islam: The House of Sa'ud from Tradition to Terror* (New York, NY: Doubleday, 2002), pp. 148–49; and Dore Gold, *Hatred's Kingdom: How Saudi Arabia Supports the New Global Terrorism* (Washington, DC: Regnery Publishing, 2003), pp. 112–16.
5. *Halqa*, literally meaning "circle", is a forum for the study of Islamic sciences, in which an *ustadh*, a teacher or preacher, gives lessons based on certain books and his participants sit around him to hear and scrutinize his lessons. It is distinct from *daura*, literally meaning "turn", which is a type of workshop held for a period ranging from one week to one month, during which its participants gather and stay in one place and follow all the designed programmes.
6. The former was a Saudi-based institution, backed by the Saudi religious establishment, operating under the supervision of the Minister of Islamic Affairs, Endowments, Dakwah, and Guidance of Saudi Arabia. This foundation, which recently came under scrutiny by the United States government because it was suspected of having ties to terrorism, was created in the mid-1980s with such aims as "establishing correct Islamic doctrines, educating new generations, confronting ideological and atheistic invasion, and calling non-Muslims to Islam." The Jam'iyyat Ihya' al-Turath al-Islami was a Kuwait-based institution set up in 1981. It operated under the supervision of the Kuwaiti government, and also received support from the Saudi religious establishment. See Jonathan Benthall and Jerome Bellion-Jourdan, *The Charitable Crescent: Politics of Aid in the Muslim World* (London: I.B. Tauris, 2003), pp. 36 and 73.

7. For the definition of sect, see Lawrence R. Iannaccone, "Why Strict Churches Are Strong", *American Journal of Sociology* 99, no. 5 (March 1994): 1192. For a comparison, see also Rodney Stark and William Sims Bainbridge, *The Future of Religion: Secularization, Revival, and Cult Formation* (Berkeley, CA: University California Press, 1985) and Thomas Robbins, Cults, *Converts, and Charisma: The Sociology of New Religious Movements* (London: Sage, 1988).
8. Alberto Melucci, *Nomads of the Present: Social Movements and Individual Needs in Contemporary Society* (London: Hutchinson, 1989), p. 109.
9. Manuel Castells, *The Information Age: Economy, Society, and Culture*, vol. II, *The Power of Identity* (Oxford: Blackwell, 1999), pp. 8–9.
10. Gabriel A. Almond, R. Scott Appleby, and Emmanuel Sivan, *Strong Religion: The Rise of Fundamentalism around the World* (Chicago, IL, and London: The University of Chicago Press, 2003), p. 30.
11. Manuel Castells, *The City and the Grassroots: A Cross-Cultural Theory of Urban, Social Movements* (Berkeley, CA: University California Press, 1983), p. 331.
12. Concerning the polemics around this issue, see Usamah Mahri et al., *Nasehat dan Peringatan [Atas Syarif Fuadz Hazaa']* (Malang: Yayasan Waladun Shaleh, 1996).
13. On al-Irsyad, see Natalie Mobini-Kesheh, *The Hadrami Awakening: Community and Identity in the Netherlands East Indies, 1900–1942* (Ithaca, NY: Cornell Southeast Asia Program Publications, 1999).
14. For a detailed discussion on Persis, see Howard M. Federspiel, *Islam and Ideology in the Emerging Indonesian State: The Persatuan Islam, 1923–1957* (Leiden: Brill, 2000).
15. Concerning the development of this institute, see, for instance, *Lembaga Ilmu Pengetahuan Islam dan Arab, Lembaga Ilmu Pengetahuan Islam dan Arab di Indonesia Pada Tahun Kelima Belas Hijriah* (Jakarta: LIPIA, 1995).
16. Barnett R. Rubin, "Arab Islamists in Afghanistan", in *Political Islam: Revolution, Radicalism, or Reform?*, edited by John L. Esposito (Boulder, CO: Lynne Rienner Publishers, Inc., 1997), pp. 196–97.
17. Concerning this figure, Bernard Haykel, "The Salafis in Yemen at a Crossroads: An Obituary of Shaykh Muqbil al-Wadi'i of Dammaj (d. 1422/2001)", *Jemen Report* 2 (October 2002); cf. Francois Burgat and Muhammad Sbitli, "Les Salafis au Yemen ou … La Modernisation Malgré Tout", *Chroniques Yemenites* (2002).
18. On this conflict, see, for instance, Gerry van Klinken, "The Maluku Wars: Bringing Society Back In", *Indonesia* 71 (April 2001): 1–26; and Lambang Trijono, *Keluar Dari Kemelut Maluku: Refleksi Pengalaman Praktis Bekerja Untuk Perdamaian Maluku* (Yogyakarta: Pustaka Pelajar, 2001).
19. For an overview of resource mobilization approach, see, for instance, Mancur Olson, *The Logic of Collective Action* (Cambridge, MA: Harvard University Press, 1965); and Mayer N. Zald and John D. McCarthy, eds., *Social Movements in an Organizational Society* (New Brunswick, NJ: Transaction Books, 1987).

20. Myra Marx Ferree, "The Political Context of Rationality: Rational Choice Theory and Resource Mobilization", in *Frontiers in Social Movement Theory*, edited by A.D. Morris and Carol McClurg Mueller (New Haven, CT, and London: Yale University Press, 1992), pp. 36–40.
21. Sidney Tarrow, *Power in Movement: Social Movements and Contentious Politics*, 2nd ed. (Cambridge: Cambridge University Press, 1998), pp. 19–20.
22. Guillermo O'Donnell and Philippe C. Schmitter, *Transitions from Authoritarian Rule: Tentative Conclusions about Uncertain Democracies* (Baltimore, MD, and London: John Hopkins University Press, 1986), pp. 20–21.
23. David A. Snow, E. Burke Rochford, Steven K. Worden, and Robert D. Benford, "Frame Alignment Process, Micromobilization, and Movement Participation", *American Sociological Review* 51 (1986): 461–81; see also Bert Klandermans, "Grievance Interpretation and Success Expectations: The Social Construction of Protest", *Social Behaviour* 4 (1989): 121–22.
24. Ja'far Umar Thalib, *Buku Petunjuk dan Latar Belakang Pengiriman Laskar Jihad ke Maluku* (Malang: Kadiv. Penerangan FKAWJ Malang, 2000), pp. 2–3; see also Ja'far Umar Thalib, "Resolusi Jihad Sebagai Jawaban Atas Pembantaian Muslimin di Maluku", *Cassette Record* (Yogyakarta: FKAWJ, 2000).
25. For a detailed discussion on these *fatwas*, see Noorhaidi Hasan, "Between Transnational Interest and Domestic Politics: Understanding Middle Eastern *Fatwas* on Jihad in the Moluccas", *Islamic Law and Society*, Theme Issue, edited by Nico Kaptein and Michael Laffan, 12, no. 1 (January 2005): 73–92.
26. Teun A. van Dijk, *Ideology: a Multidisciplinary Approach* (London: Sage Publications, 1998), pp. 26–27.
27. Pamela E. Oliver and Hank Johnston, "What a Good Idea: Ideologies and Frames in Social Movement Research", *Mobilization* 5, no. 1 (2000): 37–54.
28. See Victor Turner, *Dramas, Fields, and Metaphors: Symbolic Action in Human Society* (Ithaca, NY, and London: Cornell University Press, 1974), pp. 33–39.
29. Clifford Geertz, *Negara: The Theatre State in Nineteenth-Century Bali* (Princeton, NJ: Princeton University Press, 1980), pp. 122–23.
30. For a further discussion, see Donald K. Emmerson, "Whose Eleventh? Indonesia and the United States Since 11 September", *The Brown Journal of World Affairs* 9, no. 1 (Spring 2002): 115–26; and Noorhaidi Hasan, "September 11 and Islamic Militancy in Post-New Order Indonesia", in *Islam in Southeast Asia: Political, Social, and Strategic Challenges for the 21st Century*, edited by K.S. Nathan and Mohammad Hashim Kamali (Singapore: Institute of Southeast Asian Studies, 2005), pp. 301–24.

References

Almond, Gabriel A., R. Scott Appleby, and Emmanuel Sivan. *Strong Religion: The Rise of Fundamentalism around the World.* Chicago, IL, and London: The University of Chicago Press, 2003.

Benthall, Jonathan and Jerome Bellion-Jourdan. *The Charitable Crescent: Politics of Aid in the Muslim World.* London: I.B. Tauris, 2003.

Burgat, François and Muhammad Sbitli. "Les Salafis au Yemen ou … La Modernisation Malgré Tout". *Chroniques Yemenites*, no. 10 (2002).

Castells, Manuel. *The City and the Grassroots: A Cross-Cultural Theory of Urban, Social Movements.* Berkeley, CA: University of California Press, 1983.

———. *The Information Age: Economy, Society, and Culture*, vol. II, *The Power of Identity.* Oxford: Blackwell, 1999.

Emmerson, Donald K. "Whose Eleventh? Indonesia and the Unites States since 11 September". *The Brown Journal of World Affairs* 9, no. 1 (Spring 2002): 115–26.

Federspiel, Howard M. *Islam and Ideology in the Emerging Indonesian State: The Persatuan Islam, 1923–1957.* Leiden: Brill, 2000.

Fraser, Cary. "In Defense of Allah's Realm: Religion and Statecraft in Saudi Foreign Policy Strategy". In *Transnational Religion and Fading States,* edited by Susanne Hoeber Rudolph and James Piscatori. Oxford: Westview Press, 1997, pp. 226–34.

Geertz, Clifford. *Negara: The Theatre State in Nineteenth-Century Bali.* Princeton, NJ: Princeton University Press, 1980.

Gold, Dore. *Hatred's Kingdom: How Saudi Arabia Supports the New Global Terrorism.* Washington, DC: Regnery Publishing, 2003.

Hasan, Noorhaidi. "September 11 and Islamic Militancy in Post-New Order Indonesia". In *Islam in Southeast Asia: Political, Social, and Strategic Challenges for the 21st Century*, edited by K.S. Nathan and Mohammad Hashim Kamali. Singapore: Institute of Southeast Asian Studies, 2005, pp. 301–24.

———. "Between Transnational Interest and Domestic Politics: Understanding Middle Eastern Fatwas on Jihad in the Moluccas". *Islamic Law and Society* 12, no. 1 (January 2005): 73–92.

Haykel, Bernard. "The Salafis in Yemen at a Crossroads: An Obituary of Shaykh Muqbil al-Wadi'i of Dammaj (d. 1422/2001)". *Jemen Report,* no. 2 (October 2002).

Hourani, Albert. *Arabic Thought in the Liberal Age, 1798–1939.* Cambridge: Cambridge University Press, 1983.

Iannaccone, Lawrence R. "Why Strict Churches Are Strong". *American Journal of Sociology* 99, no. 5 (March 1994).

Ibnu Syarif al-Bengkului as-Salafy al-Atsary. "Semangat Hizbiyyah, Semangat Jahiliyyah". *Salafy,* no. 9 (1996).

Khan, Saad S. *Reasserting International Islam: A Focus on the Organization of the Islamic Conference and Other Islamic Institutions.* Oxford: Oxford University Press, 2001.

Klandermans, Bert. "Grievance Interpretation and Success Expectations: The Social Construction of Protest". *Social Behaviour,* no. 4 (1989): 121–22.

Lembaga Ilmu Pengetahuan Islam dan Arab. *Lembaga Ilmu Pengetahuan Islam dan Arab di Indonesia pada Tahun Kelima Belas Hijriah.* Jakarta: LIPIA, 1995.

Mahri, Usamah et al. *Nasehat dan Peringatan [Atas Syarif Fuadz Hazaa']*. Malang: Yayasan Waladun Shaleh, 1996.

Melucci, Alberto. *Nomads of the Present: Social Movements and Individual Needs in Contemporary Society.* London: Hutchinson, 1989.

Mobini-Kesheh, Natalie. *The Hadrami Awakening: Community and Identity in the Netherlands East Indies, 1900–1942.* Ithaca, NY: Cornell Southeast Asia Program Publications, 1999.

Mu'thi, Abdul. "Memerangi Dakwah Hizbiyyah". *Salafy,* no. 9 (1996).

O'Donnell, Gillermo and Philippe C. Schmitter.'*Transitions from Authoritarian Rule: Tentative Conclusions about Uncertain Democracies.* Baltimore, MD, and London: John Hopkins University Press, 1986.

Oliver, Pamela E. and Hank Johnston. "What a Good Idea: Ideologies and Frames in Social Movement Research". *Mobilization* 5, no. 1 (2000): 37–54.

Olson, Mancur. *The Logic of Collective Action.* Cambridge, MA: Harvard University Press, 1965.

Robbins, Thomas. *Cults, Converts, and Charisma: The Sociology of New Religious Movements.* London: Sage, 1988.

Rubin, Barnett R. "Arab Islamists in Afghanistan". In *Political Islam: Revolution, Radicalism, or Reform?,* edited by John L. Esposito. Boulder, CO: Lynne Rienner Publishers, Inc., 1997.

Schulze, Reinhard. *Islamischer Internationalismus Im 20. Jahrhundert.* Leiden: Brill, 1990.

Schwartz, Stephen. *The Two Faces of Islam: The House of Sa'ud from Tradition to Terror.* New York, NY: Doubleday, 2002.

Shahin, Emad Eldin. "Salafiyah". In *The Oxford Encyclopedia of the Modern Islamic World,* edited by John L. Esposito. New York, Oxford: Oxford University Press, 1995.

Snow, David A., E. Burke Rochford, Steven K. Worden, and Robert D. Benford. "Frame Alignment Process, Micromobilization, and Movement Participation". *American Sociological Review,* no. 51 (1986): 461–81.

Stark, Rodney and William Sims Bainbridge. *The Future of Religion: Secularization, Revival, and Cult Formation.* Berkeley, CA: University California Press, 1985.

Tarrow, Sidney. *Power in Movement: Social Movements and Contentious Politics,* second edition. Cambridge: Cambridge University Press, 1998.

Tim Redaksi. "Fatwa-Fatwa Ulama tentang Larangan Membentuk Jama`ah-Jama`ah Hizbiyyah". *Salafy,* no. 9 (1996).

Thalib, Ja'far Umar. "Akhlaqul Muwahhidin dan Akhlaqul Musyrikin". *Salafy,* no. 16 (1997).

———. "Resolusi Jihad sebagai Jawaban atas Pembantaian Muslimin di Maluku". Cassette record. Yogyakarta: FKAWJ, 2000.

———. *Buku Petunjuk dan Latar Belakang Pengiriman Laskar Jihad ke Maluku.* Malang: Kadiv. Penerangan FKAWJ Malang, 2000.

Trijono, Lambang. *Keluar dari Kemelut Maluku: Refleksi Pengalaman Praktis Bekerja untuk Perdamaian Maluku.* Yogyakarta: Pustaka Pelajar, 2001.

Turner, Victor. *Dramas, Fields, and Metaphors: Symbolic Action in Human Society.* Ithaca, NY, and London: Cornell University Press, 1974.

Van Klinken, Gerry. "The Maluku Wars: Bringing Society Back In". *Indonesia,* no. 71 (April 2001).

Voll, John Obert. *Islam: Continuity and Change in the Modern World,* second edition. Syracuse: Syracuse University Press, 1994.

Zald, Mayer N. and John D. McCarthy, eds. *Social Movements in an Organizational Society.* New Brunswick, NJ: Transaction Books, 1987.

9

FROM HANDLING WATER IN A GLASS TO COPING WITH AN OCEAN
Shifts in Religious Authority in Indonesia

Andrée Feillard

Two major Muslim organizations, the so-called "traditionalist" Nahdlatul Ulama and "reformist" Muhammadiyah,[1] are habitually said to dominate Indonesian Islam, and are thus presented as the religious pillars of the country's stability. To evaluate their influence, people tend to talk in numbers, and seem satisfied that one would have around 45 million "members", as it claims, and the other 35 million "members" (whereas it would be more appropriate to speak of sympathizers). Beyond this simplistic presentation of religious authority in Indonesia, which implies that life is still what it used to be, processes of changes are at work.

This chapter tries to discern some stages of an undeniable evolution, starting in the early twentieth century and going on until today, based both on print material and, for a major part, on interviews with several *ulama* of the older generation, whom I visited during the course of my stay in Indonesia in 2005.

First, I will describe briefly the evolution of legitimacy within Javanese traditionalist Islam in the early twentieth century, the way this authority adapted to early challenges and historical events. The impact of Reformasi on traditionalist Islam is then observed, when politics were burdened with a highly religious content. Finally, emerging new religious authorities are described as well as the *ulama*'s reaction to them.

Given the rising influence of radical Islamist literature available through translations on book markets and via Internet, the Javanese *ulama* are sought after as a natural counterweight to Middle Eastern influences. Expectations are high, but religious authority is far from monolithic within religious organizations. New actors do challenge traditional religious authority, but only a few Javanese *ulama* seemed troubled in 2005. This might be due to the fact that they faced incessant challenges before, but also because of their ambivalent judgement of the new generation.

A HISTORICAL PERSPECTIVE: KNOWLEDGE, THE *REVOLUSI*, THE CHILDREN

Religious authority has never been monolithic but it seems that modern means of communication have amplified competition. The fear of conservatism being propagated through modern techniques was present already in the 1930s. Political events later on had an impact on that competition, with a major role played by *ulama*'s sons.

ULAMA IN THE EARLY TWENTIETH CENTURY: ANCIENT KNOWLEDGE, MODERN WAYS

Until the early twentieth century, religious authority was mostly vested in personalities known for their knowledge and their reputation outside their village. The founder of Nahdlatul Ulama, Hasjim Asj'ari, had a large influence, evident in the number and diversity of origins of his pupils (*murid*, *santri*) in Jombang in East Java, who came from all over the archipelago: from Sumatra, Borneo, and also from Malaysia. To assess the importance of Kiai Hasyim Asy'ari, another criterion mattered: Muhammadiyah figures would visit him for his confirmed knowledge of the Prophet's Traditions (*ilmu hadith)* during the month of Ramadan.[2] However, this show of deference did not mean that the life of Kiai Hasyim Asy'ari was without challenges. It is important to remember that the Nahdlatul Ulama was created in 1926 in a bid to assess the authority of the traditionalist *ulama* over reformist-minded figures. The need was felt for a representation of the *ulama* to face the contesting current of thought. The hesitation of Hasyim Asy'ari to give the green light to the creation of the NU before 1926 was based on his fear of accentuating divisions, but he finally concluded it was a necessity. The NU itself emerged out of a challenge, from early on the *ulama* were used to having their authority challenged.

A few years later, the NU endeavoured to confirm its authority through modern means of communication, with printed periodicals like *Swara Nahdlatoel Oelama* (Javanese language in Pegon script) and *Oetoesan Nahdlatoel Oelama* (in Latin script) in the late 1920s. In the 1930s, *Berita Nahdlatoel Oelama* (BNO, since 1931) and *Kemoedi N.O.* (since 1937) developed their readership further. These publications propagated the *ulama*'s opinions on a wide variety of questions. In 1939, for example, the BNO sharply criticized Sukarno when he walked out of a ceremony organized by the Muhammadiyah in Bengkulu to protest against the *tabir* (room partition) set up by organizers. Sukarno qualified the *tabir* as the "symbol of women's enslavment".[3] The same year, the BNO also made clear its disagreement with Islamic reformers and the "dangers of *ijtihad*" (sacred text interpretation):

> This danger of ijtihad has to be eradicated, not only because the (opening of the) door to ijtihad is a serious and important work which is now played at by some people, so that the state of our Islamic shari'a is increasingly in a mess: this is forbidden (*haram*), this is permitted (*halal*), this is apostasy (*murtad*), this is innovation (*bidah*), and the like, and today the most stupid of Allah's creatures throws himself into the exercise of ijtihad".[4]

This argument is extremely interesting: the Javanese *ulama* are lashing out at reformists whom, they feel, do not possess the knowledge they themselves have acquired in a long process of learning, and are thus not entitled to ijtihad. However, it is not ijtihad itself that is rejected, but its exercise by the "most stupid people". The consciousness of a sharp competition over who possesses religious authority is very much present in these lines.

This BNO article was a response to the reformist-modernist current of thought, mainly represented by the Muhammadiyah, whose fear was that traditionalist *ulama* were using modern means to increase their authority. *Adil* (22/VII), a Muhammadiyah publication in Solo, had warned:

> Everywhere there are Islamic movements emerging, led by Kiai A. and Kiai B. These movement are welcomed with enthusiasm by our *santri* (religion students). And they receive support from the government. Their preachers stir things up. However we can but feel sad. Because we know that these organizations we mentioned earlier basically want to go back to the movement of Islam of the past, the orthodox Islamic movement, the Islamic movement with many innovations (*bidah*), but not everybody knows this, because these movements are well-organized. If it would be as in the past, without organization, without rules, without statutes, the danger would be small, but now these movements of archaic Islam (*Islam kuno*), of orthodoxy, which reek of innovations are using modern instruments like the radio, printing machines, white paper, etc. etc.[5]

Nowhere is the Nahdlatul Ulama mentioned in *Adil*, but the words used to discredit the *ulama* (orthodox, *bidah*, *kiai*) are a clear indication that they are the target, and they are understood as such. Indeed, it was a time when NU was increasing the number of its branches over Java. In 1935, it had sixty-eight branches, in 1939, ninety-nine branches and it was developing outside Java, in South Kalimantan, South Sulawesi and South Sumatra. And it had started its own publications.[6]

The ensuing argument against *Adil* by the BNO is most interesting:

> With the slogan: do not be fanatical! Another door of propaganda is opened in our society, and it is not only opened but its influence is also very big! One young man will criticize the Muslims (*orang Islam*) because they do not like gamelan! Another youngster proposes that Muslims work together with Christians!! Another one leaves his Muslim brothers to make alliances with all sorts of religions!![7]

In short, besides the earlier argument that they know nothing of religion, the modernists (Moeslimin-Modern) are now accused of being too tolerant of local culture and non-Muslims. The article does not spell out who exactly the modernists are but they are basically accused of being "more Western-minded than Madinah-minded". By defending local culture and religious tolerance, they are assimilated to the "West", whereas the model to follow should be "Madinah", the Middle East. It is striking that, as early as 1939, only two models were imagined, whereas local identity outside the two poles is not considered.

We see a genuine fear then that this "conservative" Islam has started to expand through modern means of communications, like the radio and machine typing. But a look at these publications show they were still at an embryonic stage. *Berita Nahdlatoel Oelama* was a small publication with only two editors, Kiai Eljas of Pekalongan and Kiai Wahid of Tebuireng. It had three co-editors, senior *ulama* Kiai Hasyim Asy'ari from Tebuireng, Kiai Abdulwahhab Chasbullah from Surabaya and Kyai Bisri from Denanyar. It seemed like a family publication with a limited audience. Until 1939, the names of all subscribers were published in each edition, with the sums received from each of them. Many were hajis, some were kiais, and most came from East and Central Java. The yearly subscription was 2.50 fl., and the price of publicity negotiable (*berdamai*). The subscribers were not numerous, but they were active readers, who could spread the message in Friday sermons and religious gatherings (*pengajian*). The combination of print publication with religious authority was starting to amplify conservative *ulama*'s influence.

It was a time when authority seemed to rest within the *ulama* circles. They were the majority at the fifteenth Nahdlatul Ulama congress, with 223 people representing local branches of the religious Supreme council (*Syuriah*) as against 121 only for branches of the executive council (*Tanfidiziyah*). Among the people invited, 251 were *ulama* as against 155 non-*ulama*.[8]

Highest religious authority was unchallenged. The respect given to Hasyim Asy'ari was so high that "Hadratus Sjech Hasjim Asj'ari" was to be the only *Rois Akbar* (Greatest Leader). When he died in July 1947, his successor Wahab Abdullah would only take the title of *Rois Aam* (Supreme Leader).

Post-Revolution: The War, Secular Education, Descent

The Japanese occupation resulted in increased influence for both the Nahdlatul Ulama and the Muhammadiyah on the national scene, with the newly created Bureau for Religious Affairs (*Shumubu*). The "*Revolusi fisik*" between 1945 and 1949, the phase of post-World War II resistance against the Dutch, was a time when some *ulama* made new following through their participation in the struggle. One example of this is little known. In the early 1980s, Kiai Asad Syamsul Arifin from East Java became a mediator between the *ulama* and the State in a conflict over the State ideology "Pancasila" (requiring belief in any monotheism, but with no specific mention of Islam), which the governement wanted to be the unique foundation for all socio-religious organizations. Many observers supposed at that time that Kiai Asad had been picked up out of nowhere by the regime, while in fact Asad had close connections with the elite in Jakarta partly because of his role during the Revolution years.[9] He thus could emerge almost forty years later with a stronger authority, reinforced by widespread belief in his supernatural powers.

Authority enhancement resulting from fighting in the Revolution could hardly be replaced by anything similar later on. The wars fought by the Indonesian Armed Forces in the 1950s after the Dutch had recognized Indonesia's independence were against local rebellions, the longest of all being the Darul Islam in West Java, Kalimantan, Sulawesi, and Aceh, in favour of an Indonesian Islamic State.

Of course, a political role for the *ulama*s was nothing new. Already before the Japanese invasion, religious figures had been moving into the political sphere. Let us take here again one example, that of Wahid Hasyim, the son of Kiai Hasyim Asy'ari. Wahid had an exceptional destiny as he was only twenty-four-year old when he became active in the Islamic Council of Indonesia (Majelis Islam A'laa Indonesia, MIAI), and before he died in 1953, at the age of forty, he had been Minister of Religious Affairs. Why was he given such a key role at such a young age? Besides being a natural leader and an intellectual who fitted into the cosmopolitan milieu of Jakarta, he was a "*gus*", the son of a major kiai.

Descent has been an important source of privilege from early on in pesantren milieu. An eighty-year-old *ulama*, a former santri in Tebuireng in the 1930s, related that the "gus" was a kind of prince (*putra mahkota*) for other students, a person to be close to in order to have access to privileges. "The sons of Kiai Hasyim Asy'ari were sought after as friends: with them, one could eat the chicken of the kiai, and take advantage of technical innovations which first came to the kiai's son, such as a typewriter."[10] When children of kiais had intellectual capacities, they had a chance to find in their "gus" status a formidable vehicle for social ascension. However, notes this former pupil of Hasjim Asj'ari,' the "gus" was not automatically called kiai, different from today when the title "kiai" is sometimes automatically used for their children, after a certain age.

The 1950s thus saw the rise of a new santri political elite, but challenge then came from within the *ulama* families themselves, expressed in political cleavages. When the Nahdlatul Ulama split from the Masyumi in 1952, Wahid Hasyim left the Masyumi but his brother Karim stayed in the party. Karim's son joined the Golkar in 1971, while Wahid Hasyim's brother Yusuf Hasyim was fiercely anti-Golkar. In the 1980s, when Wahid Hasyim's eldest son Abdurrahman became prominent, Yusuf Hasyim strongly opposed his efforts to negotiate on the pluralist Pancasila state ideology with the government.

In the 1980s, through the move to enforce acceptance of the state ideology Pancasila, the government itself expanded the authority of some key *ulama* now needed as mediating figures. Abdurrahman's first major role was to act as a co-negotiator with conservative *ulama* on the state ideology issue. Later, in 1990, religious figures were given more clout through the creation of an Association of Muslim Intellectuals (*Ikatan Cendekiawan Muslim se-Indonesia*). As ICMI members, they automatically became "intellectual" *ulama* by virtue of their belonging to the prestigious organization. This was the case for Kiai Ali Yafie, whose authority within the Nahdlatul Ulama became contested at the same time.

The fall of Soeharto in 1998 and the period of democracy that followed introduced a new era for the *ulama* and their sons. Never before had they reached such high political status and such harsh political debacles.

THE IMPACT OF REFORMASI ON TRADITIONAL RELIGIOUS AUTHORITY

Reformasi has brought into the limelight a range of political actors coming from the religious sphere: while some *ulama* have gone through the painful experience of what it could mean to be a politician, the "traditionalist" young intellectuals have seen their audience increase in a political setting where the discourse on democracy has become more and more religious.

Desacralization of the Traditionalist Kiais

When Abdurrahman Wahid was elected President in October 1999, he became the first democratically elected President of Indonesia, albeit in indirect elections. With his victory, religion was for the first time playing a major political role in so far as he was elected by a coalition of Islamic parties. This wide "Islamic" coalition, however, hides another fact: Wahid had been a candidate against the advice of his superiors in the *ulama* hierarchy. This grandson of Nahdlatul Ulama's founder decided to compete for the state's top job despite recommendations to the contrary by the religious leader (Rois Aam) of the Nahdlatul Ulama, as well as other senior kiais.[11] Abdurrahman was executive leader of the NU, but it was his family background that gave him the extra confidence. Maybe for the first time, descent superseded organizational hierarchy, age, and even religious knowledge. A "gus" stood up to a Rois Aam.

The impact of the kiais' entry into the presidential palace is a complex matter.[12] One undeniable effect was that it soon highlighted opinion differences among *ulama*, and their keen interest in politics, unknown to the average Indonesian non-santri Muslim. One case in point is the appearance of a small number of kiais as pressure groups. Less than ten kiais made an alliance in favour of Abdurrahman Wahid's presidency in their eponymously named "*Kiai Langitan*", called so after the pesantren of that name, at the same time evoking an association with "*langit*", heaven. By doing so, they challenged the authority of the NU's supreme leader, Kiai Sahal Mahfudz, who was also the Head of the Indonesian Council of Ulamas (Majelis Ulama Indonesia MUI). The "Kiai Langitan" episode will remain in memories as the symbol of a severe challenge to the supreme authority of the Rois Aam.[13] As opposition to Abdurrahman Wahid's presidency amplified in early 2001, discussions were held among *ulama* on whether demonstrations against the President were illegitimate (and thus could be crushed) as "rebellion" (*bughot*), based on religious texts.[14] But these "theological" meetings were not as widely exposed as other meetings with secular institutions. In January 2001, a few *ulama* approached Parliament to tell its chairman, Akbar Tanjung, that it should refrain from disparaging Abdurrahman Wahid who, they declared, "harboured an angel in his chest". If they did not comply, they could not stop the santris from defending the President in "their own way". Abdul Munir Mulkhan has called it the "Divine Argument" (*argumen langit*) entering a modern institution.[15] Mulkhan further comments that this showed how "smart" the "pesantren aristocrats" (*darah biru pesantren,* Coranic schools' blue blood) were then playing politics: "Like a train with Gus Dur [Wahid's other name] as a locomotive, the President, the 'saint' (wali), the sons of kiais and other pesantren elites moved to the power summit of this country."

Soon, the *ulama*'s sons became the subject of jokes, increasingly so in open forum. Let us name only a few of them here. The acronym IGGI, which stands for Intergovernmental Group on Indonesia, was now said to mean Association of Ulama Sons of Indonesia (*Ikatan Gus Gus Indonesia*); the Non-governmental Group on Indonesia (INGI) had become the Association of Daughters and Sons of Ulama in Indonesia (*Ikatan Ning dan Gus Indonesia*). One could argue that jokes are nothing new in pesantren circles, but there was indeed an innovation: earlier, jokes were more often made by the *ulama* themselves, often in self-derision, whereas this time the kiais or their sons were the very targets of painful jokes, from outside the NU circles. A gradual process of desacralization of the old religious authority had started. It should be noted however that this phenomenon did not mean a desacralization of all religious authorities. The sacralization of a new generation of Muslim preachers was taking place in parallel, as we will see below.[16]

The post-Wahid period from July 2001 heightened tensions and rivalries. By the time the Nahdlatul Ulama's thirty-first congress was convened in November 2004, a new terminology had emerged to discredit the Wahid camp. Hasyim Muzadi's supporters blamed the monarchical NU (*NU-Kerajaan*) and considered themselves "Republican NU" (*NU-Republik*). This development was new and had emerged because, for the first time, a candidate for the NU chairmanship, Hasyim Muzadi, was the son of a simple merchant, and not a "gus". He had already been elected leader of the NU in 1999, but now, he would stand without the support of his mentor, the first of all "guses", Abdurrahman Wahid. Hasyim Muzadi was finally re-elected, but his origins may have had little impact. What mattered was that his conservatism appealed more to the average kiai than the daring liberalism of his younger rival, Masdar Masudi.

The Young Traditionalist Intellectual Generation: Long Unheard, an Emerging Authority?

Is Masdar Masudi's failure to win over the chairmanship of the Nahdlatul Ulama in 2004 a sign that the young generation cannot impose itself as a new religious authority? Will the young Islamic scholars' generation share the burden of Abdurrahman Wahid's failure in presidential politics? These were recurrent questions during NU's 2004 congress, and we can so far only suggest possible answers.

Generally speaking, one could say that NU's "liberals" have long been in the shadow of Gus Dur, that they are divided, and that they have not had as much media exposure as the so-called "modernist" intellectuals,[17] who prospered under the umbrella of the government-sponsored ICMI (*Ikatan Cendekiawan Muslim se-Indonesia*) in the 1990s. Thanks to Abdurrahman Wahid's protection, they were however rather influential within the Nahdlatul Ulama itself. As a sign of this influence, take the hot debate on civil society versus *Masyarakat Madani* concepts. At the thirtieth NU congress in 1999, the young generation clearly rejected the term Masyarakat Madani in the commission on religious questions (*Bahtsul Masail*): "From the start, NU circles have rejected the term which refers to Madinah, because this period was not as ideal as it has been mystified since."[18] The concept was said to be coming from modernist Muslims (*Islam Modernis*). Given that the "Masyarakat Madani" concept is now widespread in Indonesia, and that Indonesians easily translate civil society with Masyarakat Madani, without noting any difference, we could argue that their influence did not reach far outside the limited sphere of their own organization.

Recently, they have received more serious attention from the media for two reasons. First, radical Islamism has started to capture public attention since the first Bali bombings in 2002. Second, with religion entering politics, the discourse on democracy is using references (mostly Qur'an verses and hadits) mastered only by this population group. A Muslim modernist intellectual like Dawam Rahardjo, of Nurcholish Madjid's generation, now openly places his hopes in them. Often they are graduates from Islamic public universities (IAIN or UIN).[19] These institutes of higher learning are praised and envied in some liberal Islamic circles in neighbouring Malaysia.[20]

The most thorough studies on radical salafism were published by teachers of Islamic State Universities in Jakarta and Yogyakarta. In Jakarta, Jamhari and Jajang Jahroni wrote *Gerakan Salafi Radikal di Indonesia (The Radical Salafi Movement in Indonesia)* while Agus Maftuh Abegabriel and his colleagues in Yogyakarta published *Negara Tuhan, the Thematic Encyclopaedia (God's State)*. Few bookstores dared to sell *God's State* in 2005 for fear of an Islamist reaction. Interestingly, their analyses are more critical of salafism and jihadism than those of the Indonesian National Research Institute (LIPI), whose researchers are more divided on the issue of radicalism.[21]

Not all young liberal santris come from IAINs. The rise to prominence of Ulil Abshar Abdalla, who spreads his analysis through Liberal Islam Network (*Jaringan Islam Liberal*, JIL) is a particular case: this "gus" comes from a pesantren background but was educated in a Saudi-linked Institute for Arabic Studies (LIPIA) in Jakarta. He came out as an "anti-wahhabi" militant. Other young santris may be less famous but are even more daring. Sumanto al Qurtuby challenges Islamism with the same argument used by the Islamists themselves in the 1980s to attack the government policy of enforcing Pancasila as the sole principle for all socio-religious organizations: he thus blames what he calls "*Islam Tunggal*" (Sole Islam Principle).[22]

This new liberal Muslim generation, born out of both traditionalist and reformist groups, has to face virulent diatribes from conservative *ulama* who challenge them in open debates. Within the Muhammadiyah itself, Amin Abdullah faced Persis *ulama* who challenged his tolerant text interpretation on the question of relations with non-Muslims presented in a book titled *Tafsir tematik*.[23] In Yogyakarta, his opponents came with dozens of religious books, lined up on a table in front of the audience as guarantee of their authority, while the *Tafsir* authors (mostly Muhammadiyah) pointed out that one of them was an *ulama* from a NU famous pesantren.[24] This debate, where the Muhammadiyah reformists were using traditionalist Islam as theological support in a debate against Persis radicals, was a watershed, a daring distancing of Muhammadiyah reformists from the more radical Persis organization, after a long association of the two on Indonesia's political scene.

Another case illustrates intense competition for religious authority. In 2005, Ulil Abshar Abdalla was also taken to task by salafists. In the very compound of Jakarta's famous Islamic university (UIN), in a heated atmosphere very similar to that of the Yogyakarta meeting described above, Ulil defended liberal Islam against *ulama* who openly called themselves "wahhabis".[25] Never before, probably, had religious authority been so hotly contested inside a government-run institution. In both cases, in Jakarta and Yogyakarta, "liberal" Islam, both modernist and traditionalist, was in a highly defensive position, and there was no consensus over who the "winner" had been.

Pressure from Islamist groups is increasingly felt by traditionalist students in campuses as well. For example, in Surabaya, young traditionalist Muslim female students said they now tried to avoid some mosques where militants insisted the girls had to put on longer veils that would hide their bottoms too. Out of arguments on the veil question (theirs was too short), they often ended up defending themselves by merely proclaiming a right to difference: "We are from the NU." Moreover, the strategy of the female students was to politely refuse the Hizbut Tahrir's constant demands for a meeting at the NU Surabaya headquarters.

Such pressures were reported by delegates to NU's official gatherings. During the thirty-first NU congress, a delegate from Ambon told of death threats he had received from a bunch of fighters (who had come for the jihad and remained in town) if he continued to say the habitual prayers for the dead (*talqin, tahlilan*), a practice long fought against by the reformists, albeit through more or less gentle means. But the delegate was not given a chance to speak in the plenary session, and only addressed a smaller commission. Information about such similar demands and threats circulates in Nahdlatul Ulama circles, but how much reaches the highest spheres of religious authority is uncertain.

To understand these new developments, and to try to appreciate prospects for the young liberals, it is important to look at the making of new religious authorities outside the traditional Islamic sphere.

NEW RELIGIOUS AUTHORITIES: MEDIA'S MAKING, SENIOR *ULAMA*'S AMBIVALENCE

The Nahdlatul Ulama and the Muhammadiyah remain Indonesia's dominant Islamic organizations, but they have undergone constant changes, harbour a wide variety of undercurrents, and are faced with other old but also new organizations or powerful individuals gathering more or less large followings. The NU often appears to be more divided than the Muhammadiyah, although this impression might also result from the higher sense of discipline in the latter. To measure the authority of a religious organization at a certain moment is a difficult exercise. Their sympathizers can be counted in approximate ways during national elections, whenever they are firmly in favour of specific political parties. They rarely publicize the exact number of their registered members. Numbers of pesantrens are an indication of strength. Out of the 14,556 pesantren counted by the Ministry of Religious Affairs, about 9,000 are more or less closely linked to the Nahdlatul Ulama, according to its pesantren association (*Robbithotul Maahidil Islamiyah*, RMI).[26] If that is so, the number of pesantren outside Nahdlatul Ulama's influence would total about 5,000. Given that the Muhammadiyah itself has concentrated on religious schools with general education (madrasah or not) rather than on pesantren, it is improbable that they belong to the Muhammadiyah. This would mean that the influence of the two major organizations might be overstated, this the more so as data about religious schools of other organizations, such as Mathla'ul Anwar for example, are scarce, also because such organizations have received less scolarly attention. Another interesting fact is that the number of pesantren has more than doubled in fifteen years (from 6,321 in 1990 to 14,556 in 2004). In 2005, there was no reliable official data available on the affiliation of the new pesantren.

Within the Nahdlatul Ulama itself, consciousness of the emergence of new religious authorities was clear already at its 1999 congress, where the preparatory committee included questions on the agenda concerning the appearance of new religious teachers, "beginners" (*ustad pemula*).[27]

New Actors: Individual Preachers, Political Parties, Foreign *Ulama*

The most visible "beginners" are popular preachers (*dai, pendakwah*) who are not linked to any old Islamic organization. One good example of this new type of religious authority is that of Muhammad Arifin Ilham, who leads a "*majelis zikir*". His reputation has expanded partly through wide media exposure, especially in TV religious spots. In one of these, in 2005, he urges the viewers to perform the five daily prayers ("*Sudahkah anda sholat?*"). The TV spot was carried for a long time by the rather secular and cosmopolitan channel Metro TV. A key element of his profile is not religious knowledge but secular achievement. Thus, the Islamist magazine *Sabili* complimented Ilham for his multifaceted profile: he had won a national championship for speech-making, had been ASEAN's champion for English speeches at school, badminton champion of Greater Jakarta pesantrens, running champion, and poetry-reading champion.[28] Interestingly, Ilham's discourse is also different from old-style preachers, insisting more on geopolitical than on purely religious arguments. When *Sabili* asked Ilham why the five daily prayers, especially the early morning prayer, was an important criteria in judging politicians, Ilham responded: "Why I measure (morality) from the mosque, because the Jews measure our strength from the mosque. If the number of Muslims praying at dawn is as high as those praying on Friday, then this is a tempest (for Jews). If it is not as high as during Friday prayers, then (they feel) *we can sleep.*"[29] Indeed, Metro TV viewers are not aware of Ilham's geopolitical preoccupations when they are asked to pray five times a day, but this discourse is clearly a departure from traditional religious discourse, when the Palestinian question was not linked so directly to religious duty.

Besides such popular preachers, political parties have also emerged as new religious authorities. Thus, the Muslims Brothers (*Ikhwan Muslimin*)-inspired Prosperous Justice Party (Partai Keadilan Sejahtera, PKS) struck a nerve among traditionalists when it declared in 2005 that the sacrifice day (*Idhul Adha*) had to be celebrated one day ahead of the official date. So far, the determination of religious celebration dates was a privilege of religious organizations. With this announcement, the PKS entered the sphere of religious authority, and secondly, to the distress of some kiais, it showed openly that it was following the Saudi and not Indonesia's own traditionalist guidelines. This gesture annoyed some kiais who had started to feel sympathy for the young anti-corruption party.[30]

Foreign *ulama* have also acquired an increasing impact in Indonesia's domestic affairs. The participation of the Laskar Jihad in the Moluccas conflict in 1999-2000 was partly based on *fatwas* issued in Yemen and Saudi Arabia.[31] A more pervasive impact has come from large numbers of translations from the Arabic into Indonesian of radical Islamic literature, which started in the early 1980s. Through them, one foreign *ulama*, Yusuf Qaradawi, has substantially increased his influence, as his books are sold in many bookshops, at every Islamic book fair, and treat almost every possible subject. He has become a competitor to Indonesia's star prolific writer, an Indonesian moderate conservative of Arabic descent and former Minister of Religious Affairs, Quraish Shihab. Interestingly, the fact that Yusuf Qaradawi is a figure linked to the Muslim Brothers does not prevent him from having an influence within traditionalist Islam, where his books are being read because he is still considered "a moderate among radicals".

The Response: Ambivalence, The Gains of Official Islam

During visits to Java in 2005, it seemed that the kiais' consciousness of the challenge faced by new religious actors was uneven. Some kiais turned out to have a qualified sympathy for new Islamic groups. One major kiai in Yogyakarta saw the militants of the Prosperous Justice Party (PKS) with a mixture of admiration and fear: "They have money and young people who are active."[32] This was in contrast to his disappointment with NU's own performance, "too much involved in politics". He pointed at the disastrous results of the 2004 elections in some parts of Indonesia such as South Kalimantan where, from a majority of votes in the 1955 elections, it had dwindled to only 9 per cent (for the PKB). This "apolitical" kiai was open to new groups, and explained that his pesantren cooperated with popular preacher Aa Gym to operate a local radio station. What disturbed him about the new groups like PKS was their overly moralistic attitudes for instance about smoking, a very common habit among Javanese *ulama.*

In East Java, a NU stronghold, the challenge of new Islamic actors did not seem of great concern among the *ulama* I met, and theological tolerance was cited. Thus, the regent of Gresik, son of a kiai, and himself owner of a NU pesantren with 200 pupils, did not bother much: "NU people do not enter the PKS, who are in Yogyakarta, where the Muhammadiyah is." This line of argument reflected indeed a worry among Muhammadiyah activists in

2005 about attraction to the PKS in their ranks. Theologically or ideologically, the "political" kiai refrained from criticizing PKS: "The NU accepts all schools of law (*mazhab*), including Hambali's," he explained.[33]

Further east, in Jember, one of the oldest NU kiais, Muchith Muzadi, was also taking the new preachers lightly. The eighty-year-old kiai educated in Hasjim's Asjari's pesantren said: "Indeed, we now see sudden kiais, instant kiais, like there are instant noodles. These kiais have no depth, they will last five or ten years, and then they will disappear. [....] People feel touched, but these kiais have no knowledge (*ilmu*). [....] The true kiais are those who have a complete and comprehensive vision (*wawasan*) [...]. This kind of [instant] kiais become more and more numerous."[34]

In Central Java, a few months later, the kiais' discourse was oscillating between unease and self confidence, after the National Ulama's council (MUI) had issued a number of anti-liberal *fatwas* in July. One middle-aged kiai remarked that PKS militants were now present in the villages, giving free religious education.[35] A forty-four-year-old kiai heading a pesantren was upset by Middle Eastern and bureaucratic influence in the MUI, and "strategies" of PKS militants, which had to be "watched".[36] But the most influential kiai around, oft consulted by politicians, sounded reassuring: The kiais were "very much sought after", and TV showed that everyone in Indonesia was praying the NU way, said Kiai Dimiyati.[37] One year later, in December 2006, the same kiai expressed concern at what he saw as efforts by new groups "like PKS, Hizbut Tahrir and Jaulah (a term used in Java for the Jemaah Tabligh) to reach out at Nahdlatul Ulama's people".[38] He was now feeling a new political competition.

In 2005, the kiais' general ambivalence towards new Islamic groups had prompted some young Muslim liberals to visit kiais in Central Java in search of more support, in an apparent response to their competitors who have tried to gain the old men's favour.[39] One liberal Muslim intellectual complained that the old generation was too easily fascinated by the new Islamists' action in favour of Middle Eastern issues. "We tell the kiais that our priority is to alleviate poverty in Indonesia, and not join demonstrations concerning Middle Eastern affairs."[40]

The kiais' relative ambivalence was usually explained with three main arguments: First came the long experience traditionalists and reformists have in agreeing to disagree on theological matters, which is called "*khilaf*" or divergences of opinions. Secondly, the Nahdlatul Ulama was said to favour free speech, and did not "want to follow the harsh style of Hizbut Tahrir and Prosperous Justice Party/ PKS". A third argument was the consciousness of a sheer incapacity to control much of Indonesia's religious groups. Kiai Muchith

Muzadi admitted: "What we used to manage was like water in a glass, today it is like an ocean. New people get in, but we do not see them."[41] A kind of "mission impossible" was arising as proportions were different from what they were in the early twentieth century and during the Soeharto years.

Moreover, the kiais were fully aware of their recent gains. They saw NU's own traditions being adopted in non-NU circles. This included the mere fact that many new religious teachers, formerly called ustad, were now using the title "kiai", a sign, they said, that NU culture was spreading into the non-santri population. In the 1950s, modernist figures would not have liked to be called "kiai". Today, new santris take up the title. Popular preacher Aa Gym, called ustad two years earlier, was referred to on TV in 2005 as "Kiai Haji Abdullah Gymnastiar".

Other benefits have ripened in the past five years, especially in East Java. There, kiais or children of kiais have become regents (*bupati*) or deputy regents. Nahdlatul Ulama cadres are now often solicited as partners by secular politicians.[42] In early 2005, regent candidates were actively seeking the support of kiais for their election or re-election. In Jember, in March 2005, aides to bupati candidates said they had approached about ten kiais they thought were key factors to electoral success. In Situbondo, it was a mere three kiais who were said to be able to determine the success of a candidate. In Bangil, the bupati was the son of a kiai. In Gresik, four or five major kiais were holding the keys at the regency level. Even though the June 2005 local regent election results seemed to have been more negative than expected for Gus Dur's candidates, the NU had rarely been courted that much, on all levels. It is noteworthy that almost every presidential candidate in 2004 was happy with a NU-linked partner as vice-president, and the only one who did not take a NU partner was a candidate with religious legitimacy himself, the former Muhammadiyah chairman Amien Rais. Secular politicians have thus opened the way for the kiais's continued political role, a kind of established "dual function".[43]

With such proximity to power centres, can the major Islamic organizations keep their religious authority and prestige or will they abandon it to other institutions?

Closer Ties with Official Religious Authorities

Besides non-governement organizations such as the Nahdlatul Ulama and the Muhammadiyah, two state institutions have gained in importance — or at the very least in visibility: the State Islamic Higher Education Institutes (Institut Agama Islam Negeri, IAIN, now State Islamic Universities, UIN for some of them), and the Indonesian Council of Ulamas (MUI).[44]

Their closeness to old Islamic institutions (pesantren) comes from continuity with the new institutions harbouring people raised in the old system: students in IAIN often come from NU madrasahs or pesantren, and MUI's *ulama* are partly from the Nahdlatul Ulama. But mutual recognition between the private pesantren and the public education system had never been really formalized. This changed in 2004 when, in a surprising development, the Jakarta Islamic University (UIN) gave an honoris causa doctorate title to Indonesia's leading *ulama*, Kiai Sahal Mafudz, who, besides being the head of a major pesantren in Central Java, is also the Rois Aam of the Nahdlatul Ulama and the chairman of the MUI. What seemed to be a recognition of private pesantren education in a way also amounted to self-proclaimed superiority of the Islamic public university education. Interestingly though, senior kiais were happy to see the quality of pesantren education finally being recognized in public institutions of higher religious studies. This undoubtedly formalized the bonds between the private Islamic education system and the public education system, both being reinforced in their religious authority.

The state institution which has gained most in visibility since the fall of Soeharto in 1998 is certainly the National Ulama Council (MUI). When the MUI was created in 1975 under the New Order, it was marginal, and even after it grew, it was never an uncontested source of authority. In the 1990s, as E. Turmudi pointed out, the MUI was being dubbed the Council of Indonesian Snakes (*Majelis Ular Indonesia*).[45] Abdurrahman Wahid was one of the many critics of the institution used by Soeharto among other things to promote family planning, one of Indonesia's success stories. The MUI later became a bastion of conservatism. When Abdurrahman Wahid was president he suggested doing away with the Council, but the MUI was protected by the very diversity of its components, which included the top hierarchy (rois aam) of the Nahdlatul Ulama itself.

Kiais I met in Java in 2005 seemed to agree that the MUI had more authority than it used to have. It had even acquired a new role in foreign affairs with its intervention in the Malaysian dispute over Ambalat off the coast of East Kalimantan.[46] Without any change in status, the MUI's authority has been enhanced by the high public profile of its current secretary general, Din Syamsuddin, and the low profile of its president, Kiai Sahal.[47] Interestingly, one kiai in Yogyakarta attributed the rise of the MUI's authority to the proliferation of new religious groups. For him, the Council naturally ended up as a mediator, a "unifying force".[48]

However, as pointed out by M. Machasin elsewhere in this volume, it is not easy to decide what or who actually holds the authority, as one single *ulama* with great charisma might be heeded more than the Indonesian

Council of Ulama. How much the *fatwas* of both NU and the MUI are listened to is also a matter of debate. The old wisdom was to issue *fatwas* which were applicable.[49] Although they often do have an influence, not all *fatwas* have been successfully followed, which might explain the conservative *ulamas*' demand in 2005 that they receive binding legal status.

Finally, the MUI *fatwas* might matter less than expected as religious authority has become more diffuse with the rising importance of the media, books and films: for example, as intellectual Dawam Rahardjo noted rightly, without any *fatwa*, more women have been wearing the veil since the 1990s.[50] Confirming the TV's major influence, one female religious teacher admitted that TV film series showing demons ripping off the veil of pious women were making it difficult for her to minimize (or reinterpret) the obligation of veiling.[51]

PERSPECTIVES

Debates between the members of the Nahdlatul Ulama and the reformists of Muhammadiyah or Persis show that challenges to established religious authority have been pervasive over the past century. Today, the old NU generation tries to maintain a steady course ahead of the emerging competitors, the new preachers who use, as they themselves earlier did, modern communication techniques. They gained legitimacy while the old *ulama*, busy with political squabbling, looked at them with ambivalence, uncertain of who they were. But electoral perspectives tend to push the established Islamic organizations into a more defensive reaction.

In 2005, the most visible religious authority seemed to be the National Ulama Council (MUI), with its secretary general, Din Syamsuddin, who is also general chairman of Muhammadiyah. But the Council's *fatwas* issued in July 2005 against liberal Islam and pluralism may be more the sign of an increased willingness by the conservatives to assert their dominance than an effective ruling.

Parliament is so far the ultimate "religious" authority, just as President Sukarno wanted it to be, when he said that if the *sharia* had to be implemented it could only be through a vote by a democratically elected Parliament.[52] However, members of Parliament may have become increasingly dependent on religious authority. As a result of creeping Islamization, secular politicians now tend to look at the kiais as necessary partners in a more religion-conscious Indonesia.

Despite the abrupt end of Wahid's presidency, the kiais thus do not seem to have lost their power yet. But contrary to the years 1979–84 when older kiais were blaming politicians (*politikus*, "*tikus-tikus*", the rats) for the organization's decline,[53] urging the NU to quit politics, the prospects are different today as the stakes are much higher: Political authority is — or has been — within reach. The MUI may have assumed a more prominent place in religious discourse, but political life continues for the Nahdlatul Ulama.

Notes

1. The evolution of the two organizations in the course of the twentieth century makes it harder today to keep qualifying them as traditionalist and reformist, as both harbour conservatives and modernists.
2. The Muhamamdiyah figures came from Purwokerto and Yogyakarta, and were senior: Among them was the father of former Muhammadiyah leader Azhar Basyir, and also the father of Mrs Chamamah (Interview with Kiai Muchith Muzadi, an alumni of Tebuireng during the time of Hasjim Asj'ari, 20 March 2005).
3. BNO (15 May 1939): 4. The article is signed "Imad".
4. BNO (1 July 1939): 13.
5. *Adil* cited in BNO 19 (1 August 1939): 14.
6. Haidar "Nahdatul 'Ulama dan Islam di Indonesia: Pendekatan Fikih Dalam Politik". Ph.D. thesis, IAIN Syarif Hidayatullah, Jakarta, 1991, p. 141.
7. BNO 20 (15 August 1939): 12.
8. Verslag congres Nahdlatoel Oelama jang ke 15 di Kota Surabaya, 9–15 December 1940, p. 17.
9. After Kiai Asad had fought the Dutch, on his return in Situbondo, he lost his influence to the Nationalist party (PNI) which finally dominated both the administration and the army in that area. Under these circumstances, he went to Jakarta to seek assistance from Muhammad Natsir, a leading Masyumi figure (Interview in Jember, KH Muchith Muzadi, 5 March 2005).
10. Interview with Kiai Choiron Syakur, Bangil, 20 February 2005.
11. See A. Feillard, "Indonesian Traditionalist Islam's Troubled Experience with Democracy", in *Archipel*, no. 64 (2002): 117–44.
12. Regarding this episode, see among others, Martin van Bruinessen, "Back to Situbondo? Nahdlatul Ulama attitudes towards Abdurrahman Wahid's presidency and his fall", in *Indonesia: In Search of Transition*, edited by Henk Schulte Nordholt and Irwan Abdullah (Yogyakarta: Pustaka Pelajar, 2002), pp. 15–46; Laode Ida, *NU Muda: Kaum Progresif dan Sekularisme Baru* (Jakarta: Erlangga, 2004), p. 248; Abdul Munir Mulkhan. *Kiai Presiden, Islam dan TNI di Tahun-Tahun Penentuan* (Yogyakarta: UII Press, 2001), p. 243; Endang Turmudi, *Perselingkuhan Kiai dan Kekuasaan* (LkiS, 2004), p. 348; Greg Barton, *Abdurrahman Wahid, Indonesian President, Muslim Democrat: A View from the Inside* (Sydney and Honolulu: UNSW Press and University of Hawai'i Press, 2002), p. 414; Andrée Feillard, "Indonesian Traditionalist Islam's Troubled Experience with Democracy", in *Archipel*, no. 64 (2002): 117–44.

13. Again, in March 2005, NU politicians were going to the Kiai Langitan in search of support, but for the opposite purpose of trying to undo Gus Dur's authority.
14. Regarding the detail of the argument, see Feillard 2002, pp. 131–34.
15. Mulkhan, *Kiai Presiden, Islam dan TNI*, p. 36.
16. I would like to thank Robert Hefner for this remark on the sacralization of new religious figures.
17. By "modernist" Indonesians mean mostly intellectuals closer to the Reformist Muhammadiyah organization, and to the HMI Muslim Student organization.
18. PBNU, "Rancangan Materi Bahsul Masail ad-diniyah", NU congress, Jakarta: PBNU publication seri A _05/MNU-30/99, 1999, p. 37.
19. Interview with Dawam Rahardjo, May 2005, Jakarta.
20. Interview with the feminist NGO Sisters in Islam, Malaysia, November 2000.
21. See for example Afadlal et al., *Gerakan Radikal Islam di Indonesia dalam Konteks Terorisme Internasional* (Jakarta, LIPI, 2003): 279.
22. *Lubang Hitam Agama, Mengritik Fundamentalisme Agama, Menggugat Islam Tunggal* [The Black Hole of Religion, Criticizing Religious Fundamentalism, Challenging the Sole Islam Principle] (Yogyakarta: Rumah kata, 2005).
23. Majelis Tarjih PP Muhammadiyah, *Tafsir Tematik Al-Qur'an tentang Hubungan Sosial Antarumat Beragama* (Yogyakarta: Pustaka SM, 2000), 220 pp.
24. Personal observation at the debate in Yogyakarta, 7 October 2000.
25. On the occasion of a public debate on the book, *Ada pemurtadan di IAIN* [Apostasy at the Islamic University] by Hartono Ahmad Jaiz, 16 April 2005. Personal observation.
26. Interview with RMI leader KH Aziz Masyuri, Boyolali, November 2004. Islamic University researchers put the number of NU-linked pesantren at only about half the total. No statistics are available. The RMI was created in 1954.
27. "Rancangan Materi Bahsul Masail ad-diniyah", thirtieth NU congress, PBNU publication seri A -05/MNU-30/99, p. 23.
28. *Sabili* 8, no. XI (6 November 2003): 37.
29. Ibid.
30. Interview with Attabik Ali, 28 March 2005, Krapyak, Yogyakarta. The conflict is an old one with the traditionalists who prefer to use vision of the moon in Indonesia to determine the time of celebrations.
31. On these *fatwa*, see Noorhaidi Hasan, "Between Transnational Interest and Domestic Politics: Understanding Middle Eastern Fatwas on Jihad in the Moluccas", in *Islamic law and Society* 12, no. 1 (2005): 73–92(20), edited by Nico Kaptein.
32. Interview with KH Attabik Ali, 28 March 2005, Krapyak, Yogyakarta.
33. Interview with Regent Robbah Ma'sum, 4 April 2005.
34. Interview with Kiai Muchith Muzadi, East Java, 20 March 2005.
35. Interview with Kiai Khafidzin, Kaliwungu, Kendal, 24 August 2005.
36. Interview with Kiai Solahuddin bin Humaidi bin Irfan, Kendal, 24 August 2005.

37. Interview with Kiai Dimiyati, Kendal, Central Java, 24 Augusut 2005.
38. Interview with Kiai Dimiyati, Kendal, Central Java, 8 December 2006.
39. Interview with Kiai Dimiyati, Kendal, Central Java, 24 August 2005.
40. Interview with A. Baso, Jakarta, February 2005.
41. "Dulu, yang diatur adalah bagai air dalam glas, sekarang bagai lautan, ada yang baru masuk, tidak kelihatan". Kiai Muchith Muzadi, Jember, 5 March 2005.
42. Interviews in Gresik, Jember, Bangil, 4 april 2005.
43. The expression is from an Indonesian intellectual living in Europe who wrote: "NU should through mature discussion from down to top decide to apply a dual function, that is to become a political party and at the same time a religious, cultural and educational organization, for the stake of this country and our nation." (BDG Kusumo, Ceko, 28 October 2004).
44. On the question of *fatwas* and religious authority in Indonesia, see Nico Kaptein, "The Voice of the 'ulama: Fatwas and Religious Authority in Indonesia", in *Archives de Sciences Sociales des Religions* 2004, 125 (January–March 2004): 115–30.
45. Endang Turmudi, 2004, p. 267.
46. In March 2005, Din Syamsuddin visited Malaysia's Prime Minister (*Republika*, 15 March 2005).
47. Some senior kiais defend this low profile, and believe that giving few *fatwa* (*hemat fatwa*) may enhance credibility.
48. "Sebagai pemersatu", interview with K.H. Attabik Ali, Yogyakarta, 28 March 2005.
49. Ms Zakiah Drajat, a senior woman member of the MUI said (17 May 2005 on Metro TV) it was useless to ban Indonesian women from wearing bikinis, "because people would not listen to us", when asked about a controversial beauty pageant.
50. Interview with Dawam Rahardjo, 27 May 2005, Jakarta.
51. Interview with N. Muktharom, a female religious teacher, granddaughter of a major *ulama*, Boja, Central Java, 6 December 2006.
52. Deliar Noer, *Gerakan Modernen Islam di Indonesia* (Jakarta: LP3ES, 1980), pp. 301–306.
53. See Mitsuo Nakamura "The Radical Traditionalism of the Nahdlatul Ulama in Indonesia: A Personal Account of Its 26th National Congress, June 1979, Semarang", in *Journal of Southeast Asian Studies* (June 1980). At the 2004 thirty-first congress, Kiai Sahal did give a general reminder but it was different from 1979.

10

RELIGIOUS AUTHORITY AND THE SUPERNATURAL

Kees van Dijk

Many topics have been discussed by staff, researchers and visiting exchange fellows of the "Islam in Indonesia: the Dissemination of Religious Authority in Twentieth Century Indonesia" programme. In accordance with the subdivisions of the programme, their studies were clustered around four main themes: *ulama* and *fatwa*; tarekat; education; and dakwah. The results are diverse. Some scholars have focused on Islamic education and the changing role of the *ulama* in Indonesian society. Other research has concerned the issuing of *fatwa* and the impact of such authoritative rulings on society at large and on specific organizations or religious communities. Other topics pursued have been the importance of the Middle East for religious developments in Indonesia; the Shia community in Indonesia; the role of Islam in early nationalism; and individual Islamic organizations from the moderate to the radical, and those in between. As planned, two conferences have already been held; one on *fatwa*, the other on dakwah, and this gathering is the third, concluding one of the programme. The researchers affiliated with the programme were also present at many other scholarly meetings. Dr Nico Kaptein has calculated that they have participated in more than a hundred seminars and conferences in Indonesia, the Netherlands and elsewhere in the world.

Much of the research carried out within the framework of the programme has been of a sociological or historical nature. This may be one of the reasons why the spiritual factor has not been a main topic of research and has been touched upon only in the passing; unavoidable as in many instances it is to mention God-given and sanctioned authority and correct behaviour. In a sense we have, so to speak, forgotten God. Nevertheless, in Islam the rewarding and punishing God is the ultimate religious authority. For some Muslims, He is so in a very direct and concrete way. A striking example is provided by the well-known case of the stoning of a member of the Laskar Jihad found guilty of raping a thirteen-year-old girl in Ambon in March 2001. The man in question, Abdullah, was said to have undergone his punishment voluntarily. He had been given the opportunity to withdraw his confession, but refused. In the absence of four male witnesses (of good characters) to the rape it would have been impossible to sentence him had he retracted. His crime would have become a matter "between him and God" (Shoelhi 2002, p. 75). His consideration was said to have been that by evading justice on earth, the punishment in the Hereafter would be much more severe. It "was better to receive the mentioned sentence passed to be free of sin and the threat of torture in the Hereafter" (Shoelhi 2002, p. 73).

Whenever misfortune strikes, such pious Muslims consider it a punishment by God for the human disregard of religion. A prime example is Abu Bakar Ba'asyir. He and other leaders of the *Majelis Mujahidin Indonesia* (the Indonesian Jihad Fighters Council) are convinced that not obeying Islamic law inexorably brings disaster. A few months after the MMI had been founded on 7 August 2000, they sent a letter to President Abdurrahman Wahid with copies to a great many politicians, social and religious leaders, and editors of mass media. In it, Indonesia's "multi-dimensional crisis" of that moment was blamed on the being in office of a secular government and the wrath of God that not upholding Islamic law had evoked. All that had gone wrong — the severe economic crisis at that time, the widespread poverty, the large-scale violence in Aceh, the Moluccas, Kalimantan, and elsewhere in the country — was attributed to the absence of an Islamic government in Indonesia, though on other occasions Ba'asyir and MMI did not fail to mention "the Jewish foreign currency adventurer", George Soros and Zionist and Christian scheming as causes of Indonesia's misfortunes (Anshari 2002, pp. 68–75, 79, 102). Proof that with the introduction of Islamic law problems would almost automatically disappear they descried in contemporary developments in Aceh. Reading the signs wrongly and disregarding statements by the *Gerakan Aceh Merdeka* (GAM), Free Aceh Movement, claiming its struggle was a political and not a religious one, they thought that the

Acehnese no longer wanted independence. After all, Aceh was the first and only province in Indonesia which had been given the right to implement Islamic law (Anshari 2002, p. 90). The automatic salvation by God which the introduction of Islamic law will bring is presented by more Muslims as a strong argument in favour of its introduction. Outside Indonesia, Abdul Hadi Awang, president of the *Parti Islam SeMalaysia* (PAS), was sure that when Islamic legislation was in place it "would create 'willingness to surrender', as Muslims believe that punishment under Islamic laws will cleanse them of their sins" (Malaysia 2003, p. 121).

One of the other moments Ba'asyir testified to his image of God was shortly after the bombing of the Australian embassy in Jakarta on 9 September 2004. He explained that the explosion was a warning by God to the Indonesian nation for not having introduced Islamic law, and reiterated that this very oversight was also the reason for all the other disasters that had befallen Indonesia in previous years. Ba'asyir, who condemned the bombing, which he asserted, had been planned by the United States and Australia, expressed his sympathy to the relatives of the victims, taking the opportunity to say it had been God's will that the innocent passers-by had been killed by the explosion. They would have died anyway on 9 September, but maybe at a different time of the day.[1] (*Rakyat Merdeka*, 14 September 2004)

Ba'asyir is not alone in his view that what in old-fashioned Dutch is called *rampen van boven*, disasters from above, are punishments inflicted by God on a society which does not adhere to His commandments; though not all of them would include the Asian financial crisis of the late 1990s and protracted communal violence on the list. Still others, though sharing Ba'asyir's basic assumption, refuse to agree with the path he propagated making the government responsible for taking the lead. In their eyes it is not primarily a matter of the state proclaiming and enforcing Islamic law, but first and foremost of an ever-increasing number of individual Muslims following the prescripts of Islam. But whatever approach is chosen, the firm conviction that once Islamic law according to the scriptural interpretation such protagonists embrace is in place, the ideal society will be attained, strongly motivates their way of life. The introduction of Islamic law remains their answer to the question of how to appease God. Yet others may feel that sacrifices and special prayers are in order to avert further disasters. They may do so blaming the absence of a legal basis for the upholding of Islamic law for the tragedies that befall their nation, but can also think reconciliation rituals are in order, without making such a connection.

Religious convictions provide guidelines for Muslims and Christians to arrange their lives, and in some instances, to opt for a radical way of life. The governments of Malaysia and Singapore are well aware of this, organizing religious rehabilitation programmes for detained Muslims belonging to what is usually described in these countries as deviant religious teachings (*ajaran sesat*) or who allegedly had been hard-core members of the Jemaah Islamiyah. Perhaps we have not focused on the spiritual factor because for a religious person, whether he or she is a Muslim or a Christian, the ultimate authority of God is an obvious reality, which requires no discussion; while for an atheist who does not believe in God, it is difficult to grasp the meaning and implications of the belief in God for the life of individual believers. Yet another factor why God's authority has not been a central issue is that, at least where it concerns the examples presented in this paper, the religious beliefs adhered to are not exactly prime examples of a modern, enlightened Islam. Religious people share the belief in the ultimate authority of God, but only a minority, and we can find them in every religion, holding views which inspire them to embrace violence or even propagate it in their efforts to attain the society they envisage as one which is properly religious.

Participants in the "Islam in Indonesia: The Dissemination of Religious Authority in 20th Century Indonesia" programme have described concrete mechanisms influencing the religious life of individuals and groups and contributing to religious continuity and change. Maybe the time has come to initiate a second, follow-up programme to focus on the less tangible, transcendent aspects, turning away from the relations between human beings in the terrestrial world to those aspects of life which are concerned with the supernatural and the otherworld.

THE RELIGIOUS FACTOR

Whenever there are outbreaks of religious violence in Southeast Asia, the tendency among local political and religious leaders and in the scholarly community is to downplay its religious nature. At times it is even argued that what is taking place has nothing to do with religion. An explanation is sought by highlighting poverty, a high level of unemployment, poor education, economic and social discrimination and other such factors, or by casting suspicion on political manipulations. Even when religion is mentioned as a source of inspiration, it is these non-religious factors which are stressed in the explanation. Redressing social evils is presented as the solution with the same certainty and at times with the same zeal as that displayed by Muslims who propagate upholding Islamic law as the one and only answer to all that goes wrong. Such an approach may even backfire, as it has done in Thailand, by being perceived by part of the Islamic community as too materialistic.

Sometimes ignoring the religious aspect is politically wise and incontrovertibly the social realities mentioned are important and do play a role in creating the circumstances under which dissatisfaction may erupt. However, whatever is said and done, the dynamics of religious motivation remain. It is impossible ever to be completely sure and conditions differ from region to region and through time, but perpetrators of violence committed in the name of religion and those participating in religious conflicts do have a religious frame of reference. In their opinion, and in that of a wider group of Muslims, the civil wars in the Moluccas, in Poso, in south Thailand, the southern Philippines and Arakan in Myanmar, to confine ourselves to Southeast Asia, are religious conflicts (Samudra 2004, p. 189). They (and jihadists preaching violence are an example) may even overrate the appeal of religious concepts and sentiments and be scornful of the suggestion that social conditions lie at the root of the problems. People also do not act as they do only in pursuit of social and religious prestige and the desire to fit in with their social surroundings, or because some temporal religious authority tells or motivates them to do so.

The importance of the "religious factor" has been acknowledged in some recent studies about Christian violence. In the scholarly debates on the early crusades, a turning away from the materialist approach is to be discerned. Nowadays the religious motivation of the crusaders and the religious context of the crusades are taken far more seriously than in the past (Janse 2005, p. 72). Piety, the fear of God's punishment in the Hereafter, and penance are accepted as real driving forces which motivated devout Christians to become crusaders. Material considerations take second place: "The generalizations about motivation for profit, which always rested on insufficient evidence, look less and less convincing the more we know of the circumstances in which the early crusaders took the cross" (J.S.C Riley-Smith, *The First Crusaders and the Idea of Crusading*, cited by Janse 2005, p. 84). Popular perceptions lag behind this scholarly trend. Among the questions most frequently submitted to the website of the Society for the Study of the Crusade and the Latin Near East by secondary school students who have to write an essay about the crusades is a request for information to demonstrate that the crusades were not religiously motivated (Janse 2005, p. 71). In a similar vein, Ridley Scott's recent film, "The Kingdom of Heaven", drew heavy criticism from Christian fundamentalists exactly because Scott would have portrayed crusaders as being "driven by greed rather than piety" (*Sunday Times*, 24 April 2005).

The images believers nurture of God and of the life Hereafter, or more broadly their religious beliefs, are equally important, as are the immaterial aspects of the interaction between leaders and their followers or audience; for instance, the degree to which there is any room for doubt and discussion. The practices and beliefs touched upon in this chapter are not the exclusive property of radical groups. They are shared by many, but it is usually in a hard-line environment and only under specific circumstances that they may have undesired consequences, and may even lie at the root of violence. Scores of religious and non-religious organizations are characterized by strong internal cohesion and a high degree of loyalty of the members to the leaders and an unwavering commitment to the tenets of the group, but usually such traits do not constitute a threat to law and order. As Snouck Hurgronje (1857–1936) already argued in his recommendations to the Governor-General of the Netherlands Indies and the Ministry of the Colonies in The Hague when he wrote about mystical brotherhoods, the strict discipline within such institutions was usually confined to the sphere of religion, and only very rarely did it form a threat to law and order in the Netherlands Indies, or as he chose to rephrase this on other occasions, assumed a political nature (Gobée and Adriaanse 1957–65, pp. 1173, 1206).

What has struck me about the words and deeds of some contemporary Muslims is the firmness of their belief. People must have strong convictions to be prepared to commit suicide for their cause and their religion. Their commitment can be so intense that it even baffles their fellow fighters. In Iraq, one insurgency commander recently told a journalist of *Sunday Times* (8 May 2005) that he had difficulty in understanding the Arab suicide bombers he deployed: "They come with a belief and ideology that is non-negotiable and inflexible .... The mind and spiritual levels required are already there."

Not so many years ago such acts were associated with the Palestinian struggle; giving members of one of the largest Islamic organizations in Indonesia, the Nahdlatul Ulama, cause to discuss whether or not suicide bombings were permitted by Islam. They could do so because it was considered unthinkable that Southeast Asia would become the scene of suicide bombings. At that time, even extremists were still of the opinion that Southeast Asian Muslims were not ready for such a sacrifice and that groups in Southeast Asia contemplating suicide attacks were dependent on Muslims from the Middle East to carry out their plans. When the Jemaah Islamiyah was preparing its simultaneous attacks on the embassies of the United States and Israel, the High Commissions of Australia and Great Britain, and other targets in Singapore, scheduled to take place shortly after 11 September, the plan still called for the recruitment of Arab suicide bombers to drive the seven trucks which had to be detonated (White Paper 2003, p. 27). For a similar reason, a key Jemaah Islamiyah operative, Omar al-Faruq, is said to have been forced to cancel a suicide attack against three American warships and a Coast Guard vessel docked at Surabaya in May 2002 during a CARAT (short for Cooperation Afloat Readiness and Training) American-Indonesian naval exercise. The plotters were unable to recruit a sufficient number of Arabs to carry out the job (*Times*, 23 September 2002, p. 49). Reality at that moment may have been different. It is not beyond the bounds of possibility that part of the revelations about the plans of the Jemaah Islamiyah presented in the *Times* issue, of which the Surabaya plot is one, are untrue either because of a deliberate act of disinformation on behalf of the CIA or because Omar al-Faruq told his interrogators a number of lies.[2] Whatever the case, since the Bali bombings of 12 October 2002, we know that the situation has drastically changed and that radical Indonesian Muslims do carry out suicide attacks.

A firm belief in God also allowed one of the perpetrators of the Bali bombings, Abdul Aziz, better known as Imam Samudra, to build up a solidly wrought mental construction to justify his deeds. Using quotations from the Qur'an and examples from the Hadith, and when necessary recalling events in early Islamic history, he attempted to demonstrate that he is right and did nothing wrong, and that his interpretation of Islam was the correct one. Imam Samudra was also convinced that jihad fighters are closer to God than religious scholars because they are in constant danger. The latter confine themselves to studying religious texts and giving lectures and sermons. The former felt that they could die any moment and hence their hearts were in the process of being cleansed. Jihad fighters, he writes, were assured of God's guidance which implied that their religious rulings (*fatwas*) and opinions were closer to the truth than those of others who did not share their experience (Samudra, pp. 172–73).

Imam Samudra's other motivation — which he shares with a wider group of Muslims — is an equally rock-solid belief that the Americans and Jews are waging a crusade to dominate the world and destroy Islam and that, in reaction to this, the Americans and their allies may be attacked anywhere in the world (see Samudra 2004, pp. 149–50, 188). Somehow Imam Samudra succeeded in convincing himself that the Western tourists killed in Bali were non-civilians. He regrets that Indonesians were among those killed in Bali, but calls this an "error" (using the English word) which can happen during a war. "Because man indeed was created with all his weaknesses" (Samudra 2004, p. 154).

GROUP COHESION

The Jemaah Islamiyah responsible for the bombing attacks in Indonesia provides plenty of material for reflection. In the early years of its existence, before the hunt for its members was on, it was a tightly organized hierarchical group. Social cohesion within the group was strong. Observers have pointed out the kinship and marital ties which connect the core members to one another. The Jemaah Islamiyah formed a close-knit community in which the forging of marriage ties was one of the ways to cement relationships. Kinship ties fortified this still further. Brothers, fathers and sons, and sons-in-law and fathers-in law all found their niche in the group; as did of course sisters, mothers and daughters, but they had a less prominent role to play.

The Jemaah Islamiyah is not alone in showing these characteristics. Family ties play a conspicuous role in the Abu Sayyaf, or Al Harakatul al Islamiyah (Islamic Movement) as its members prefer to style themselves, a terrorist group operating in the southern Philippines, though in this case this trait is also palpable because the Abu Sayyaf is essentially a local group, with a specific home base: Basilan, Jolo and adjacent islands. The founding father of Abu Sayyaf was Abdurajak Abubakar Janjalani, a fundamentalist ustad, of whom it is said that he "disapproved of TV, movies, dancing, songs on radio, even laughing with bared teeth" (*Asiaweek.com* 5 May 2000). After he was killed on the island of Basilan in an exchange of fire with the police in December 1998, his younger brother, Khadaffy Abubakar Janjalani, took over. In February 2004 yet another Janjalani brother, Hector, was sentenced to life imprisonment for his role in the kidnapping of an American, Jeffrey Schilling, in August 2000. He was arrested in Manila in December 2000 for illegal possession of drugs. Another relative, Khadaffy Abubakar Janjalani's cousin, Alhamzer Manatad Limbong, alias Commander Kosovo, was arrested in March 2004. He was said to have commanded an armed assault on the Dos Palmas beach resort on Palawan in May 2001 and was believed to be the person who had beheaded an American, Guillermo Sobero, kidnapped during the raid by the Abu Sayyaf, in June 2001.

Marriage within the group itself is a typical feature of exclusive communities considering themselves to be a vanguard in society, even the more so in a society where an arranged marriage or marriage without prolonged courtship is not an unfamiliar and alien feature as it is in the West. For that matter, it can be observed in the higher echelon of the Indonesian army and other elite groups, including those in which members consider themselves to be a religious elite. Indonesian pesantren are a good example. In this environment the selection of a son-in-law on the basis of his religious qualifications is not uncommon.[3] Radical Indonesian Muslims likewise have no problem with arranging marriages with members sharing their own social and religious status. The director of Abu Bakar Ba'asyir's Al-Mukmin pesantren near the city of Surakarta, Farid Ma'aruf, was quite frank about this: marriages between male and female religious teachers and male and female pupils of the pesantren were preferred (Qodir 2003, p. 73). Arranging marriages was also practised in the Laskar Jihad, where the bride was usually selected by the wife of the religious teacher of the husband-to-be (Noorhaidi 2005, p. 219). Laskar Jihad leaders justified such a custom as following the tradition prevailing in the time of the Prophet Muhammad (Baker n.d., p. 19). We should also not forget that, for the future bride, the religiosity of the man she is going to marry may be one of his major assets. To give an example, the second wife of Noordin Mohamad Top, a girl from Malang in East Java, had known her husband only one day before marrying him. After she had been arrested for hiding her husband, who is a JI bomb expert wanted for his role in the Bali and JW Marriot Hotel bombings, the Indonesian police explained that she had married her husband because she considered him to be a good Muslim.[4] Though arranged marriages are not uncommon in religious circles, the Jemaah Islamiyah seems to have carried the principle almost to the extreme. Indonesian intelligence officers were surprised by the number of such marriages within the Jemaah Islamiyah community, a practice which they suspected was also intended to foster ties between Indonesian and Malaysian members, and, to a lesser extent those in the Philippines (*Straits Times Interactive* 8 September 2004). They had charted more than a hundred of them.

THE OATH OF LOYALTY

Absolute loyalty to the leader has formed another characteristic of the Jemaah Islamiyah. On entering the organization members swear an oath of loyalty (*bay'a, bai'ah, bai'at*). Imam Samudra even swore an oath to the person who had recruited him before he left for Afghanistan. He promised that he would be faithful to the commands of God and the Prophet, would be faithful to his leaders as long as they did not act in contravention of the commands of God and the Prophet, and would give precedence to waging holy war over personal, family or group interests (Adisaputra 2006, p. 71). Members of the Jemaah Islamiyah have taken the swearing of such an oath of loyalty very seriously. In an interview with Malaysian TV, detained Malaysian Jemaah Islamiyah members have said that no one dared to break such an oath out of fear of the wrath of God. As a former leader who left the Jemaah Islamiyah explains: leaders and preachers of the Jemaah Islamiyah stress that a person who breaks his vow of loyalty to the leader of the Jemaah Islamiyah has to account for this in this world and, as God has been a witness to the swearing of the oath, in the Hereafter (Abbas 2005, p. 313). Abbas (2005, p. 314) also observes that members of the Jemaah Islamiyah are of the opinion that leaving the organization means leaving Islam. Consequently, one of the "misunderstandings" addressed by religious teachers in Singapore, who counsel arrested Jemaah Islamiyah members and their families, is that breaking one's oath of loyalty does not mean that one is no longer a Muslim (*Straits Times Interactive* 18 October 2005).

In this respect the Jemaah Islamiyah could also link up with a long-standing religious tradition. The taking of such an oath of loyalty, and equally important of secrecy, is a well known practice in the Islamic world and in Indonesian Islam. Mystical orders are one of the institutions in which the oath-taking is practised. Snouck Hurgronje's observations about the non-political nature of Indonesian mystical brotherhoods were made in relation to the oath-taking and the ensuing obedience to its leaders. He unkindly overstates his case by describing the initiate as *perinde ac cadaver* and as members becoming "like dead persons" in the hand of their spiritual leader (Hurgronje 1923–27 I, pp. 275–76).

Probably borrowing from this tradition, the oath was an equally popular practice in local chapters of the Sarekat-Islam, the first large Indonesian nationalist movement in colonial times. In Cirebon it was believed that people who broke their pledge would immediately go insane. They might even die (Sarekat 1975, p. 75). In Banten, death in the near future was also believed to be punishment for violating one's oath (Sarekat 1975, p. 6). In Kudus, new members first had to recite the confession of faith three times, after which they had to take a sip of water. Thereupon they had to state that if they did not honour their promise they would burst into pieces like the water they had just drunk (Sarekat 1975, p. 131).[5] At times, an oath was thought to function as a special means to cement relationships between members, creating ties "stronger than those of blood" (Sarekat 1975, p. 291).

The swearing of an oath functions in two ways. Its strengthens cohesion and obedience and at the same time makes an organization more exclusive and membership more thrilling. In a way it supplements the feeling of exclusivity, which can lead to the shunning of non-members, and even, the early history of the Sarekat-Islam provides examples of this, to a complete boycott of them extending to such important life events as burial rites. It has to be noted that Muslims with the strictest interpretation of monotheism object to the swearing of an oath of allegiance. Among them are the members of the Laskar Jihad, but in this group the God-sanctioned devotion to their own flock and aversion to the outsider contributes to an equally strong cohesion (Noorhaidi 2005, pp. 164–66, 183).

The Sarekat-Islam was a manifestation as well as a catalyst of a sudden upsurge in expressions of dissatisfaction among Indonesians in the first decades of the twentieth century, which echoed in the emergence of an unruly, defiant Malay-language press. Confronted with this changing mood, Dutch people felt uncomfortable, even afraid. Not only had a modern Indonesian mass organization emerged, an institution hitherto unknown, but that same organization continued to embody some traditional traits, which, they knew, could spell danger. Troubled by similar apprehensions, Snouck Hurgronje, who in some of his recommendations had argued that mystical brotherhoods very rarely formed a threat to law and order, had not always been overly confident about their peaceful nature. Writing about such institutions operating outside Indonesia, he explained that when leaders of such brotherhoods thought that they could profit from political upheavals, "their statement that the time for the 'holy war' has come is a divine command for their pupils" (Snouck Hurgronje 1923–27 IV, p. 75). He made his observation in an article "An Arab Ally of the Government of the Netherlands Indies" (that is, *Sèjjid Othmân ibn Jahja al-Alawi*) published in the *Nieuwe Rotterdamsche Courant* of 14 and 16 October 1886. In his article, Snouck Hurgronje draws attention to the sudden eruptions of Islamic risings against European colonial powers which more often than not had taken the authorities by surprise and the role mystical groups played in them.[6] As people familiar with Indonesian history know, the article appeared in the NRC less than two years before the "peasants" revolt' in Banten erupted, an uprising so well described and analysed by Sartono Kartodirdjo (1966). In the rebellion, which aimed at the establishment of an Islamic state, mystical brotherhoods, *tarekat*, played a vital role. The collective excitement of its members, who "could at any time be mobilized as active crowds to engage in a common undertaking, i.e. the actualization of the millenarian ideas" served to "integrate unrest and discontent" (Kartodirdjo 1966, p. 26). In his study, Sartono occasionally does mention the oath — in Javanese *bengat* — defined by him as the "official contract between *guru* and *murid*" (Kartodirdjo 1966, p. 362). Maybe because of the definition he chooses to give, Sartono stresses the "blind obedience" and the *perinde ac cadaver* already mentioned by Snouck Hurgronje, but it may also be that he just takes Snouck Hurgronje's observations for granted (Kartodirdjo 1966, pp. 159–60).

Sartono does not touch upon the supernatural aspects involved in the swearing of an oath; the fear of punishment by God that follows breaking it. Only in one place does Sartono gives a glimpse of what is at stake. He does so when he discusses the initiation rites of the *Ilmu Tarik* brotherhood established in 1866 by Tubagus Djajakusuma, leader of an insurrectionist movement at the end of the 1860s, but at that time still Patih of Lebak. Discussing the "vow of solidarity with the teacher" a new member had to pledge, Sartono emphasizes "the absolute obedience to his spiritual superior" the pledge entails and continues: "No wonder that the people interrogated by the colonial government did not say anything about Djajakusuma's plan" to raise in rebellion (Kartodirdjo 1966, p. 131).

The oath and the fear of breaking it is not some antiquated custom. At present it is practised not only in the Jemaah Islamiyah, but also in a variety of other religious organizations. One is the equally scriptualist Negara Islam Indonesia (NII), Indonesian Islamic State, of which the so-called IXth region, the NII Komandemen Wilayah IX, is perhaps the most sect-like of all such groups active in Indonesia nowadays, with stories circulating about members being brainwashed and being forced to collect money for the groups in whatever way they could, legal and illegal, for instance, by deceiving other Muslims and even their parents, or stealing from them (Abduh n.d., p. 123, *Media Indonesia*, 18 February 2002). And, however routed and scattered the Abu Sayyaf may be at the moment, the oath taken by its members apparently enforces its command structure and their willingness to fight. In March 2005, when twenty-two people were killed when the police stormed a prison in Manila where Abu Sayyaf inmates had started a revolt, the spokesman for the Abu Sayyaf, Abu Solaiman, said that when "we took our oath to be part of this group, there are only two ends for us, victory or martyrdom" (INQ.net 17 March 2005). He added that those who had died during the retaking of the prison "got the ultimate victory we are all dying to have", that is they had become martyrs.

The importance of the oath is also underlined by the fact that some authors list the belief that danger will befall a person who breaks his pledge of secrecy among the characteristics of contemporary deviant sects in Singapore and Malaysia (Hassan 2003, p. 174). Contemporary examples are not difficult to find. The taking of an oath, for instance, had a very prominent place in a Malaysian group which acquired notoriety recently: the traditional healing and *silat* group, *Pertubuhan Persaudaraan Ilmu Dalam al-Ma'unah* (The Brotherhood of Magical Power al-Ma'unah). The Al-Ma'unah Brotherhood, which had been registered by the Selangor Department of Islamic Affairs in April 1999, had its headquarters in Kelang in Selangor, but also had members in other Malaysian States. By July 2000, membership would have reached 1,700 (Mohamed 2003, p. 181). Among them were police and army officers and civil servants. Al-Ma'unah's leader was a lorry driver, Mohammed Amin bin Mohammed Razali, who had previously been employed as a radio operator in the army, but had been discharged from service because of the use of drugs (Mohamed 2003, p. 176). The members called him Ustad Amin or simply Sheikh.[7] He made no secret that he believed Islamic law should come into force in Malaysia.

Amin had drawn attention to al-Ma'unah by advertising in the PAS magazine *Harakah*. During meetings and training sessions he had prepared his followers for a jihad, stressing that at all times a Muslim should be ready to wage such a war. Holy war was also propagated on the group's website, <al_maunah.tripod.com>. Drawing his examples from Bosnia, Chechnya, Afghanistan and the Moluccas, Amin told al-Ma'unah members that the reason Muslims in these regions had been slaughtered was that they had not prepared themselves in advance to ward off an assault that was an ever-present threat. Members of al-Ma'unah should be able to fight, not only because they might have to join the jihad in Ambon, Chechnya and other places outside Malaysia, but also to be ready should an enemy attack the Muslim community in Malaysia (Mohamed 2003, pp. 79, 102).

On entering al-Ma'unah and before being instructed in the esoteric knowledge taught by Amin, new members had to take an oath and swear that as long as Amin obeyed God and the Prophet, they would obey him (Mohamed 2003, p. 180). Amin's authority was undisputed. Followers thought he was a *wali*, a saint. They were terrified that they might lose his blessings (*berkat*) or that the esoteric knowledge (*ilmu*) he had taught them would weaken or not work at all should they disagree with Amin or question his words (Mohamed 2003, p. 180). He also persuaded them to buy from him special, magically endowed twin swords (*pedang kembar*), probably a reference to the two-pointed sword, *Dhu al-Faqar*, given by the Prophet Muhammad to Ali, which he made them believe were a gift from saints in heaven (Mohamed 2003, p. 262). The swords were an additional means to enforce his authority. If members disregarded their religion and ignored a call to a jihad by Amin, the swords would turn against them (Mohamed 2003, p. 183). His followers were also sure that the magic swords would strike them if they were to break their oath of loyalty (Mohamed 2003, p. 183).

The author of the book from which I have these facts, Zabidi Mohamed, was able to understand such behaviour and such fears very well. He himself had been a senior member and legal advisor of al-Arqam (and in 1994 had been put under Internal Security Act (ISA) arrest for this), a popular scriptural mystical sect which had been banned by the Malaysian government in 1994. In his years in al-Arqam, he himself had been a fanatical, gullible member. He had been part of an organization in which pupils had to surrender to their teacher as a "corpse", as he chooses to express this (Mohamad 2003, p. 312). He had continued to follow al-Arqam's leader, Ustad Ashaari bin Muhammad, even after the latter had told his flock that they could call him *Rasulullah,* Apostle of God (Mohamed 2003, p. 94).[8] Members accepted Ashaari bin Muhammad's directives, however illogical they might seem, without any reservation. God would later reveal the wisdom (*hikmah*) behind them (Mohamed 2003, p. 310).

Disguised as soldiers and army officers, al-Ma'unah members raided two military armouries in the state of Perak and stole over a hundred rifles and a number of rocket launchers in July 2000. After having accomplished this they fled into the jungle, where Amin told his followers — of whom some probably had had no idea in advance of what he intended to do — that the holy war to establish an Islamic state in Malaysia had begun. "People above", Amin also explained to one of his adjutants, wanted them to act quickly. The person in question, thought that by "people above" Amin meant the saints in the world of spirits (*alam ghaib*) (Mohamed 2003, p. 186). Amin's warning was clear. Those who tried to desert would be killed. Their blood was *halal,* they could be killed (Mohamed 2003, pp. 231, 235).[9] Though doubt crept in among some of his followers, initially they did not dare to surrender to government troops. The swords, stuck in the ground around their camp were two-edged: an effective barrier against an attack by the army and police, and instrument of punishment for those who deserted Amin's jihad (Mohamed 2003, p. 267). Afterwards some seemed to have no regret that two non-Muslim prisoners taken had been killed. That was fate. God would later reveal the hidden purpose (*hikmah*) of their execution and of the whole event (*hikmah*) (Mohamed 203, pp. 316–17). After their arrest, members were incarcerated in the Pudu Prison in Kuala Lumpur. Zabidi Mohamed (2003, p. 112) tells us this prison is a special one. He claims that no matter how much *ilmu* a prisoner might possess, his powers would disappear after he had entered Pudu Prison.

In neighbouring Thailand the authorities are very much aware of the importance of the oath sworn by Muslims. In the past years, a number of times they have called upon the highest Islamic official in the country, the Sheikul Islam or Chula Ratchamontri, to counter the oath sworn by Islamic insurgents fighting for an independent Patani State in the south of the country. The Thai authorities do so in a situation in which they are at an utter loss how to maintain law and order. Dormant for years, resistance to Bangkok rule in the southernmost part of the country has taken an unprecedentedly violent turn since the beginning of 2004. Killings take place on a daily base. The prime targets are policemen, soldiers, village defence volunteers, teachers and village and district officials, but garbage collectors, railway personnel and other government employees have also fallen victim. Construction workers, rubber-tappers, food hawkers, high school pupils and other ordinary citizens have also been attacked. Some victims were hacked to death with machetes, were knifed, or had their throats slit. Others were shot. Most attacks are carried out by assailants riding pillion on motorcycles. Bombing attacks have also become frequent; not yet quite daily but almost so. The Thai authorities fear that tens of thousands of young Muslims are involved. From the interrogation of those detained, it was surmised that many of those who had joined the insurgency movement had sworn an oath of secrecy. Because people who had been arrested were tight-lipped, it was speculated in July 2004 that the Sheikul Islam planned a trip to the south, to administer another oath, to revoke the other "separatist" one (*Bangkok Post*, 8 July 2004). The idea resurfaced in April 2005 when the Southern Border Provinces Peace-building Command, the institute established in March 2004 to coordinate security efforts, said that it would contact the Sheikul Islam "to free young Muslims from an oath of secrecy they swore to separatist insurgents" (21 April 2005).

INVULNERABILITY MAGIC

As the belief in the swords Amin sold to his followers indicates, the supernatural had a very important place in al-Ma'umah's thinking. People were drawn to the movement because they were impressed by Amin's supposed magical and healing powers. Once a member, the stories they told about him became more fantastic. It was rumoured that Amin could walk on water and fling away and kill an enemy just by lifting his eyebrow (Mohamed 2003, p. 176).[10] The members themselves began to believe in invulnerability magic (*ilmu kebal*) and were convinced that bullets and fire could do them no harm. They also acquired lesser abilities. The group's website showed photographs of members who put their hands in boiling oil or had tree trunks thrown onto their chests to demonstrate the magical powers they possessed: scenes not uncommon in such sects.

This belief in invulnerability and other magical powers is yet another element worthy of consideration. It is a trait that runs through Indonesian and Malaysian history, and has manifested itself in Singapore and South Thailand, where resistance against expanding Thai Buddhist state power in the early decades of the twentieth century linked up with the same combination of mystical groups, belief in invulnerability and the use of amulets as in colonial Indonesia, and has, as the al-Ma'unah affair already indicates, its present-day counterparts. Sartono Kartodirdjo (1966, p. 321) notes that belief in invulnerability is an "outstanding feature" of the millenarian movements he studied. Presenting an overview of its occurrence in colonial and contemporary Southeast Asia would be a lengthy, time-consuming exercise. Taking in account the related wider belief in magical powers would take even more time and space. Nevertheless, one example, again taken from Sartono Kartodirdjo (1966, p. 232), will be presented here to indicate how powerful a force it could be in the past and has been in the present. Sartono describes how on the morning of 10 July 1888, one of the leaders of the peasants' revolt, Haji Mohamad Asik, ordered his followers who gathered together in great numbers at Bendung in Banten "to drink holy water in order to make them invulnerable in battle". Thereupon he blessed the assembled crowd. Elsewhere, at Trumbu, insurgents held "purification rites".

Since World War II, groups of which the members were sure that they had acquired invulnerability and other magical fighting powers have caused trouble in Malaysia, Singapore, Thailand and Indonesia a number of times. In Thailand and Malaysia, some of the confrontations of the central government with such groups over time have become "historical landmarks", symbols feeding Muslim discontent with concrete examples of cruel suppression by the state. In Thailand, distrust nourished by the authorities of villagers who combined the belief in magic with martial arts may well have been the reason why Thai government forces acted against villagers of Nyior in Narathiwat on 28 April 1948, killing more than a hundred people, according to some recollections as many as 400.

In Malaysia, the confrontation with al-Ma'unah was not the only one of its kind in recent history. Fifteen years earlier, in November 1985, there had been an even bloodier encounter between security forces and Malaysian Muslims aspiring to set up an Islamic state. The consequences of what happened then can be witnessed to this day. The incident became part of the propaganda war between the two main Malay political parties in Malaysia, PAS, propagating a fundamentalist Islamic state, and UMNO, keen to present an Islamic state in which tolerance and reason prevail as the ideal antidote to this. It also provided Islamic preachers who were the founding fathers of the Jemaah Islamiyah with a strong argument to win over their initial following.

The scene was Memali, a village near Baling, a PAS stronghold in the state of Kedah, where a religious teacher and PAS leader, Ustad Ibrahim Mahmood, better known as Ibrahim Libya, had taken refuge. Ibrahim Libya, who had studied in Libya, India and Egypt, was accused by the authorities of preaching the establishment of an Islamic state by violent means. An Internal Security Act arrest warrant had been issued in 1984, but in September of the following year a first attempt to arrest him had been foiled by the villagers who had rallied to Ibrahim Libya's defence. Ibrahim Libya and his followers had prepared themselves for a harsher second confrontation that was bound to come by wearing amulets and drinking medicine to achieve invulnerability (Metzger 1996, p. 82). On 19 November 1985, the police made a new attempt to apprehend him. A five-hour fight between villagers armed only with simple weapons and the police equipped with M-16 rifles and deploying armoured cars followed. Shots were fired and tear gas was used. Ibrahim Libya and thirteen villagers, all male, and four policemen died.

In Singapore, sect-like groups of which the members were sure they were invulnerable had a share in the racial riot which erupted on 20 July 1964, on the Islamic holiday of Maulud, costing the lives of twenty-three people. A few years later, the then-Prime-Minister, Lee Kuan Yew, called to mind how people prepared for the riots by "getting into a trance, 'believing they were invulnerable to machetes and bullets after undergoing certain rituals' " (*Straits Times Interactive* 18 February 2002). He added that in 1987, anticipating new racial riots, members of a martial art group equipped themselves with sashes believed to make the wearer invulnerable.

Most recently, the belief in invulnerability took centre stage in the escalating violence in South Thailand, where Muslims are striving for an independent state. Among the most shocking manifestations of the upsurge of violence since January 2004 is what happened on 28 April 2004. In the early morning of that day, hundreds of young men, many of them clad in black and wearing red headbands, attacked some ten police posts and government buildings in Yala, Patani and Songkhla, in what was supposed to be an attempt to seize weapons. During the assaults they shouted "God is Great", "It's time for liberation", "We are ready to die for God" and other such slogans (*The Nation* 29 April 2004). Most were armed with only machetes and knives. A few had firearms. Security forces lay in waiting. The authorities had known of the attacks in advance through the interrogation of prisoners. The outcome was a bloodbath. One-hundred-and-eight insurgents, most of them young men in their teens and early twenties, were killed. Among the dead was an entire football team from a village in Songkhla. Only seventeen arrests were made.

Afterwards politicians and commentators expressed their bewilderment about the suicidal nature of the attack of the "jihadists". Due to the utter unfamiliarity with Islam of Buddhist Thais, and Prime Minister Thaksin Shinawatra and other Thai politicians must be included in this observation, the point was missed that not all the blame should be laid, as often is done in Thailand, on a growing Wahhabi influence among Muslims in the country and that the young men who participated in the attacks were of a different type to the al-Qaeda and Middle Eastern suicide bombers. The assailants may not have had death in mind.[11] Many of them wore amulets. One of them who later turned himself in, revealed that after evening prayers on 27 April, one of the insurgents' leaders, an ustad, a teacher at an Islamic school, had instructed him to drink "sacred water" which would make them safe and "invisible to police and soldiers" (*Bangkok Post* 13 May 2004). Another one admitted that he had attended a camp where he learned special prayers and techniques making him invulnerable to bullets. The instructors had a convincing way to show that the magic worked. They held a loaded revolver to his head which did not discharge a bullet when the trigger was pulled (*NST Online* 13 September 2005). The Commander of the 4th Army (the troops stationed in the south) also claimed that some of the assailants had been told "not to fear anyone after drinking the holy water, that they would be invulnerable and invisible to soldiers and police" (*NST Online* 5 May 2004). To attain extra security, at least in the case of one attack, consecrated sand was scattered just before the attack was launched to thwart operations by the army and police (Krue Se 2005, p. 1). Ismail Rayalong, one of the separatist leaders, headed a mystical group — the Tarekat Hikmatullah Abadan, the Divine Wisdom (Magical Power) Order — teaching the art of invincibility and other supernatural powers (*The Nation* 1 September 2004). Members had to swear an oath of secrecy. Later it was also reported that an alleged separatist had been arrested in Malaysia who convinced people that a special ceremony of bathing with water would make them invisible. He had asked 350 baht for the cure. Among those who he could count as his customers would have been a number of 28 April assailants (*Bangkok Post* 16 August 2004).[12]

In Indonesia, the belief in invulnerability and other magical powers has also occasionally entered the political arena in recent years. One of the moments it did was in the summer of 2001, at a time when it had become very likely that Abdurrahman Wahid would be impeached and deposed as president. When part of his Nahdlatul Ulama following flocked together in East Java and threatened to travel to Jakarta to prevent this from happening, they were taught a variety of skills. How to climb a barbed-wire fence and how to knock down a concrete wall with bare fists were but two of these (indications, by the way, that the powers on offer adjust to changing times and new inventions). Both would have been needed should the demonstrators have had to storm the Congress Building where Abdurrahman Wahid's fate would be decided. In the end, the furious Nahdlatul Ulama supporters did not get the opportunity to display their skills in Jakarta. Abdurrahman Wahid and other Nahdlatul Ulama leaders had succeeded in persuading their hot-headed supporters not to execute their plans and to stay in East Java.

Another example of the mobilization of people who were alleged to possess invulnerability skills took place about a year later in March 2002. This time the person that had to be rescued was an equally important politician, the general chairman Akbar Tanjung, of one of the largest political parties, Golkar, who had been accused of misusing state funds and faced arrest. A number of people announced peaceful demonstrations in his support, which in the political constellation prevailing at that time might well end up being not particularly peaceful. One of the persons who did so was Fahri Andi Laluasa, chairman of the youth wing of Golkar, the Angkatan Muda Partai Golkar. Fahri said that among the demonstrators would be *pendekar* (which, though this is not the correct meaning because of what I read about demonstrations in Jakarta, I tend to associate with magically endowed sword-waving rowdies from Banten) who were invulnerable to stabbing (*anti bacok*) and bullets (*Rakyat Merdeka* 7 March 2002).

There is an uneasy relationship between obtaining magical skills and displaying them. People who believe they have acquired supernatural powers are tempted to test their skills and show off in public. In this context I like to refer to an observation made by the military commander of Central Java about some of the clashes which took place in his province between supporters of two Islamic political parties, the PKB and PPP, in the run-up to the general election of 1999. The blame for the disturbances was put on inflammatory speeches given by local religious leaders. The military commander of Central Java suggested an additional reason for the violence. He claimed that invulnerability mantras had been handed out by *kiai* on both sides and, when fighting broke out, people had wanted to put their newly acquired magical power to the test. The result had been that "many hands were cut off by swords" (*Jakarta Post* 5 June 1999).[13]

In theory, showing-off is not done. Practitioners of magic may be of the opinion that a display of invulnerability skills is not permitted, or that esoteric knowledge, as a gift from God, can only be taught to a select group of followers, to those leading a devout life. The Indonesian founder of al-Ma'unah, who had to avoid falling into disrepute because of the behaviour of Amin's sect, professed to be quite shocked when he heard about the public display of their skills by the Malaysian al-Ma'unah members. In an interview he was adamant that such skills could only be mastered with the help of God and thus should not be exhibited. They could also not be a source of pride. What Amin practised was black magic (Mohamed 2003, pp. 140–41).

Other teachers tell the same story. In the introduction to an Indonesian book on *ilmu kebal*, the "science of invulnerability", published a few years ago, the author recounts the reaction of "*pendekar pesantren*", the teachers of *ilmu kebal*, to his request for information. Many refused to cooperate. They did not want their knowledge to become public and were not prepared to provide information for the book he intended to write. One of them mentioned as the reason for his refusal the fact that "*santri*" possess only *ilmu selamat*, which the author admits is a very wide term, but judging from the text can be translated as knowledge to protect (from danger) (Masruri 1999, pp. 5–6) *Ilmu kebal* was for the "*jagoan*", a word which this author in another section of his booklet uses in the meaning of a *silat* fighter (Masruri 1999, p. 25).

Masruri (1999, p. 40) cannot deny that displaying magic gives prestige (*gengsi*).[14] The illustrations in his own book testify to how rewarding showing-off is. Another point is that a person convinced that he is invulnerable gains extra confidence. And, what is the use of having acquired special skills when these cannot be tested or displayed? An exception, of course, are those who teach or sell the techniques of acquiring supernatural skills and the paraphernalia that go with them and receive veneration, esteem, and financial rewards in return. The flesh is weak and the temptations are great. For some bravado and showing-off seem almost as important as mastering esoteric knowledge. This certainly holds true for some of the Nahdlatul Ulama members rallying in support of Abdurrahman Wahid. They did display the strength and skills they had acquired in public. People had cars driven over their bodies while lying on the ground. The most peculiar aspect of their mobilization, at least to me, brings the bravado even more sharply into focus. It was the setting of the training; a combination of scenes from a spy movie with an apparent love of everything that is military. People trained in secret camps hidden in the forest. Journalists who were allowed to visit the training ground were blindfolded so that they could not reveal the location afterwards. The trainees were dressed in camouflage kit. Their faces were blackened. Branches with leaves to make them even more part of their surrounding completed the outfit. To prepare them for battle in broad daylight in downtown Jakarta, they received training which equipped them to fight a war in the forest. The fact that they called themselves *Pasukan Berani Mati* (Troops Who Fear No Death) is another indication of the combined attraction of invulnerability beliefs, military posturing, and playing at being soldiers.

CONCLUDING REMARKS

In the examples presented here, it has been social and political circumstances which ripened the climate in which people came to resist state power, but it was religious ideas which made them prepared to act: magic, belief in invulnerability, and the defence and promotion of the Faith. The role belief in magic played in the uprisings against colonial rule and in a number of recent examples of religious-inspired dissent spilling over into violence falls within the sphere of religion. It concerns behaviour confined to that segment of the larger Islamic society which is usually described as the traditionalist Islamic community, but as such classifications do not fit reality completely, also go beyond it. The cultural embedment is that of the devout Islamic community, in Java often denoted with the term *kaum santri*, even that of those who are prepared to fight for their faith. In his famous book, *The Religion of Java*, Clifford Geertz tends to dissociate magic and all that is akin to it from this religious sphere. Though he recognizes that beliefs in "curing, sorcery, and magic centering around the role of the *dukun* ... are spread throughout Javanese society", Clifford Geertz (1976, p. 86) places them in the realm of the *abangan* religion. It is time for a reappraisal. Geertz' assessment may be true for some manifestations of the belief in the supernatural, but the main actors do belong to the santri community. The "santri variant" of such beliefs may even have a far greater political impact, and is worth studying in more detail.

The scope is wider than the phenomena described above. *Ilmu kebal* is akin to the practice of magic both white and black. In a volume on witchcraft and sorcery in Southeast Asia, Roy Ellen describes the latter as "mystical aggression" and "the supernatural harming of others" (Watson and Ellen 1993, pp. 5–6). In Indonesia and Malaysia, belief in the *dukun* (a word that can denote a great many professions from the midwife to the seller of amulets and the sorcerer) or *bomoh is* widespread. In Indonesia, some *dukun* have never been so busy as they have been since the economic crisis struck in 1997. Nevertheless, in the field of Southeast Asian studies the subject is relatively unexplored. Rommy Nitibaskara (1993, p. 125) points out that "there is no established body of case material we can rely upon to document and analyse these beliefs". Judging from the bibliographical survey of Islam in Indonesia compiled by Boland and Farjon (1983), it was indeed a subject barely dealt with, let alone analysed, in colonial days. Post World War II literature also seems disappointingly scarce, with a brief, sudden upsurge in interest when the *dukun santet* murders were at their height. A notable exception is Bertrand's *Indonésie: La Démocratie Invisible*, published in 2002. One of the reasons for this lack of studies is the secrecy that surrounds the supernatural practices. What is on display are the outward and visible manifestations of the skills, not the way in which these skills are acquired and the thoughts behind them. Another stumbling block is the disinterest the scholarly society has shown in explaining this subject in any depth. In the light of the upsurge in killing of people believed to be practitioners of black magic in the latter half of 1998 in Indonesia and the role of invulnerability beliefs in popular uprisings, the subject definitely deserves more attention.

Notes

1. Similarly, the wife of Heri Kurniawan alias Heri Golun alias Igun, the suicide bomber, said that it was God's will that her husband had died. When Heri Kurniawan committed suicide his wife was pregnant. In a letter he asked her that if she bore a son to name him Rahmad Jundullah.
2. The leaking of this information to *Times* formed part of an American offensive to have President Megawati Sukarnoputri order the arrest of Abu Bakar Ba'asyir in September 2002. Omar al-Faruq had been arrested in Indonesia in June 2002, handed over to the Americans, and transported to Bagram, the American air base in Afghanistan.
3. For marriage practices and family relations of families running pesantren, see Dhofier (1982), pp. 61–78.
4. She was sentenced to three years in jail in June 2005.
5. The taking of an oath by new members of the Sarekat-Islam may have been a familiar tradition, the widespread practice of drinking water as part of the initiation certainly was an innovation. Though the drinking of holy water was not an unheard of practice, it may have been the combination with an initiation rite that made some Muslims frown. Making a connection with the Christian baptismal ceremony, they disparaged the custom for using "Christian water", see Kaptein (2005).
6. For *Sèjjid Othmân*, see Kaptein 1997.
7. Ma'unah can be translated as an extraordinary quality a person can acquire through the help of God. The group was in fact a splinter of an Indonesian organization. The Indonesian Al-Ma'unah, said to have been founded by a descendant of one of one of the saints who spread Islam in Java, Sunan Gunung Jati, was headed by Ibnu Abbas. Ibnu Abbas explained the word Ma'unah as *pertolongan Allah* (the help of God), see Mohamed (2003), pp. 136–39, 177. In Brunei an Al-Ma'unah — *Persaudaraan Ilmu Dalam al-Ma'unah Malaysia Seni Bela Diri Warisan Islam (Sumber Kekuatan Batin)* — is also active, see Mohiddin (2003), pp. 90–94.
8. Ashaari bin Muhammad was arrested in Thailand. Followers had such faith in him that they were sure that as Ashaari bin Muhammad had told them he would soon become Prime Minister of Malaysia, they mistook the police cars which suddenly appeared in front and behind the al-Arqam bus in which they and Ashaari Muhammad were travelling for an escort of honour (Mohamed 1998, p. 86).
9. Other incidents in Malaysia have been an armed confrontation with security forces by members of a group called Empat Sahabat in Kelantan in October

1974, and a raid on a police station in Johor in October 1980 by a group headed by Ahmad Nasir Ismail, who claimed to be the Imam Mahdi (Hassan 2003, p. 168)

10. In a similar vein, leading Jemaah Islamiyah operatives, though they themselves must have abhorred such stories, also became the subject of magic folklore. One of them, Fathur Rohman al-Ghozi — sentenced to between ten and twelve years imprisonment for the illegal possession of explosives in the Philippines — literally walked out of the detention centre of the Philippine National Police headquarters, supposed to be a maximum-security prison, took a taxi to a bus station and disappeared. It was said that he had a talisman which had opened the door of his cell. Of two other leaders of the Jemaah Islamiyah on the run, Azhari Husin and Noor Din Moh. Top, it was believed that their magic was the reason the police was not able to locate and arrest them. <Philstar.com> 22 November 2003, *Rakyat Merdeka*, 1 November 2003).
11. A most striking example of this unfamiliarity is that a booklet *Berjihad di Patani* found on the body of one of the Muslims who had participated in the 28 April attacks was mistaken for a "new version" of the Qur'an. Prime Minister Thaksin Shinawatra said that the Thai National Security Council would "invite Thai and foreign Islamic scholars to scrutinize the Qur'an to ensure only the original version of this Islamic bible would be publicised" (*Bangkok Post* 6 June 2004). This gave rise to the "misunderstanding" that Bangkok wanted to "rewrite" the Koran. The newspaper heading "Government Not Seeking Review of Muslim Bible" must have come as a relief (*Bangkok Post* 8 June 2004).
12. Belief in the supernatural meant that as it were alongside a physical war was fought another war. On their part, Buddhist soldiers hung themselves about with amulets, many carrying scores of them. Their commanders asked them not to wear them too conspiciously in order not to offend local Muslims (*Bangkok Post* 21 July 2004). To attain immunity, Buddhist soldiers also armed themselves with sacred tattoos.
13. Belief in invulnerability and other supernatural powers may also explain (or at least is used by Indonesians to explain) some of the extreme cruelty of mob justice in Indonesia. Masruri (1999, p. 12) relates the case of a person, who during the dukun santet hysteria in the month following Soeharto's fall was suspected to be a "ninja" and was sprayed with petrol and set on fire because he was believed to be invulnerable to cuts by knives and other sharp objects. Nitibaskara (1993, p. 131) mentions a case in a village in Cianjur in which a father and a son had their heads cut off. Both were thought to possess a spell to ensure eternal life. By cutting off their heads the villagers wanted to assure that the two could not come to life again.
14. He relates how, when still a pupil at secondary school, he had tested his invulnerability skills in the privacy of his room (his teacher had wisely ordered him to do so because should the test fail nobody would witness his failure). In his own room the invulnerability magic did work. When the temptation became

too great and he wanted to show a neighbour what skills he had acquired, he received a deep cut in the arm (though the wound did not bleed when he was taken to hospital by motorbike).

References

Abbas, Nasir. *Membongkar Jamaah Islamiyah: Pengakuan Mantan Anggota JI Nasir Abas*. Jakarta: Grafindo Khazanah Ilmu, 2005.

Abduh, Umar. *Pesantren Al-Zaytun Sesat? Investigasi Mega Proyek dalam Gerakan NII*. Jakarta: Darul Falah, n.d.

Adisaputra, Asep. *Imam Samudra Berjihad*. Jakarta: Pensil-324, 2006.

Al-Anshari, Fauzan. *Saya Teroris? (Sebuah "Pleidoi")*. Jakarta: Republika, 2002.

Baker, Jacqueline. "Laskar Jihad dan Mobilisasi Umat Islam dalam Konflik Maluku". n.d. <www.acicis.murdoch.edu.au/hi/field_topics/jbaker.doc>, (accessed 3 April 2005).

Bertrand, Romain. *Indonèsie: La DÈmocratie Invisible. Violence, Magie et Politique à Java*. Paris: Karthala, 2002.

Boland, B.J and I. Farjon. *Islam in Indonesia: A Bibliographical Survey 1600–1942 with Post-1945 Addenda*. Dordrecht: Foris, 1983.

Dhofier, Zamakhsyari. *Tradisi Pesantren: Studi tentang Pandangan Hidup Kyai*. Jakarta: LP3ES, 1982.

Gobée, E. and A. Adriaanse. *Ambtelijke Adviezen van C. Snouck Hurgronje*. s-Gravenhage, Martinus Nijhoff, 1957–65. Rijks Geschiedkundige Publicatiën, Kleine Serie 33, 34, 35.

Geertz, Clifford. *The Religion of Java*. Chicago and London: The University of Chicago Press (Phoenix Edition), 1976.

Hassan, Muhammad Haniff Hassan. "Penyelewengan Kebatinan di Singapura". In *Kebatilan dalam Ajaran Kebatinan*, edited by Abdullah Muhammad Zin, Haji Mohd. Alwi Yusoff, Muhammad Haizuan Rozali. Kuala Lumpur: Kolej Universiti Islam Malaysia, 2003, pp. 98–180.

Hurgronje, C. Snouck. *Verspreide Geschriften*. Bonn und Leipzig, Kurt Schroeder & Leiden: E.J. Brill, 1923–27.

Janse, Antheun. "De Kruistochten na Runciman: De Religieuze Factor". *Leidschrift* 20, no. 1 (2005): 71–92.

Kaptein, Nico J.G. "Sayyid 'Uthman on the Legal Validity of Documentary Evidence". *Bijdragen tot de Taal-, Land- en Volkenkunde* 153, no. 1 (1997): 85–102.

———. "Being a Muslim in a Colony: Sayyid 'Uthman and the Sarekat Islam". Draft paper presented for the conference on *Political Legitimacy in Islamic Asia*, Asia Research Institute, National University of Singapore, 25–26 April 2005.

Kartodirdjo, Sartono. *The Peasants' Revolt of Banten in 1888, Its Conditions, Course and Sequel: A Case Study of Social Movements in Indonesia*. 's-Gravenhage: Martinus Nijhoff (KITLV Verhandelingen 50), 1966.

Krue Se. Krue Se mosque incident: Militants met to plan attack, *The Nation*, 26 April 2005.

Masruri. *Ilmu Kebal: Agresif & Defensif.* Solo: Aneka, 1999.
Metzger, Laurent. *Stratégie Islamique en Malaisie (1975–1995)*. Paris & Montreal: l'Harmattan, 1996.
———. La minorité musulmane de Singapour. Paris & Montreal: l'Harmattan, 2003.
Ministry of Home Affairs. *White Paper: The Jemaah Islamiyah Arrests and the Threat of Terrorism*. Singapore: Ministry of Home Affairs, 2003.
Mohamed, Zabidi. Arqam. *Tersungkur di Pintu "Syurga": The Untold Truth and Inside Story of Al-Arqam & I.S.A. (Detention Without Trial)*. Kuala Lumpur: Zabidi Publications, 1998.
———. *Rahasia dalam Rahasia Maumah: Kebenaran yang Sebenar* [The Naked Truth]. Kuala Lumpur: Zabidi Publications, 2003.
Mohiddin, Awang Suhaili Haji. "Al-Batiniyah dan Pengaruhnya di Negara Brunei Darussalam". In *Kebatilan dalam Ajaran Kebatinan*, edited by Abdullah Muhammad Zin, Haji Mohd. Alwi Yusoff, Muhammad Haizuan Rozali. Kuala Lumpur: Kolej Universiti Islam Malaysia, 2003, pp. 77–97.
Nitibaskara, Ronny. "Observations on the Practice of Sorcery in Java". In *Understanding Witchcraft and Sorcery in Southeast Asia*, edited by C.W. Watson and Roy Ellen. Honolulu: University of Hawaii Press, 1993, pp. 123–33.
Noorhaidi. "Laskar Jihad: Islam, Militancy and the Quest for Identity in Post-New Order Indonesia. Ph.D. dissertation, Utrecht University, 2005.
Qodir, Zuly. *Ada Apa dengan Pesantren Ngruki*. Bantul: Pondok Edukasi, 2003.
Samudra, Imam. *Aku Melawan Teroris!* Surakarta: JazÍra, 2004.
Sarekat. *Sarekat Islam Lokal*. Jakarta: Arsip Nasional Repiblik Indonesia, Penerbitan sumber-sumber sejarah no. 7, 1975.
Shoelhi, Mohammad. *Laskar Jihad Kambing Hitam Konflik Maluku*. Jakarta: Pustaka Zaman, 2002.
SUARAM. "Malaysia: Human Rights Report 2002, Civil and Political Rights". Petaling Jaya: SUARAM Kommunikasi, 2003.
Watson, C.W. and Roy Ellen. *Understanding Witchcraft and Sorcery in Southeast Asia*. Honolulu: University of Hawaii Press, 1993.
Zin, Abdullah Muhammad, Haji Mohd. Alwi Yusoff, Muhammad Haizuan Rozali, eds. *Kebatilan dalam Ajaran Kebatinan*. Kuala Lumpur: Kolej Universiti Islam Malaysia, 2003.

Websites and Newspapers
Asiaweek.com
Bangkok Post <www.bangkokpost.com>
INQ7.net (an Inquirer and GMA Network Company)
Jakarta Post and the online, *<Jakarta Post.com>*
Media Indonesia
The Nation
New Straits Times Online (NST Online)
<Philstar.com>
Rakyat Merdeka
Straits Times Interactive

INDEX

T

www.ingramcontent.com/pod-product-compliance
Lightning Source LLC
Chambersburg PA
CBHW020811100426
42814CB00001B/22

* 9 7 8 9 8 1 2 3 0 9 4 0 2 *